THE

COACH

He is one of the best!

maddog!

THE
COACH
MANAGING FOR SUCCESS

RIC CHARLESWORTH

MACMILLAN
Pan Macmillan Australia

For Mum and Dad
who gave me a start
and Kate, Libby, Jonathon and Oscar,
the best reason to keep going

First published in Australia 2001 in Macmillan by Pan Macmillan Australia Pty Limited
St Martins Tower, 31 Market Street, Sydney

Reprinted 2001 (twice)

National Library of Australia
Cataloguing-in-Publication Data:

Charlesworth, Richard.
The coach: managing for success.

ISBN 0 7329 1106 0.

1. Hockey — Coaching. 2. Hockey coaches — Australia —
Biography. 3. Success — Attitudes. 4. Coaches (Athletics) —
Australia — Biography. 5. Charlesworth Richard.
I. Title.

796.355092

Typeset in 11/15 pt Sabon by Midland Typesetters
Printed in Australia by McPherson's Printing Group
Cover design by Liz Seymour, Seymour Designs
Front cover photograph by Corinne Reid
Back cover photograph by Greg Ford, Sport The Library

Every endeavour has been made to source the photographs and to contact copyright
holders to obtain the necessary permission for use of photographic and quoted material
used in this book. Any person or organisation that may have been inadvertently
overlooked should contact the publisher.

FOREWORD

You admire from afar many people in the public domain – actors, politicians, academics, authors, entertainers and sports men and women. Few do you really get to know. Fewer retain the initial level of admiration once embraced and unveiled.

This is the story of a man who I admired for many years from a distance. An athlete who excelled in more than one sport at both national and international level. A coach who moulded a group of hockey playing women into a team which dominated their sport for nearly a decade. A person who I've got to know over the past few years as a colleague in coaching, and still respect enormously.

This book provides fascinating insights into the man, Richard Charlesworth. Few people can claim such a varied experience pre-coaching. His life as an athlete, university student, doctor of medicine, father, husband and Labor politician, somehow forged a defining philosophy and a specific set of values which underpin his coaching career.

Ric has high expectations – of his athletes, but of himself too. He speaks his mind. He is empathetic, but refuses to allow sentiment to interfere with objectivity in decision making.

My reading round sporting performance, and in particular coaching, has been prolific. There are many publications which interest, inspire and educate. But none in my opinion do it better than *The Coach*. Ric's thoughts on competition, flair, individuality, game analysis, team selection and leadership will initiate debate throughout the sporting world – with athletes, administrators, spectators, commentators and, of course, coaches.

While there is much for the coach and the hockey enthusiast in these pages, there is equally as much for the Australian lover of other sports, and those like me who are intrigued by the sport/business relationship.

David Parkin, four times AFL Premiership Coach with
Carlton and Hawthorn and lecturer in the School of
Health and Life Sciences at Deakin University

CONTENTS

PART THREE

AFTERWORD

APPENDICES

INTRODUCTION

Why write a book? During the past couple of decades there have been two occasions when I came close to doing so. In 1988 as my career as an athlete was coming to an end I started a project with the journalist Warwick Hadfield. We proposed to write about a parliamentarian – me – preparing for the Olympics. Our disappointment in Seoul, when we failed to win a medal, and the depression which followed snuffed out my enthusiasm. Anyway, I had not been certain anyone would be interested in that story. The drafts of the project were sighted in one of the many boxes of stuff that I unearthed when I moved house late in 1999. I think they found their way to the tip.

In 1996 I considered another project. This book would be more autobiographical and contain some of my philosophy of coaching. The full spectrum of my experiences in sport and politics would be part of the story. Alas my busy lifestyle and the frenetic pace of my job with the Hockeyroos gobbled up the time and a few snippets of that project were all that remained when I revisited it at the end of 2000.

Once I arrived back in Perth after our Sydney 2000 Olympic

success I was approached by various publishers. Their interest suggested to me that maybe this time I could write a book that would have broad appeal. I believed I had a fair bit to say about coaching and what was important and what worked for sports teams. Perhaps, as well, there was an interesting autobiography to be written. Also I wanted to tell the story of the Hockeyroos. In the end I have endeavoured to do justice to all three aims. This book tells some of the story of the Hockeyroos, but more importantly it encapsulates what I believe about coaching. It draws on my experiences as an athlete in cricket and hockey as well as reflecting on the influences of my training and short career in medicine and my decade in Federal Parliament. All of these things have played a part in making me the coach I became and the person I am today.

In Part One I outline some of the ingredients that contributed to my development. Chapters on medicine and politics briefly review those parts of my life and how they contributed to my sporting philosophy and approach. I also discuss those who influenced me during my time as a player.

Part Two deals principally with my coaching approach. Some chapters give templates of ideas which provide the core of my approach to coaching, selecting and keeping a team fresh. Others deal with my views on captaincy and leadership, the dangers of playing conservatively, flair – an overrated commodity – and problems of selection. I discuss the need for a holistic approach to training and competition and highlight some of the contradictions and distractions that can interfere with performance. I also reflect on the need for coaches to see past the score, which in any single encounter can deceive and distort what actually happened. Coaches should not fall for analysing the game according to the score.

All chapters in this Part reflect a philosophy and approach to coaching which I hope will be of interest. I have endeavoured always to illustrate my assertions with anecdotes and in doing so have given a flavour of the Hockeyroos saga and of my own experiences as an athlete, coach and interested observer of many sports.

However the material in this Part is descriptive rather than detailed. In order to coach well one has to attend to all the details which in sum make for a consistent, consolidated team performance. An account of the really fine detail of coaching is not for this book. It is the substance of a coaching manual. But if you set in place a structure and develop an appropriate culture for your club or team then you are on the way to building success. This book deals mainly with those broadbrush structural issues.

Part Three contains a discussion about some of the great champions I have seen and known in sport in general, and for the hockey enthusiast I make some observations about the greats I have known in hockey.

During the past five years I have increasingly found myself in demand to talk with business people about the parallels between sporting teams' practices and those operating in commerce. The obstacles and problems businesses face in order to compete successfully – to become champions – are remarkably similar to those of sporting teams. Accordingly I have included my thoughts on what the Hockeyroos and other champion teams can teach business. I outline a philosophical view of how I see sport and where it may be heading, and take the opportunity to outline what is emerging as a new direction for me.

In trying to talk about my Hockeyroo experience and how I got there, at times I have been autobiographical. In recording my coaching approach I have not dotted every 'i' and crossed every 't', but I have certainly described the core issues. I have done it this way because I believe that the personal insights, sporting anecdotes and experiences and the story of a great team can make my messages more palatable.

My time with the Hockeyroos has been one of the best periods of my life. It was a wonderful experience to see the group grow and develop during the past eight years. Being with outstanding athletes who aspired to be world champions was a good place to be. I am immensely proud of what the team achieved. I am delighted that they have gained some of the recognition they deserve. They will never be individually famous like Greg Norman, Pat Rafter or even Wayne Carey, Brad Fittler or John Eales. Yet some of them are pound for pound every bit as good as those male athletes.

Their greatest achievement, however, was in the building of a team which dominated their sport. Not for one year, not for a couple, but for the best part of a decade. In major competitions during that time they turned up to win. It was in the World Championships in 1994 and 1998 and the Olympics in 1996 and 2000 that we saw them at their best. Like all of those who contributed to our program I take credit for playing a part in the Hockeyroos performance, but I know that in the end the athletes were the ones who did it. Without quality athletes such a record can never be achieved. Accordingly, to the extent that this book recognises the accomplishments of those outstanding athletes, I am delighted.

I have had a very fortunate life. My parents encouraged me to seek excellence and provided an environment in which I could thrive. Many others – coaches, teachers, colleagues, friends and family members – gave me encouragement and support. If some of the events of my life are of interest to others then I am grateful. I have tried to represent faithfully those influences and events.

Finally, I came to serious coaching late in the piece. Perhaps it was a great advantage to have enjoyed the many influences that shaped my life up to my fortieth year before I teamed up with the Hockeyroos. My preparation for the job was practical as well as theoretical, and its diversity gave me a solid platform on which to base my views about sports teams.

Sport has always been my greatest passion. It is not an activity fit only for philistines, as high-brow commentators often suggest. I have always seen it as an intellectual exercise as much as a physical one. Indeed it is because it is one of the few activities that embraces both requirements that I have found it so challenging.

The ancients understood the truth of the saying '*Mens sana in corpore sano*' ('A healthy mind in a healthy body'). It is no less relevant today. But team sports have another – a third – element to them. Complex, integrated activities, they require co-ordinated, co-operative effort in order to succeed. The ethic of being able to work co-operatively is understood by successful enterprises the world around. I believe there is no more important message that we can teach our young people. If the reader learns anything from this book I hope it is that in sharing and working co-operatively we can achieve our aims, and at the same time obtain satisfaction beyond what we could ever imagine for ourselves or by ourselves alone.

PART ONE

1

An Olympic Dream
in Sydney

With a minute to play, Jenny Morris intercepts in our defence and Nikki Hudson runs the ball wide and unchallenged for 60 metres in a manner we have so often discussed – smart play! Our 3–1 lead is safe. With the ball out of our defence and away from danger we cannot lose. The gold medal is won. Those sitting on the bench know it. Bob Haigh, our assistant coach, sits calmly as is his way. I am relieved. It is over. We have done it. The game runs out in front of us and at the end, as in Atlanta, the players forget the ball and start to celebrate with a few seconds left on the clock.

It had been a stressful day, at the end of a stressful fortnight, nine months into a stressful year. I have never understood how coaches can assert their team will play well on any day. I can never confidently predict the outcome. Perhaps I have seen too many upsets. I know the vagaries of sport all too well. I knew if we played at our best we would prevail over Argentina at their best. But teams seldom play at their best. You usually have to accept less. Argentina had four brilliant players, all capable of doing something special if given the opportunity. We had to be vigilant.

We had scored early after wasting a couple of very good chances in the first five minutes. Alyson Annan, lurking about the goals, as she does so well, took advantage of a fumbled cross from Lisa Carruthers. She poked the ball past the Argentinian goalkeeper who was trying to close her down. Argentina appeared very nervous and we really should have won it in the first twenty minutes. Our first penalty corner worked perfectly, the goal was open and Alyson fired the ball over the goal. All tournament this play had been withheld to be used, if appropriate, on the final day. The execution was perfect except for Alyson's final shot. Proof that the best laid plans don't always work. You need more than one plan. You trust the others might work if your best plans fail.

On the next corner we try another play. Again perfect, till the ball ricochets off the goal-post. Thankfully Juliet Haslam scores a reflex rebound to give us a 2–0 lead at half-time. It is her only goal in the tournament: a typically alert, brave goal. She scored a similar goal in the World Cup final in 1998. Juliet's sharpness in such situations had been in our minds when we considered her for selection in August. She had missed our final selection matches suffering from pyelonephritis, a kidney infection that put her out of action for two weeks. During our final Sydney trial she was laid up in hospital. I suspect for her the few days after leaving hospital and being selected were very anxious. The same kidney infection had proved sufficient to finish swimming star Samantha Riley's Olympic dream a few months earlier.

Two–nil is a scary score at half-time. It's not enough to be secure, but enough for some teams to fall into complacency. I was not worried about complacency with this group on this day, but being ahead in some ways is harder than being behind. When you are behind you have real definition in the task. When ahead, teams are often indecisive, unsure whether to continue attacking or to close the game down. In the Olympic final you worry about getting ahead of yourselves in such a situation. Don't think about the gold medal! That is what you must guard against. Our strategy had always been to play the same whatever the situation, but that is easier said than done.

Three minutes after half-time we score from a corner. We call the corners from the bench and I mess the call, but thankfully Jenny Morris just smashes it into the goal. Three years earlier almost to the day I had been watching as Jenny collapsed screaming with pain during a finals match in Perth. I went into the operating theatre to watch her knee reconstruction. The brutality of the surgery surprised me that day. After a few decades out of medicine I had forgotten what orthopaedic surgery is like. They saw and drill into the bones with great force. I watched during the next two years as Jenny faced many setbacks to her recovery.

We introduced and developed alternative players and we learned to play without her. I was not confident that she could make it, but as 2000 arrived Jenny was there and playing better all the time. Authoritative, powerful, highly skilled and courageous she earned her spot, and that night at that moment it was her shot that put the game beyond Argentina's reach.

For the next five minutes we dominate and could finish the game off but we are held out. Against the run of play Argentina score through brilliant play by Karina Masotta and Vanina Oneto. With twenty minutes left they have plenty of time and, for the first time all day, some belief. They press hard. The clock appears to slow down and there are two or three very messy goal-front situations. Another goal to them would have tested our character. Fortunately we are able to hold them out and as the clock speeds up again we reassert ourselves, but cannot kill them off with another goal.

During the twenty minutes between Argentina's goal and knowing the game is safe there are many heroic moments. Rachel Imison in goal makes a couple of crucial blocks. Alison Peek, Renita Garard and Angie Skirving all make critical interventions, but none is more reliable than Kate Starre. Throughout the tournament she had been consistently excellent. Aerobically outstanding, Kate had been troubled by a recurring back injury for more than a couple of seasons. I had often wondered if she would make it to Sydney.

I truly believe it was her professionalism that got her there. Fastidious in following her 'special program', she was wonderfully aggressive yet controlled at the Olympics. This feisty and often controversial 'bad girl' of club and interstate competition showed composure and calmness time and time again. During that period when the game could have slipped away on that most important night she was wonderfully in control.

No, we didn't play at our best. We had made enough chances to score a couple more times, but as the last minute runs out it does not matter anymore. I closed my notebook on the game. I didn't run to join in the hugging. I watched, a spectator, acknowledging the feelings that Bob and I felt for each other and the team. Twenty-four years earlier we had been losers together on such a day in Montreal. I hugged Wendy Pritchard, our manager, and after a time made my way to congratulate Sergio Vigil, Argentina's coach, on the performance of his team. In spite of losing, his team would be heroes at home. This was their first medal at the Olympics in hockey and one of only a handful for the country in Sydney. Sergio had criticised me in Amsterdam some months earlier after I inadvertently failed to shake hands after a game. I would not make that mistake again.

I found my way out onto the field and hugged each of the players – they were excited, overwhelmed and delighted. They were Olympic champions, each in her own way was special, and each had a story to tell. Together they usually combined selflessly and relentlessly to achieve their dream.

As a player it had also been my dream to win Olympic gold. I knew only too well how such a dream could slip away and be lost in the helter-skelter of competition. I had three chances at a gold medal in my career as a player and three disappointments. I don't believe, as is the public perception, that we were chokers, whatever that means. What I believe is that we were never properly prepared and never really a resilient team, and each time we made mistakes in crucial games.

I have tried to be the coach I would have liked to have had. I always wanted the Hockeyroos to have the organisation, discipline, and team identity that those Australian men's hockey teams lacked. I hoped as a coach to ensure we would avoid some of the mistakes those teams had made. I think over time we came close to my ideal team.

Of all the players, Katie Allen was the most emotional. I cannot remember what I said to her, but her year had been a roller-coaster ride of emotion. Extremely close to selection in Atlanta four years earlier, outstanding in the 1998 World Cup, then omitted from the Champions Trophies teams in 1999 and 2000, she had spent the year uncertain about her chances of selection. Perhaps the most physically courageous athlete I have ever known, she earned a spot by her performance and played throughout the Olympics as if her life depended on it. Katie was sobbing and yelping alternately. Her release of emotion was palpable, overpowering and left me in tears too. (I've included Katie's story later in this book to give a player's view of sport's highs and lows.)

Everyone associated with the team was happy – there was lots of backslapping and high emotion. The ritual of victory was played out by the players, the medal ceremony awaited and I felt predominantly . . . *relief*. Perhaps there was some satisfaction sneaking through, but also already emptiness. Over the weeks and months that followed, the realisation that the Hockeyroo experience was over would sadden me with regret and loss, while at other times the satisfaction of achievement would take centre stage.

During the previous thirteen days two of my three children, Libby and Jono, with my partner, Carmen, had been through the anxiety of close matches and the tension and the build-up to this match. They were relieved too. They were sitting behind our bench, close by. It was great to have them there. Kate, my eldest daughter, had enjoyed her Olympic experience watching soccer at the MCG and then had relaxed on a skiing holiday with her boyfriend, Sam Cuneen. After most matches I had seen the family for a few moments before walking back to the village alone.

Libby, Jono and Carmen were staying with Carmen's sister Diane Bramuzzo. Carmen, who was eight months pregnant, had to tolerate an uptight and stressed partner. Rarely over the previous months had I not been absorbed in hockey matters, team strategy and player issues. The family had no doubt all felt neglected, but had always been supportive – they knew better than anyone how much the Olympics had dominated my life in 2000.

Each evening after our match as I walked back to the village, my mind would be full of strategy, replaying in my head events of the game just completed or evaluating what I had seen or knew of our next opponent. I would plan the next day's program and consider what I would emphasise at our team debriefing, which would take place when I arrived back at our quarters.

Usually I would make my way up Olympic Boulevard through throngs of excited Olympic visitors. Emerging from various venues, chatting with one another about their experiences, they set the night abuzz with activity. I would turn left and skirt around the main stadium where it was quiet and descend past the media centre towards the village. Ahead, across Haslams Creek, was the village with all its drama and activity. Immediately before me was the artificial hill – a rubble pile shaped by bulldozers and covered with blue and white flags which fluttered continuously, sounding like a flock of birds. That last 600 metres to the gate was silent time. I needed that. In the village it could only be found in the early morning hours.

I imagine that I will go to Homebush again and watch hockey played there. It will probably be a strange feeling. When I look back at my Olympic experiences I remember the pitches well. The magnificent grass fields in Munich became community open space with the odd soccer field and some housing. Molson Stadium in Montreal with its steep grandstands reverted to gridiron, as did East Los Angeles College after 1984 in Los Angeles. Seongnam Stadium with its athletic track and concrete grandstands was, like Los Angeles, a place with unfortunate memories for me.

The fields in Atlanta became more gridiron pitches too, with the massive concrete stands seating college football fans. Most of those stadiums would look the same if I revisited them now. When I go back to Homebush, however, the vast temporary stands will have been removed and the special atmosphere of those two weeks in September 2000 will have gone. I expect that if I sit quietly I will perhaps be able to remember what it was like on 29 September at the end of the millennium.

That evening I did not go to the press conference after the match. I had decided that once the game was over my work was finished, and I had said I would not be there. I believed it would be a good opportunity for the players to have their time. Generally at press conferences 70 per cent of the questions were directed to me and I knew if I was there the same thing would happen. Equally, I might have got carried away and said things I might regret! Better to allow the on-field deeds to speak for themselves.

The players had come through their trial magnificently. The coaching staff and others helping had played their roles so professionally that there was good reason to be proud of what had been achieved. You couldn't say things went according to plan; there are always ups and downs along the way and any program must have the flexibility to adjust. When you enter the tournament you can never be sure how it will unfold.

Quite often before I had thought about what I would do on that night. I saw myself dining out in Sydney with Carmen, Libby and Jono – perhaps somewhere in Darling Harbour or The Rocks area. That way I could be just another spectator watching other Olympic revellers as they enjoyed the last couple of days of the Games.

It did not turn out like that. The kids had decided that they'd like to join all the other hockey supporters at the Lidcombe Catholic Workmen's Club, where a celebration was planned. I was too tired to disagree and transport to Sydney would be difficult anyway. The Workmen's Club was only one station away on the railway line.

I did not go back to the village but walked with my kids and Carmen through the thousands of visitors at the Olympic precinct. We arrived at the club well before the players, who had gone back to the village to change. My night was spent signing autographs and talking with excited, fanatical, loyal and often inebriated supporters. Once the players arrived there was thankfully less attention paid to me. The kids met friends and supporters from all over Australia and seemed to slide easily into the party. Jonathon, his spiked hair defying gravity and resplendent in green and gold, was right into it. Only fifteen years old, he even had a few beers, I suspect!

In the early hours of the morning we headed back to Annandale where the family had been staying. It was my first night outside the village. Carmen and the kids would return with me to the village in the morning but this was life again as a civilian. It was quiet, there was not the excitement and activity of village life. My duty had been discharged and I felt as though I had been discharged too. Yes, I was relieved. Yes, I needed and had craved a break, but I also knew that I would miss it and that I was close to the end of my time with the Hockeyroos.

The Closing Ceremony was the embodiment of that ending, the formal completion of what had started with those faltering steps in 1993 when at Homebush against Korea I had first been in charge of the team. Back in Perth there was a parade and a couple of functions, but soon life was pretty normal and a new rhythm began. The members of the team that had been built over years and that had played in Sydney would never play together again. Perhaps in our game we would not see the likes of such a team for a good while. I was planning a break from hockey. Maybe I would be involved again in such a quest. If not, then it was a good way to end.

Exactly four weeks later on another Friday afternoon, this time in Perth, Oscar was born. He is a happy, healthy, beautiful little boy.

Throughout the year the Olympics had filled my life to the point of obsession. Oscar's arrival was a grounding event, reminding me of what was most important to me. The Hockeyroos came second in my life to only one thing, my family. Carmen and Oscar were the new part of my family. Kate, Libby and Jono were my family from my time with Frances, two decades earlier. All were vitally important and precious to me.

Despite the great adventure of the Olympics and as central to my life as the quest for gold medals had been, my greatest pleasure and my greatest success is seeing my children develop. While there have been times in my life when this perspective has slipped through my consciousness, I felt in 2000 that Oscar's birth had helped me keep my balance. Thanks Oscar!

2

Beginning with the National Team

The journey to Homebush Bay began in mid 1992. As the member for Perth in the House of Representatives, I decided I would not contest the forthcoming election but would leave the political arena behind. Interesting job, worthwhile endeavour but horrible lifestyle, was my conclusion about political life. The election was looming late in 1992 or early in 1993. After that I would be out of a job.

Sharon Buchanan called me one morning in September 1992. It was years since I had spoken to her. Captain of the team that had felt the disappointment of fifth place in Barcelona, she asked whether I would be interested in coaching Australia's women's hockey team. Might I like to apply for the job that was being advertised? It was an option from left field. I had contemplated a range of possibilities – a return to medicine, being a student for a while, perhaps writing. Nothing was concrete except for a commitment to assist Stephen Smith who had won the preselection tussle for the Perth electorate. I felt obliged to ensure that the seat remained safe for Labor.

During the previous couple of seasons my coaching experience had extended to the local Westside Wolves Under13s and Under15s, where my eldest daughter, Kate, was a player. The step from Under 15s to the national job would be substantial. Brian Glencross had coached the Australian team for the past decade and was keen to continue. Brian and his assistant coach, Peter Freitag, were both applicants for the job. I suspect they suffered the fate of coaches the world over when their teams under-perform. Peter returned to teaching at Scotch College and Brian would work with me as a valued high performance manager where his experience and contacts were put to good use.

On reflection, it was my first formal job interview: a newly qualified doctor automatically got work as a resident and the preselection process with the Australian Labor Party, while more daunting, is not the traditional job interview. The election itself is hardly a normal job interview either. My resolve was to say what I thought; it has always been my view that candour is the best policy. At least then they knew what they would be getting; there would be no misunderstanding. I was not nervous. I expected to get the position and the prospect was becoming more attractive as I thought about it. Women's Hockey Australia agreed that I should start immediately after election day. Informally, things were already taking shape in late 1992.

I sent all players a questionnaire, those from the junior teams as well. I was interested in what they felt about Barcelona – what had they felt was lacking? What were the backgrounds of the up and comers? How did they see the future? Who would continue? Which players were in the offing?

In March 1993 I began. Little did I know what would unfold during the next seven and a half years. There would be major competitions in Amsterdam, Dublin, Mar del Plata, Atlanta, Delhi, Seoul, Berlin, Utrecht, Kuala Lumpur, Brisbane and Sydney. We would win in all those places. Many hundreds of athletes would be scrutinised, assessed and considered. I would have an involvement with coaches and players throughout Australia and overseas. I would feel the jubilation that goes with victory and the intense angst that goes with playing poorly or having to leave athletes out of teams. I would be the one whose judgments would crush the hopes and aspirations of some very deserving and talented athletes. In my time as coach, 54 players would represent their country playing for the Hockeyroos.

I had not seen the women play since Seoul in 1988. There, they scrambled through the round games but played emphatically in the semi-final and final to win gold. Subsequently, they had placed second in the Sydney World Cup in 1990 and slipped to fifth in Barcelona in 1992. They were a team in transition and I suspected big changes would be required. Teams get tired and need refreshing. They can be refreshed with new ideas, new players, a different way of playing and with new and different challenges. It was a good time to start and why not try to do everything.

My first assignment with the Hockeyroos (they did not adopt that name until 1994) was a series of matches against Korea in May 1993. I had not had much contact with the players as the Australian Institute of Sport (AIS) program in Perth was catering for the Junior World Cup squad that year and many of the senior players were based elsewhere. During 1993 and 1994 I was national coach but Brian Glencross remained AIS head coach. This was not ideal and would change when I assumed both roles in 1995. Taking on the job as high performance manager Brian did less coaching and more administration. Korea at the time were very good. They had been stung by a fourth place in Barcelona, going down surprisingly to Britain in the bronze medal match. Very fast, athletic and skilled, the Koreans were a stern test for us. In the first match we trailed 0–3 at half-time before recovering to draw 3–3. A subsequent win and loss tied the series. There was much to be done. A couple of issues were clarified by those three matches.

First we needed more pace. To adequately counter the skills and athleticism of our opponents this would be essential. Watching tapes of the games the team played in Barcelona, I had been concerned about our lack of dynamism in movement. Not only was raw speed necessary, but craft and agility also counted. One who had this but appeared under-used in Barcelona was Alyson Annan. Another two players who interested me there were Michelle Andrews and Nova Peris. As 21 year olds in 1992 they were not eligible for the Junior World Cup in 1993.

Indeed Nova was recommended to be dropped from the AIS squad when I arrived. The view was that her skills were too erratic to make up for her obvious athleticism. I disagreed, I had seen her instincts were good and her competitiveness exceptional. She was raw in her skills but I liked her balance and she was very quick in a straight line. In club matches we would look at her some more. Michelle was fast but had two other attributes that you cannot easily find. She was fiercely competitive and aggressive, and a gifted goal scorer. Unorthodox but effective, she would eventually play nearly 150 matches for Australia and score on average in every second match.

My second observation was that I thought the players were too comfortable in their formation. We needed more flexibility in each player's game, more flexibility to cope with the variety of ways of playing worldwide and more flexibility in our own team game. In Japan in June 1993 we would try some things that were different.

Not only did I believe we needed to challenge the team with a new structure, I believed we needed to do the same thing with individuals in the team. I like a team full of all-rounders. If I had been successful as a hockey player, it was because I had tried to become an all-rounder. I wanted players comfortable on the right or left, able to defend and attack, and quick in transition. There can never be enough players in your team who want to score when the chance arises; if they aren't thinking about it and practising it then it will not occur. People who were pigeonholed in any position would have to move on if they wouldn't or couldn't adjust to the new challenges. Inevitably in every squad there are some players who are on the periphery, nearly there but still not quite. In the games against Korea and in our competition in Japan I included a number of those players. I suspected that they might not be what was required, but they warranted the opportunity to show what they could do.

In June we went to Japan to play in the Prince Takamado Cup. Spain (the Olympic champions from Barcelona), Japan, Korea and Australia made for a quality competition. We played each team in Tenri, and then in Osaka. In Tenri, we stayed in student accommodation in a hostel. Sleeping on the floor in traditional Japanese style and helping to prepare food in the kitchen was a chastening experience. Communal bathing facilities caused many a modest Hockeyroo to see the world in a more expansive way! Undefeated in Tenri, we beat Spain for the second time in Osaka and with the score tied with only seconds to go against Japan had the tournament won as there would be no final. Pressing for a winner we were scored against on a counter-attack with seventeen seconds remaining. That loss to Japan and subsequently losing 0–3 to Korea the next day gave the Koreans the Cup.

In the first three months we had played nine matches for five wins, one draw and three losses. This was not a particularly auspicious beginning. Our tenth match, against the Netherlands, saw a 0–0 draw in a windswept game in Breda, a place best known for its cheeses. So after ten matches we still only had a 50 per cent winning record. Indeed had it continued at that rate our win–loss record would have looked very different at the end of eight years.

The two major events of 1993 lay ahead of us. The Champions Trophy in Amsterdam in August would pit the top six nations against one another, and then in September the Junior World Cup would be held in Terrasa, Spain.

In Japan we had trialled a new way of playing. Instead of the traditional structure of three lines – attack, midfield and defence – we would try to play with four lines. For the first time we played with two strikers, two attacking midfielders and two defensive midfielders in front of a goalkeeper and four defenders. To play without a traditional centre-forward or centre-half was experimental. It required aggressive play by the midfielders in order to get forward as well as to provide width as our two strikers did not play like traditional wingers. Indeed they were asked to play well inside the sidelines and cross over in lateral movements as often as possible. They needed to be able to play both left and right sides of the field.

Our two all-out attackers (or strikers) and four midfielders (two attacking and two defensive) were expected to be interchangeable, and whenever possible any of the four defenders could also go forward. This structure was developed as much to challenge and test the athletes as to give us more flexibility. It also gave us a chance to use our abundance of midfielders. They could best serve the team by giving us dominance in the middle of the park.

One of the requirements of the new structure was a high level of fitness. Already I had my eye on Atlanta, where the 1996 Olympics would be played in hot and humid conditions. The consequences of an extremely high work rate would need to be carefully evaluated.

It was fortuitous for our new style of play that the introduction of interchangeable reserves occurred around the same time. This allowed us to use a fresh player in each line, to rest players and ensure the work rate was maintained. I was keen to develop a culture of regular interchange to replace the prevalent view that to be brought off was a sign of failure or indication of coaching displeasure. Additionally, it appeared to me that the new interchange rule offered a unique opportunity to expand the experience of the group in an inclusive way. By using all sixteen players every game and sharing the workload, many more players got to play in internationals and the starting line up–bench dichotomy was broken. By doing this every time we played the players began to realise that coming off could be a plus rather than a minus. It allowed them to recharge their batteries, to discuss tactical issues with coaches, to rehydrate more effectively and to reset their goals as well as see the game from a less intense perspective. Over time it was to become a preferred way of playing for the whole team. Indeed many players, if asked to play the whole match, found it extremely difficult as they were accustomed to a high-tempo game and couldn't last a full 70 minutes.

The transition in our way of playing had hardly been a riveting success in Japan, yet I had seen enough to suspect that it could work well for us. We had started to break down the shackles of many years of traditional playing, and even though our best players had not all been available, we had done OK. While some of the older players had reservations, they, to their credit, embraced the paradigm shift. Every coach has a honeymoon period and, thankfully, in that time major changes are often relatively easily effected.

In August 1993, we took eighteen players to Amsterdam for the Champions Trophy. On the way we played two games against the Netherlands in Breda and Vught and two games against Great Britain at Bisham Abbey. This gave us a further chance to try out our new approach. Only sixteen could play in the Champions Trophy but two players, Morris and Annan, were due to play in the Junior World Cup which would follow Amsterdam. Accordingly we allowed Jenny and Alyson to travel a week later than the rest of the team and we included in our eighteen two players who had missed selection for the junior team. Both Katie Allen, nineteen, and Nikki Mott (later Hudson), seventeen, would become significant players in Sydney seven years later. They played in the sixteen for the lead-up games but Alyson and Jenny took their places in the team on their arrival a few days before the competition started.

As the newly appointed national coach I had no say in the selection of the Junior World Cup team in 1993. The omissions of Allen and Mott in my view were very unfortunate, so I was delighted to include them in the senior party for Amsterdam. I have no doubt that the experience and involvement made a big difference to the development of Allen who, a year later, would make our World Championship team as a late replacement. The younger Mott would blossom into an outstanding player as the years went by.

In Amsterdam, we played emphatically to be undefeated through the round-robin competition. On the final day we met the Netherlands in the main game. Both teams had disappointed the previous year in Barcelona and appeared to have recovered form a year later. I thought we were in control in the final at Wagener Stadium, Amstelveen, but an enthusiastic Dutch crowd remained buoyant as we were unable to get two goals ahead. Against the run of play the Dutch scored and despite some good chances we were unable to do justice to our possession. The score was 1–1 at full-time; the game would be decided on penalties.

Three years earlier Australia had missed more than a handful of penalties in matches in Sydney at the World Cup. Many of the players were reluctant penalty takers as the memory of those matches lingered. In some ways this first penalty shoot-out would be a watershed experience for the group. Successfully negotiated it would help redefine the group's belief in itself. Its ability to handle the pressure and intensity of a shoot-out would be instructive.

There are two aspects to a shoot-out: making your own shots well and saving the other team's. The five penalty takers are crucial of course. You must have players who want to do it, who are competent at the task and confident. Sometimes your final choice will hinge on who played well in the game if other things appear equal.

As was our method we had asked each of the players that morning if they wanted to take a penalty shot, should the game come down to that. Of the eight or nine who nominated themselves we settled on Michelle Andrews, Jenny Morris, Kate Starre, Alyson Annan and Juliet Haslam, in that order. None had been in Sydney in 1990. Haslam at 23 was the oldest. Perhaps the more difficult task is to select the goalkeeper. Karen Marsden and Justine Sowry were both good at saving penalties. Marsden was big and quick. Sowry was more a stay-at-home keeper, smaller but with great reflexes. I chose Marsden whom I felt, because of her size, was more imposing.

Out they went to do battle. Imagine my surprise when Sharon Buchanan came up to me and said she thought Sowry would have been a better choice. I was not offended. In fact I thought it was a measure of Sharon's maturity, and indeed the maturity of a relationship we were developing, that she felt able to speak up. I said I thought they were both good but opted for Karen because of her speed and size. We sat and watched.

The shoot-out was anticlimactic. We won 4–2 without requiring our last penalty taker. Marsden made two terrific saves (nearly three) and we could take home the trophy. Significantly the younger players, including Annan and Morris who were off to the Junior World Cup in Barcelona, scored their penalties.

That night the senior team flew back to Australia. I ate out in the Leidseplein with Alyson Annan and Jenny Morris. Amsterdam was a lively and exciting place for these two twenty year olds who would be leading athletes in the team for the rest of the decade. I remember the evening well as we talked at length about the possibilities ahead. Alyson and Jenny, although excited about joining their team mates in the Under 21 team, would find it difficult to play another tournament so close to the Champions Trophy. I warned them not to expect an easy time ahead.

The Junior World Cup team was immensely gifted with Katrina Powell, Renita Farrell (later Garard), Clover Maitland and Louise Dobson, as well as Alyson and Jenny, all going on to become Olympic gold medallists. Kate Sage, Tammy Cole, Rachel Durdin and Allison Lippey would play senior matches for Australia. Of the reserves in that age group, Katie Allen and Nikki Mott would be gold medallists in Sydney, and Bianca Langham, Kerry Crawford, Simone Wallington and Nina Bonner would all play senior hockey.

I had a week to kill before the tournament started. I caught the train to Graz in Austria where I would spend a few days with friends before flying down to Barcelona to watch the junior team coached by Don Smart, one of our best ever players. In Graz I had quiet time and a chance to chill out. An old university town in the south, Graz was close to the border of Slovenia with its spectacular scenery. I visited the university where Kepler had taught while preparing his three laws of planetary motion in support of Copernicus. I could only marvel at the men who observed the planets and made such brave and insightful predictions at a time when most were wedded to theories that placed earth at the centre of the solar system. Hockey coaching really is an easy thing!

After my break, I arrived in the cosmopolitan port city of Barcelona, a major cultural centre and a focus for Catalan separatists seeking independence from Spain. Gaudi's idiosyncratic architecture was all around and I enjoyed many hours walking the streets looking at the unusual and often bizaare buildings. The way of life in this Mediterranean land in many ways reminded me of home, but with more style and panache.

I found my way out to Terrassa, a sleepy industrial town nestled in the hills outside Barcelona, a centre of the textile industry. The site of the Olympic hockey tournament, it is also the centre of hockey for the Catalans. The game was brought to the region by British textile workers in the nineteenth century and remained an important part of the local scene. Within Spain there is intense rivalry between the Catalans and the rest of the country. A few rich benefactors and wealthy sporting clubs such as the Polo Club in Barcelona, where hockey is also played, underpin hockey's existence. Always competitive in the men's game, Spain has recently produced very competitive women's teams from a relatively small base of players. Their gold medal in Barcelona was unexpected, but given their organisation and resilience in that tournament not undeserved.

Interestingly, Jose Braza, the coach of that winning team in 1992, gained much, it seems, from a connection with Australia. Following Australia's gold medal in Seoul, Braza spent many months in Perth observing activities at the AIS Hockey Unit, before setting up a parallel structure in Madrid where he prepared his team for their Barcelona triumph.

The Australian girls played soundly in the early games in Terrassa and after disposing of the Netherlands were assured of a place in the finals. However Korea upset them in the last round match and so they were faced with a tough game against Germany in the semi-final. I expected Korea to dispose of Argentina in the other semi-final. But upsets were abroad and unexpectedly the dynamic Koreans fell to the patient Argentinians. Australia trailed Germany all day, scored late to go to penalties and beat Germany in a shoot-out to reach the final.

In the tough final game Argentina scored twice from limited chances to win. Many of the Argentinians would be in the senior team a year later when we would meet them in the World Cup final. That game would give our Under 21 players a chance to exorcise the demons that took hold that afternoon in Terrassa. Against a patient team that counter attacked I though we had not been aggressive enough. A late flurry of activity did not get them back into the game and the players were crestfallen at the final whistle. The Argentinian form reflected the growing popularity of the sport in the Spanish-speaking South American land.

When I was in Buenos Aires eight months later I would seldom travel on public transport without seeing young girls carrying hockey sticks to or from school. While soccer was a national obsession for the boys of Argentina, we would play hockey against young women from as far west as Mendoza in the shadow of the Andes. The game introduced by British railway workers had penetrated that vast southern land as surely as their railways struck out westwards across the pampas.

As I made my way back to Australia after the tournament, I reflected on my first six months in the job. It was bigger than I had thought it would be. I found that it absorbed much of my time even away from the pitch. Do all coaches find themselves sucked into the vortex of total involvement? I could see this happening to me. But I also enjoyed it after a decade of defending the decisions of others. I was in a discrete job which allowed me to measure my worth. I liked that.

Our junior team, although talented, had lost to Korea and Argentina and only beaten Germany on penalties. The Dutch senior team was very impressive and Korea at that level could be dynamic. Those four countries would cause us angst during the next seven years. They would at different times be our opponents in major competition finals. I would need to keep my eye on them all.

I returned to Australia with an emerging view as to how we should play. I had the luxury of knowing that I would be able to include the junior players in our main squad and we would thereby be able to try a variety of new players. The resources of the Australian taxpayers through the Australian Sports Commission formed an important part of our program budget and would enable us to play nearly 40 matches in 1994.

On arriving in Australia, I was very disappointed to hear that Sharon Buchanan had decided to retire after the Champions Trophy win in Amsterdam. She had been a brilliant player and I had tried to persuade her to continue through 1994. I thought she still had a role in the team, though I told her I could not be confident beyond 1994. Some athletes go on too long, but not Sharon. She lacked explosive pace but had developed her ball control and passing to such an extent that she was able to escape close marking and penetrate the best defences. In 1993 she was still a valuable player. I spoke again with Sharon but her mind was made up so her decision had to be respected. A gold medallist in Seoul, she had played perhaps her most brilliant game when the Australians upset the Netherlands in the Olympic semi-final. In scoring twice Sharon had ensured a place for Australia in the final against Korea.

Sharon moved on to hockey administration and has recently moved to Brisbane with her husband, Phillip Reid. During the Sydney Olympics she was an expert commentator for Channel 7 and in December 2000 she became the mother of baby Jesse. She has often attended major hockey competitions in her role with the media. Whenever I see her I am reminded of how I came to be in my coaching job. I am very grateful that she thought of me.

3

Medicine – An Art According to Judgment

For the past decade I have made a living from sport. As a school leaver such a possibility never entered my mind. Medicine offered a variety of pathways (clinical, teaching, research); it was science with a human touch. I was fascinated by the body's complexity and capacities and medicine was a way of finding out more.

The fundamentals of a medical education were later to prove complementary to the task of coaching. I learned the value of thoroughness and vigilance, the gains made through good teamwork, the necessity of prioritising and allocating my time within a busy schedule. While studying I would get my first taste of international competition and the Olympic Games, and I would see, at close range, the horror of terrorism in Munich in 1972. All these influences helped me to put my sporting obsession into perspective. Sport was a wonderful escape from the serious work of medicine. It was an exciting and challenging activity which measured my capacities both physical and mental. But it was sport, it was not life and death. It had its place.

Hippocrates is considered the father of medicine. He introduced a scientific approach to healing by seeking physical causes of disease rather than magical or mythical explanations. He compiled case records evaluating treatments and developed the art of ethical bedside care. Medicine is an amalgam of art and science, and practised without balance between the two it is not practised at its best.

In getting this balance right there are many similarities between coaching and medicine. Increasingly coaches are bombarded with a plethora of scientific advice on how to do their jobs. Yet the coach's job, in my view, is still more art than science.

One part of the oath of Hippocrates declares: 'I will prescribe regimen for the good of my patients, according to my ability and my judgment and never do harm to anyone.' This also sums up the coach's task.

He must optimise athletes' capacities with a training, learning and counselling regime. For this his judgment and talent is put to good use. His task is not simply a scientific one, for the subtleties and nuances of coaching are best learned by experience and through wide consultation. The coach must absorb scientific data and apply it to the best effect using judgment and finesse.

As for the never do harm to anyone component of the Hippocratic oath, that too is part of the coaching contract. The wrong advice or direction or over-coaching can be detrimental to performance and development. Equally a coach should know when to give an athlete their head, and leave them alone. It is often the coach's task to lift pressure from athletes and allow them the freedom to express themselves. This is analogous with providing optimum healing conditions so the body can heal itself.

I entered medical school in March 1970 unsure about where it would take me. How does any seventeen year old know where they want to go? Which career is best for them? My school days had been full of sport and passing exams. What richness there had been early on in middle school had been taken away when I, like my peers, was directed towards matriculation and career orientation.

I had done well in history and geography and enjoyed languages, but if one studied maths and physics and chemistry there was no room for humanities. I chose German as my last subject and so my earlier interest in the arts fell by the wayside. As one who has recently seen my own children wrestle with the same issue I cannot understand why we do not promote a wider range of subjects and experiences for our teenagers. Many today take only five subjects into their final years of school. I am not an expert educator but I think a simple sense of balance would have one question this system.

Similarly, since I studied medicine I have come to believe that it ought to be exclusively a post-graduate course. Students entering medical school in their twenties would know better where they wanted to go, and be more mature and ready for what medicine entails. The pre-clinical years (as they were when I studied) of dry science with very little clinical connection and no patient contact did little to enhance an experience few seventeen year olds are prepared for. It was only in my fourth year that the relevance of what I had studied came into focus. I had to examine patients and communicate with them. Suddenly I, and my fellow students, were faced with illness and trauma and often with death. The raw emotions which go with this can be overwhelming for those just out of their teens.

The course is better now and there is more contact with patients much earlier, but most students are still starting as seventeen year olds and that is the crux of the problem as I see it. Still only twenty when clinical work begins, they have not seen enough or lived enough to really know their minds. It is often a turbulent and con-fusing time and a period of concentrated self-interest. In my view young people need to grow through this stage before being ready for a medical education and career.

Notwithstanding this, my university days were halcyon times. I could stay out late, come and go at home with more freedom, and for the first three years at least my holidays lasted for four months each year. There was free time during the day – seldom were you missed in crowded lecture halls, and there was plenty of time for socialising and sport.

Unfortunately the latter activity occupied too much of my time during my third year at university. In January 1972 I received one of the greatest surprises of my sporting life. I was playing cricket at Abbett Park for University against Scarborough when Brian Glencross appeared on the boundary line as we fielded in the mid afternoon sun. During the drinks break Brian, the captain of the national hockey team, informed me that I had been selected for the Olympic team to compete in Munich in August–September of that year.

I had not even known a team was being selected at the time. It came completely out of the blue. In 1971 I had played for Western Australia for the first time in interstate competition in Brisbane. We had finished an undistinguished third and my performance had been good at times but inconsistent. I had not been selected in the national team that travelled to the World Cup in Barcelona later that year and so I had no aspirations of Olympic selection in 1972 even though my season in club hockey in Perth had been very good. I had led the goal scorers and scored the crucial goal in a winning grand final effort, but that could not have been enough even if it had been noticed by the national selectors. Perhaps it was my very good Under 21s form in Adelaide later in 1971 that had been viewed by national coach Arthur Sturgess. Who knows?

As I joined my University team-mates after the drinks break I could not keep the news to myself. I was overwhelmed and excited beyond imagining. I cannot remember exactly what happened in the cricket that afternoon but I seem to remember getting a second innings hit and playing with wild abandon not typical of the man Phil Wilkins of the *Sydney Morning Herald* would describe as the 'master of the nick and nudge'.

Thus 1972 proved a very difficult year as I wrestled with the complexities of anatomy, physiology, biochemistry and neuro-anatomy while preparing for an Olympic journey that would take me overseas for the first time in my life and open up a world that until then was quite out of reach. In May we travelled to New Zealand, where I played my first international for Australia at centre-forward. It was the only time I would play in that position in 227 matches. We played in Whangarei not too far from that beautiful area north of Auckland known as the Bay of Islands. According to the *Whangarei Observer*, 'Young Charlesworth played with alacrity in his first international . . .' I only remember being disorientated in the new position and not really sure where to go.

People often ask me about Munich and of course the terrible events of 5 September when eight Palestinian terrorists broke into the Olympic village and made their way to the dormitory of the Israeli team. Two Israelis were killed immediately and nine hostages later perished at the airport during a botched rescue operation. The Games were suspended for more than a day and I took part in the memorial service in the main stadium.

Until then the atmosphere had been idyllic. The sun was shining, the taverns throbbing, I enjoyed shopping in town and the West Germans enthusiastically welcomed visitors from all over the world to their beautiful Bavarian city. The Olympic facilities, in my view, were only surpassed by those in Sydney. A visit to the former concentration camp at Dachau was the only reminder of a less peaceful time three decades before.

On more than one occasion I had scaled the Olympic village fence as terrorists did on that fateful morning. A tracksuit was often sufficient to gain village entry and security was low-key.

As we ate our cereal on the morning of 5 September we could see tracksuited figures climbing on buildings outside. We had no idea what they were doing – was it some prank? After breakfast it became obvious that something serious was happening as we were unable to take our normal constitutional to the shopping mall. Only when we returned to our rooms and turned on the American armed forces radio did we realise what was going on.

I suspect there was little difference being in Munich or anywhere else from then on. We watched with the world as the events unfolded. I was careful not to stand at the open window of our room only 500 metres from the siege. When the athletes and terrorists left the village we were hopeful of a good outcome. With hindsight, it seems the decision to allow the terrorists and their hostages safe passage to the airport, was expedient for the Games to continue but not good negotiating practice.

I was horrified by the events, but in my heart of hearts I hoped the Games would continue. Selfishly, I wanted nothing to interfere with this adventure. Of course things were different during the last week of the Games. Security increased exponentially and at every Games since it has been greater and more restrictive. Our aging team (I was the youngest at twenty) just fell short of a semi-final place and finished fifth.

Having gone as a reserve and ending up playing every match, I returned to Australia with a new confidence in myself, with great stories to tell and with a sense of perspective that I had previously lacked. Australia was a long way from the centre of the world. Going to Europe by flying over Asia had changed my outlook immediately. But there were still exams to pass and with a Sheffield Shield tour between my return and supplementary examinations in January, my time for reflection was short. My first selection to play cricket for Western Australia came in December and meant I would be away for most of the month. It was a thrill but with the exams looming I went with mixed emotions.

It was around that time, in the clinical years, that the medical course started to make sense. I think the challenge of putting the puzzle together made diagnosis exciting. I learned that given the opportunity the patient will tell you all there is to know in their life histories. That is 90 per cent of the diagnosis. Doctors must know how to listen and observe.

Of course young children, unconscious or non-communicating patients or those telling fantasy stories provide different problems! The theory of the earlier years started to make some sense as we came face to face with practical problems. I enjoyed talking with patients. Their lives, their details of family and work and friends painted pictures to which I could always relate. My status as a sportsman very often helped to break the ice and ease me into their confidence. Almost everyone has an opinion about sport and we all love to talk about it.

It was when studying surgery at St John of God Hospital that we students came into contact with George Pestall. We were among the first students to be taught as part of the surgical program at the private hospital. The old buildings in Subiaco with their wide verandahs were still staffed by sisters and when working at night we shared their quarters close to the railway line.

George was a surgeon in the old style. Immaculately attired he must have been horrified by the way we rocked up for rounds. On Mondays, he would greet us with his favourite saying, 'What is the price of life?' The answer, we soon learned, was, 'The price of life is eternal vigilance, Mr Pestall.' It was a bastardisation of the famous quotation of John Philpot Curran, the Irish justice and politician made in 1790: 'The condition upon which God hath given liberty to man is eternal vigilance . . .'

However, the message served this student well. For surgery one needed to prepare diligently. One needed to know the anatomy, know the pathology, be ever vigilant about the various possibilities and capable of dealing with them. In recovery, vigilance was necessary to detect any telltale signs of problems.

George Pestall exemplified this ethos in his own work. He was a perfectionist, at times pedantic and laboured but always careful and thorough. I would never follow through on that early training in surgery, but the imprint was indelible. Eternal vigilance was a message for all life, sport included. It matched lessons my father had always underlined.

As time passed I learned that there were other ways of doing things. Bryant Stokes, whom I worked with as a resident in neuro-surgery, was theatrical and far removed from the stolid efficiency of

Mr Pestall. A chain smoker, he was a slick operator and brilliant technician yet a volatile and enigmatic personality. Bryant was completely dedicated to doing his work thoroughly and well, yet in personality and demeanour a world away from George.

In medicine you deal at times with life and death. Usually good can be done, sometimes harm is caused. Such outcomes focus the mind on the process and getting it right. Thankfully, sport usually doesn't have these concerns attached to it. But if one wishes to do well then preparation, the right processes, the execution of skills and one's capacity to work co-operatively in a team all impact on the outcome.

During my time in medicine I learned more about teamwork than at any other stage in my formative years. I played team games and they required co-ordinated, co-operative efforts to produce a result, but often in the heat of battle the efforts became individualised and chaotic and the practice of teamwork was sometimes greater in perception than reality.

In a typical ward one saw the co-ordinated, co-operative efforts of doctors, orderlies, nursing staff, pharmacists, physiotherapists, occupational therapists, catering staff and many others. The contributions of all those people made for good patient care. While the doctors thought they were in charge and did in fact control critical technical areas of patient management, the nursing staff were the practical people who kept things moving. They were the glue that held everything together.

In the operating theatre the effort was necessarily even more slick and co-ordinated. Time was precious, and before, during and after procedures surgeons, anaesthetists, nursing staff, orderlies and sometimes others such as radiographers or radiologists all needed to work co-operatively. If the anaesthetist didn't get it right then the surgeon (and the patient) would find it difficult. Everyone had responsibilities that required co-operation. Teamwork was what it was all about. Without each other it was impossible to get the job done.

Successful sporting teams know about co-operation and trust and work hard at ensuring a culture which embodies these things. They don't come easily and they require work, discipline, good structures and processes to be part of the team culture. My medical training provided many good examples of such processes and structures that could be transplanted into sporting teams.

My time in medicine also gave me experience in interacting with a wide variety of people. Colleagues, patients, ancillary staff and families of patients were all part of the experience. This stood me in good stead when, as a coach, I had to deal with athletes from vastly different backgrounds, not to mention administrators, support staff and the media. I found out quickly about on the job training, too. One's formal vocational training is only the beginning of the journey to competence.

Only a few formal coaching avenues are open in Australia, but this is not necessarily a bad thing. Practical, on the job experience and knowledge in the hands of someone with commonsense is often sufficient. Many successful coaches have very little formal training but come from a physical education background or are former players.

However as coaching has become more professional and the number and character of the support staff increases, the job of co-ordinating and selecting the best and most relevant input has become more complex. Every coach given these inputs needs more than just practical experience and commonsense. My unusual training, which would be embellished by experience in politics, was in a way an ideal background for my time as a coach.

Studying medicine had given me invaluable insights into physiology, psychology, counselling, physiotherapy, pharmacology and other disciplines vital to high-performance sport. I also learned that cutting corners to fit everything in may result in inadequate preparation and a failure to do things really well. Our best lessons often come from our failures. My experience in 1972 where I struggled through supplementary exams alerted me to the fact that I had tried to do too much in that year.

After two or three years of hospital jobs I started to work in general practice. My sporting interests frequently took me away from Perth, so I worked in a variety of practices and with a mobile locum service. If there was anything in my medical background that led me to politics it was my experience in that mobile locum service. Working nights, I would visit a dozen different houses every shift. In a unique way I saw how people lived and shared their anxiety about sick or injured loved ones. Often after the consultation I would sit in the kitchen or living room to discuss treatment, medications and maybe have a cup of tea.

I worked this way for two to three years. In that time I would have entered thousands of homes in suburbs all over Perth. Sometimes the contrasts I encountered between rich and poor were very stark, far more so than the impressions I gained when door-knocking as a candidate or politician.

For me the inequality in our society was symbolised by two teenagers I met studying for university entrance. In Lockridge in the eastern suburbs of Perth a young student was trying to study on the kitchen table of a Housing Commission flat while mum prepared a meal, dad had a beer after work and the other kids watched TV in the same living area of the small flat. There were two beds to a bedroom and no desk or study facilities.

The equivalent student in Cottesloe in the western suburbs had a sizeable bedroom with a desk and bookcases full of books. Today they would have their own laptop computer. The bedroom was in a quiet part of the house with the kitchen, TV and other distractions far away. This teenager attended a private school which had access to every resource and advantage.

If we really believe in equality of opportunity in our society then Lockridge ought to have the best equipped school, most sophisticated equipment, the most experienced teachers and everything else that could redress the imbalance present from birth. Instead state schools in less privileged areas are often rundown, starved of funds and short of experienced teachers. Such contrasts were common and disturbing. My background at home had not been political although my father was pretty reactionary and tended to criticise whoever was in government. During the 1960s that meant the Liberals and Menzies.

I think my experience in the locum service helped me clarify my views on society's inequalities. I saw close up the desperation and helplessness of those without work. Surely there must be some way in which the world could be a fairer place. Surely the problems of the parents ought not be transferred to their children.

I believed equality of opportunity should be the underpinning principle of good government. Redistribution of resources to provide core services in health, education, housing and income support should be fundamental aims. Eventually I would pursue a political career. My decision to do so was not made suddenly, but over the years my interest grew. My experiences in medicine were part of my motivation.

Also I came to a stage where I did not want to continue in general practice. The alternatives were further specialisation in medicine or a change of direction. It was then that the political option became more interesting to me and a 'live' possibility. During the last twenty years at various times I have considered a return to medicine. However with absence I had become deskilled and a return seemed further away. Had I not got into coaching in the early 1990s I suspect it may have occurred. Now it is unlikely although I do enjoy discussing cases with my daughter Kate. A fourth-year medical student, she keeps a check on the state of my medical knowledge.

4

Politics — Interesting Job, Terrible Lifestyle

My decade in politics extended from 1983 to 1993. It was born in hope and enthusiasm, grew weary with travel, workload and wrangling and closed down with resignation and relief. My already healthy scepticism was reinforced at times, yet I saw at close range some very good people working very hard to make our country a better place. I saw the antithesis of teamwork in operation on some occasions but I also learned better to listen to both sides of an argument.

Interesting job, terrible lifestyle. This was the reasoning that underpinned my retreat from politics. I was in a safe seat and was confident I would eventually make the front bench. My judgment was that the price I was paying was too high. My young children were growing up and progress in the job would have exacerbated my absences from home. I never regretted the decision, indeed there was a freedom in the release. The fact that I had somewhere to go was comforting but not crucial. Life as a private citizen was pleasant compared with life as a public figure.

*　　*　　*

During the 1970s politics was never central to my life but always a thing of fascination. Gough Whitlam inspired and appealed to me. He made sense, he was an advocate of change; and for the university student of the time Vietnam was a defining issue. I, like many students, worked on polling day to elect Labor. With victory, conscription was halted and the troops came home from a futile and ill-conceived involvement. Whitlam preached values which I believed in, and education and national health, sexual equality and multiculturalism were causes worth fighting for. Inexperienced and overzealous, his government made mistakes but perhaps given more time Hayden's last budget could have resurrected Labor's fortunes. The Dismissal only served to fuel my political interest. Wasn't the governor-general supposed to take the prime minister's advice? It contradicted my sense of fairness and confirmed my anti-royalist sentiments.

I remember 11 November 1975 well as I was driving to Royal Perth Hospital listening, as was my way, to the ABC so I could capture Parliament. I heard the member for Werriwa moving a motion of no confidence in the Government. I was perplexed. Why would Gough be doing this? Unknown to me the governor-general Sir John Kerr had installed Malcolm Fraser as caretaker prime minister earlier that day. Whitlam moved no confidence in Fraser. He had the parliamentary numbers but he was no longer the prime minister.

The excitement of the rallys and the rage of Labor supporters was not matched throughout the electorate. Doorknocking for Labor in November 1975 was uncomfortable and those who read the signs knew the fate that election day would bring. Labor was overwhelmed and Fraser's tactics were legitimised in the eyes of many.

There would be one more event that solidified my political position. In 1976 in Montreal a silver medal had left me hungry to go further in Moscow. Our team, inexperienced and raw in 1976, was mature and ready for the challenge in 1980. The Moscow Olympic boycott following the Soviet invasion of Afghanistan had a very personal effect on me.

In a career of about a decade most who aspire to Olympic glory get two or three chances at it. At 28 I was at the peak of my powers as an athlete. I believed our team was well prepared and capable of going one step further than in Montreal. Alas we would never get the chance to find out if we could win gold in Moscow.

As captain of the men's hockey team I lobbied strenuously in support of the Australian Olympic Committee's right to go to Moscow. We athletes received scant financial support from the government and felt little enthusiasm for the political posturing of Fraser and Reagan. We were elated when the Australian Olympic Committee made the correct but controversial decision to attend the Moscow Games, despite governmental opposition.

A week later the Australian Hockey Association broke its promise to the players and unilaterally decided to toe the government line. The men's hockey team would not compete in Moscow. The women had given in earlier. We were crestfallen. With the threat of funding cuts held to their head and the promise of goodies for acquiescence, the hockey association succumbed. This was not a decision of principle, it was steeped in manipulation and was politically based. To me it was more of the 'all the way with LBJ' philosophy that had embroiled Australia in the Vietnam War.

Of course the question of what a Labor government would have done might be asked. I suspect it would have been much less aggressive in influencing individual sports with what amounted to bribery even if it agreed with the broad Western position. The Waterside Workers, for instance, ensured the water polo team could compete by providing financial assistance to Western Australian team members.

Close up, Liberal principles didn't impress me in 1980. While I did not know it then, three years later I would be part of the vanguard which would remove a tearful Malcolm Fraser from office. Nothing could replace the Olympic opportunity I had missed in 1980, but election night in March 1983 was a joyous one. Mind you, my *bête noir*, Malcolm Fraser, these days appears to be a much more liberal Liberal. I doubt there would be a place for him in a Howard Cabinet.

In the early 1980s I joined the Labor Party. There was a tide of political change emerging in Western Australia. Since my days at the West Perth Cricket Club my political persuasion had been known to Bob McMullan, then the state secretary of the ALP. Bob played in the Second XI and his father, Jim, was a great stalwart of the club. When Michael Beahan took over from Bob, who was heading east to become federal secretary, Michael and I discussed a parliamentary career for me over lunch. Around the same time I became involved in the Kimberley Justice Appeal which raised money to defend those charged by the state coalition government with electoral offences in the north of Western Australia. Over many months I thought about the possibility of a career in politics.

Without an extensive history in the party – I was still in my twenties – my profile in sport would certainly be a help, especially if I were a candidate in a marginal seat. Indeed without my profile I know my rise in the party would have been slower. There were possibilities for me to be involved at either state or federal level. I saw the federal scene as the 'A grade' and eventually took my chance in the federal seat of Perth, a seat that traditionally swung with government. We would need it to ensure a Labor victory.

The preselection process was one of the most exhausting and stressful experiences of my life to that time. Facing the state executive with a handful of other candidates I only just got over the line. Throughout 1982 and the early part of 1983 I was a candidate doorknocking the electorate, trying to raise funds and still doing locum work.

In February 1983 when Malcolm Fraser called the election I was working with Dr Tony Galvin in his city practice. I told him I would not be back again – the last month would be frenetic with no time for medical work. Thirteen years later Tony would be the doctor with our team at the Atlanta Olympics. He had a distinguished record of service to Australia's men's and women's teams from the early 1980s to 1996.

I knew I had a good chance of winning my seat and indeed with Labor's landslide win I became the member for Perth, defeating Ross McLean who had held the seat since 1975.

I soon found I had underestimated the lifestyle shift involved. I spent some time early on endeavouring to bring about change in the parliamentary sitting arrangements which were very difficult for those living outside the Canberra–Sydney–Melbourne triangle. Some improvements were made but the schedule for distant members was still extremely demanding. To cope with parliamentary sitting times and committee work, a Western Australian member could be required to fly across the country 35–40 times a year. Over time it was easy to become disconnected from family, home and the electorate. By the time I decided to leave politics I had been in the job nearly nine years and was separated from my wife, Frances. Much of my children's early lives had passed me by. I did not want to further lose out on their childhoods. If I stayed I could see no solution to this situation. I had to weigh up whether I had the drive to continue, especially through a long period in opposition which appeared to be coming Labor's way.

I also discovered that the backbencher's life can be pretty frustrating as much of one's time is spent defending and presenting government policy. That policy may not always be perfect, but backbenchers are expected to be team players. During the first half of my time in Parliament I still played competitive sport so had little time for political machinations within the party. However, between 1984 and 1988 I only travelled overseas twice to play hockey for Australia and as there were eleven tours in that time my sporting career was winding down.

After I finished with sport I stepped up my political activity in order to further my front bench ambitions. Unfortunately renewal was not on the Labor Party's agenda in any substantial way and like many an aging team the signs of decay were appearing in our government. After the 1990 election I would start to assess my chances of progress. I suspected time might be running out for our team.

One of the best things about Labor's front bench in 1983, when I first entered Parliament, was the quality of the people on it. Some who come to mind are Bob Hawke, Paul Keating, John Button, Neal Blewett, Lionel Bowen, Don Grimes, Ralph Willis, Mick Young, Peter Walsh, Gareth Evans, Kim Beazley, John Dawkins and Barry Jones. It was an eclectic group by any measure. What I was impressed with was their energy, purpose and desire to be part of a good government. In the early years the pace of activity was rapid. Every portfolio had its achievements and priorities and there seemed to be daily announcements. There was the Taxation Summit, the Wages Accord, the dollar was floated, Medicare was introduced; there was electoral reform, changes in Social Security, the protection of the south-west Tasmanian wilderness and even a Russian spy! The list went on and on.

Those I knew best were in the Centre Left faction of the party, where I found myself most comfortable. In the early period Neal Blewett had stewardship of Medicare, a reform which is still central to our high-quality health care system. Diligent and decent, his progressive handling of the AIDS epidemic has subsequently saved many lives. Peter Walsh as finance minister was one of the rocks of government. Parsimonious and rigorous in the best traditions of the job, this man's integrity ensured the government's fiscal position was sound. John Button was wise and experienced, and his initiatives in industry policy were creative.

The Western Australians, of course, travelled together across the country and were often in each other's company. That way I got to know Kim Beazley, who may soon become prime minister. He certainly has the intellect to be outstanding in that position. Some suggest he doesn't have the ruthlessness of Paul Keating or Bob Hawke. To me that is not necessarily a deficiency. What Kim does have is warmth and a genuine concern for all Australians. He loves his job and wants to serve his country. He is a really decent man.

Of all those I came into contact with in Parliament Paul Keating was the most charismatic and powerful. He could be utterly charming one minute and ruthlessly cutting the next. I supported his leadership challenge against Bob Hawke, and after getting to know him a little better when I was chairman of the Economics Committee of caucus, I appreciated even more that this man really wanted to lift Australia out of its conservative slumber. His vision excited me, but unfortunately for Paul Australia was not ready to go with him. The time for a change of government was closing in.

One of the most disturbing experiences that one can have in Parliament is to be persuaded by the arguments of the Opposition. It wasn't a rare experience yet the adversarial parliamentary system did not allow one to agree with, let alone support, Opposition positions. Thankfully in committees and sometimes on parliamentary delegations I was afforded the opportunity to share common views and experiences with the 'enemy' on the other side of the house.

I learned quite quickly that there were two sides to most arguments and many of those on the opposite side of the house were decent, thoughtful Australians with ideas and philosophies held for valid reasons. How could a real democrat object to unions having secret ballots? Shouldn't wealthy Australians take out private health insurance to lighten the public burden? Both parties believed in broadening the tax base, just by different means. There were always two sides to each issue.

In September–October 1990, I was the leader of a parliamentary delegation to the Soviet Union, Mongolia and Japan. Such tours afforded a practical educational experience unobtainable anywhere else. My deputy on that trip was many years my senior. The old war-horse of the National Party, Ian Sinclair proved to be a charming, hard working and fundamentally decent man. Sharing the evening in a yurt in the middle of the Gobi Desert revealed the irrelevance of our political labels and the rigidity of political ideology on both sides. Ian Sinclair had a reputation as a parliamentary head-kicker, but I suspect most of his antics were more theatrical than anything else. After all, most entertainers know how to get a headline. But only by getting to know the man better as we travelled together did I really appreciate where he was coming from. He was an agrarian socialist!

On our journey through the Soviet Union and Mongolia we could not help but compare the coherence and quality of our political system with the enormous difficulties faced by the Eastern Bloc nations emerging from behind the Iron Curtain. One of our aims was to assist the area's new parliamentarians by sharing our democratic experiences. I hope we provided some useful information. We certainly saw first hand their difficulties and also improved some of the understanding between parties within our own democracy.

While in Parliament I decided to embark on some further education. In 1990 I enrolled in a Bachelor of Arts course in philosophy and history at the University of Western Australia. Ever since I'd arrived in Canberra I had been sure to avail myself of the numerous educational opportunities available to backbenchers. The parliamentary library held regular tutorials in economics, and foreign affairs issues papers were always crossing my desk. Ministers frequently provided briefings for the various committees, but most of this related to political detail. Politics was all about making arguments and in Philosophy 100 I studied 'critical thinking' which required me to build arguments and take them apart, examining their fallacies, strengths, weaknesses and explanatory powers. I enjoyed this part of the course and found it useful when constructing arguments for debate or assessing Opposition views.

Only rarely did issues of conscience arise which required us to consider the ideological underpinnings of policy-making. Much of the time, our energy was devoted to ensuring that policy could be 'sold' to the electorate; arguments were more about how to 'sell' what was proposed than whether it was the best policy. For example, the rights and wrongs of our involvement in the Gulf War were not canvassed, but we discussed at length how much military assistance we could commit to the US coalition forces without appearing too hawkish at home or wimpish abroad.

I may seem ideological and impractical, but I thought that rather than finessing through public opinion, government ought to devote much more energy to leading public opinion. Encouraging and sponsoring informed debate and arguing cases strenuously were the stuff of real democracy envisaged by our forefathers. Paul Keating took a stance on Mabo. He believed in reconciliation between Indigenous and other Australians and tried to lead public opinion and stimulate discussion. Unfortunately, John Howard has not seen fit to follow through on Reconciliation. There is little generosity, empathy or tolerance in his position. Similarly, his government's position on refugees is without compassion. A few thousand boat people cause great distress to our wealthy nation, yet a country such as Pakistan with its poverty and difficulties harbours three million Afghan refugees with hardly a whimper.

Now John Howard tells us that economic rationalism is the best way forward. But why is it good for us? Surely economic policy must be useful in the context of the community. The term 'rational' means being rightly adapted to its purposes. Surely the purposes of government ought to entail fairness and sharing of resources? The public good and equity are relevant and important considerations. I believe that most people want to live in a decent society that shares the load as well as allows people to realise their potential. Altruism and unselfishness are not irrational and the 'greed is good' mentality can be pretty frightening.

In studying philosophy and economic history, even at undergraduate level, one develops a different perspective indeed. Adam Smith, David Ricardo and John Stuart Mill were first educated in disciplines such as philosophy and so came to economics from a different foundation – a foundation that in my time in politics seldom bore consideration. Adam Smith's 'invisible hand' that gives markets some decency required perfect access to knowledge and equal access to those markets. Our present-day sharemarket entrepreneurs usually succeed because of special or inside knowledge. These markets aren't fair or decent.

What about the rationale for our taxation policy? How far does our responsibility to the poor really extend? Should our taxation system be used as a tool for wealth redistribution? If so, how? How far should we go in interfering with the lives of strangers? Privacy issues are important, but would an 'Australia Card' really represent an infringement of liberty? Too often such issues become bogged down in political point scoring. We seldom gave such issues the time they deserved.

The present government, of course, is not without ideology. John Howard is convinced that the family is all important, yet his definition of a family is narrow and limited. Howard's great achievement is the broadening of the taxation system through the introduction of a goods and services tax, but unfortunately he chose to do so without adequately compensating the poor and those on fixed incomes or pensions. His government, like a succession of previous governments, ignores an obvious source of taxation revenue. Intergenerational transfer taxes, or death duties, are underpinned by the belief that we are all born equal. When we die, the state claims a proportion of our estate for redistribution to the most needy areas of our society in the form of funding for education, health and welfare. I remember reading debates in the British House of Commons where the right-wing Maggie Thatcher argued for death duties to be increased. Such taxes would clearly increase equity in our society, yet no political party in Australia will go near the issue. Even to raise the debate is political suicide. As for legislation to discourage tax sheltering through trusts and other vehicles it always seems to be coming. Our Labor government should have acted in this area; the Liberals are still dragging their feet.

Perhaps the thing that disappointed me most about the political process was the widely held view that the pork barrel worked. Handouts in the months before an election were calculated to paper over failures in the previous years. Looking from the outside I notice that the present government of John Howard is again this year hastily making peace with the disaffected and neglected via this well-rehearsed route.

In sport, teams prepare best for major events by thorough and diligent work over the years, rather than via last minute efforts. In the same way governments cannot ignore major areas of policy for years and expect to be supported. Usually the voters are smarter than that. John Howard claims he is now 'listening' to the electorates and responding. It begs to question as to what he was doing during the previous two years. I suspect the 'listening and caring' of today is merely a mirage.

Most Australians are capable of understanding notions of public good and what is fair. We are lucky that our public institutions have generally delivered better than many countries in education, health and justice, but increasingly the moral arguments for these institutions, for co-operation and sharing are being diluted by a 'me first' ethos and it is governments that often lead this. It is seldom that government will do other than what is popular.

As long as people who earn millions of dollars, whether they be in business, entertainment or sport, believe they are worth it, we have a problem. Excessive salaries in these areas of endeavour, just like sharemarket fortunes made overnight, are seldom earned. Worse, they are made usually at the expense of others, whether in a Nike sweatshop, or by hopeful punters who buy at the top. They are no more earned than a lottery win. Does anyone really deserve millions of dollars for being able to hit a golf ball well?

At the turn of the last century J. P. Morgan, one of America's greatest financiers and capitalists, observed that very high salaries at the top disrupt the team. They make even high-ranking people in a company see their own top management as adversaries rather than colleagues. Pretty soon the company 'we' is replaced by a 'me' ethos.

It is my view that in order for teams to function well there must be unselfishness and sharing. Given that team games are only able to be undertaken by co-operating with others, their place in our learning of values can be very important. They can influence our demeanour in business, in our families and in our civic life if we are so inclined.

Athletes competing in individual rather than team sports also must be co-operative and tolerant. They only achieve consistently with support from family, coaches, other athletes, managers and medical and paramedical staff. It is never a one-person show. Most would acknowledge the parts played by others.

It is encouraging to see the philanthropy displayed by many of our successful athletes. Pat Rafter, Ian Thorpe and Steve Waugh can all afford it, of course, and they may be embarrassed by their wealth, but notwithstanding that their generosity underpins a basic decency which is commendable. He may be an Aussie icon but Greg Norman's $100 million boat is an indulgence that displays a lack of perspective.

Professional sports teams present a great challenge for the coach. Often, spoilt and over-indulged athletes are required to perform together to produce a result. I do not profess to be an expert in such situations as money played only a small part in the Hockeyroos story, but the potential for disharmony was still there. Interestingly, as revealed in his book *Sacred Hoops*, Phil Jackson, the coach of the Chicago Bulls, appeared largely to rely on the decency and professionalism of Michael Jordan to be the catalyst for successful play in his team. Often the very best players *are* the very best players because of their understanding of these issues and their ability to make others around them shine.

Bob Hawke knew something about teamwork. His life had been dedicated to developing a consensus in the industrial landscape of

Australia. He prided himself on being able to bring people together. He realised the importance of Cabinet solidarity and consistency. If his government were to do well and survive this would have to be a crucial ingredient. Unfortunately solidarity only extended to the Cabinet. Bob only had half of it right. Little attention was given to including the backbench. Perhaps there were just too many of us. Perhaps we were seen as incompetent. I suspect it was just too difficult for Cabinet to consult and discuss issues with us, but eventually, like all those excluded we would have grievances.

Abraham Lincoln was constantly concerned with the 'enemy within'. The greatest threats to America were within society, he said, not from across the sea. Given his fate, his paranoia proved well founded. It is no less true today. Governments can decay from within when those with ambition are unfulfilled and not included. With a large caucus, those excluded from the decision-making process may be quiescent for a while but will eventually become restless. Managing this environment would be a job for an experienced coach. Alex Ferguson might have thought that the egos of Manchester United were a difficult cocktail to mix into a winning combination. I suspect that effectively managing the caucus and its tensions and stresses would be a job far more demanding and difficult!

One could take the analogy further and look at the coaching provided for caucus members. What degree of teamwork is developed and nurtured? How much individual coaching, mentoring or advising occurs? My experience tells me that there is very little of this. I cannot remember any individual mentoring ever taking place. It was the factions and their tribal character that filled the void. All too often the politics of personality and ideology overshadowed merit and clarity of purpose or thought. Certainly with more attention to individual counselling members would have functioned more efficiently.

I also believe that governments coached in process and teamwork would function better and be more inclusive. They would be more productive and better places to work. Already the demands on parliamentarians are such that electorate responsibilities and policy and law making compete for the member's time. A coach or manager could help solve such conflicts for individuals and the group. More importantly more direction is necessary regarding performances, priorities, stress management and, in general, all the skills that make a good legislator.

A member of a national sporting team has the resources of coaches and assistants to call on. Specialists are available to evaluate performances, teach mental skills and advise on every aspect of the competitive environment. Counselling in life skills and support when stressed or under pressure is available. No such resources are available for those in the team selected to run the country!

If you were to be on *Who Wants to be a Millionaire* there is no one you would want to have as your 'friend on the telephone' more than Barry Jones. Barry Jones is a fascinating character. His volcanic mind erupts with ideas and knowledge. He is passionate, always informed, humorous and cutting.

I remember soon after I arrived in Parliament, Jones speaking in the debate on the Franklin Dam in Tasmania. He described the Tasmanian politicians pushing the construction of the dam which would destroy a World Heritage wilderness as standing 'for the politics of Tiny Town . . . They stand for the world in which appeals to larger long-term issues are regarded as a form of political death . . . The issue can no longer be discussed rationally – it is a matter of faith not susceptible to rational analysis.' (Hansard, 1983 May 4, p 222) These were words I identified with!

Barry Jones stood for much of what Australia needed and needs now. He may not have been a political operator, was not Machiavelli dressed in a suit, not the man to dot the i's and cross the t's. He was a man of ideas and a man who saw what Australia might become. He was beaten by the wear and tear of the political system. He was downtrodden by lesser men who were jealous of his intellect and who thought in the short term. He was dismissed as the 'quiz kid', an interesting curiosity. What a shame.

In 1990 I stood for the ministry following our election win. In my faction, the Centre Left, I received only modest support and my name did not go forward. Barry lost his ministerial position in the same ballot. I voted for myself but I also voted for Barry. While disappointed with my loss, I could not in conscience see myself as more worthy than he was. But he was being phased out. In a more creative government he could have been one of Australia's most influential agents for change. I think it was about that time that I knew I would not be around after the next election.

I do not think I am being optimistic to expect more of our political leaders. Their positions put them in the best place to lead opinion and benefit society. Business leaders will continue to hide behind their shareholders' interests, and the self-made millionaires without shareholders to answer to often admire their makers too much to usefully contribute to society.

The capacity of national governments to influence global issues is an emerging concern in world politics. Already seen as ineffectual in local governance, national governments can only influence global issues if they work co-operatively with one another. The environment and AIDS are examples of global crises where single nation states cannot by themselves put in place effective policy. Transnational businesses and powerful media conglomerates wield increasing power on a global scale. Without governments being able to demonstrate willingness to co-operate on trade and other global issues we will be left to rely on big business and the media to show ethical leadership.

That prospect does not leave me with much optimism. However, we can all endeavour to work locally and decently to make our contributions and display as much moral leadership as possible.

Ordinary individuals without access to the media can and do usefully influence individual lives, but unfortunately larger changes seem to require wider exposure. Those who control the media seem to be easily able to justify not contributing to ethical debate.

One of the great joys of the past eight years has been the opportunity it afforded me to influence the lives of the athletes who were in our program. One can feel like one is making a difference at a micro level. The problem of macro change and influence is the greatest challenge and it is certainly the most difficult. To usefully effect such change, the media and politicians must be morally and ethically committed to seeking truth, even if it isn't good for the ratings. That unfortunately may be a bit of a dream!

5

My Early Influences

If I am an accomplished coach, it is because I have taken something from each of the experiences that have made up my life. As a student, as an athlete in both cricket and hockey, in medicine and during my time in Parliament the lessons learned, the frustrations and triumphs, the successes and failures helped to fashion a philosophy that I brought to my coaching. Though it was never my aim to become a coach, when I fell into the job in 1992 all of those episodes of my life added something to the cocktail I began to mix.

By the time I took over the Hockeyroos I had coached many teams. Those experiences gave me a measure of confidence that I could do the job. I coached my first team in 1971 when, as a second-year university student, I coached the Under 14 boys at my hockey club, Cricketers, so called because the club began in the 1930s when a group of Claremont cricketers decided to play hockey together in winter. It was a club that would be pre-eminent in Western Australian hockey until it was subsumed into the giant amalgamated western suburbs club now known as Westside Wolves. Those

Cricketers days were different times. I had played for the club since I was twelve years old and as I was playing in the senior team there was an expectation that I would help with the junior boys as senior players had helped me.

The Under 14s played on Saturday afternoons, as did the senior team. Accordingly I often wasn't able to make the game. However helpful parents filled in for me and I usually managed to catch some of the action. Three of the boys in that team eventually played for Western Australia with me and one of them, Peter Haselhurst, was to become a great friend and a team-mate in the national team in the 1980s. His omission from the team in 1988, due to fitness concerns, was in my view one of the reasons that team lost its potency in the weeks leading up to the Seoul Olympics. Before the Games started Peter was producing 'best on ground' performances for his club team in Perth. He was fit to play and should have been in Seoul. The selection process failed Peter and that Olympic hockey team.

I coached the Under 14s for two seasons. Twice I took away the state Under 21 team (in 1977 and 1978) and was coach of my club's first team in 1976, 1977 and 1978. (We were twice premiers and once runner-up.) In 1975 as a 23-year-old captain of the state senior team I also assumed the coaching duties when our coach, Merv Adams, was unable to tour with us. It was a daunting and difficult job as the team contained a number of former captains and national players who were many years my senior. With their support, in a freezing cold May in Canberra, we successfully retained our national title. Given the requirements of coaching today, it would no longer be possible to compete and do justice to the coaching role. That year we muddled through. In 1990, 1991 and 1992, when I was no longer playing, I coached teams in which my daughter Kate played. The Under 13s and the Under 15s were keen and we had some great fun. In cricket I was captain and effectively coach of both University and West Perth cricket clubs at different times while I played for them.

While my own coaching experiences played a part in shaping my approach to the Hockeyroos job, I was more strongly influenced by the ideas and practices of the many coaches I had played under. Each coach from my earliest days offered something that would fashion my philosophy and method.

As a youth at my club, Cricketers, my coach was the redoubtable Doug McKenzie. Twice a week I rode my bicycle to train at College Park in Claremont. Mr McKenzie emphasised skill and fair play and saw to it that we understood tactics and structure in our play. Often we played forwards versus backs. On Saturday's, after footy in the morning, I would ride my bicycle to Mr McKenzie's house in Dalkeith Road and we would travel to games all over Perth in his car.

That was not my first hockey experience, however. In the 1960s primary schools in Western Australia did not have hockey on the sporting calendar. You played footy in winter and cricket in summer. The girls had netball and softball. Fortuitously for the kids at Dalkeith Primary School, the Year 7 teacher, Wilfred Thorpe, had a passion for the game and devised and oversaw a hockey program for us. After school he organised training across the school ovals. We had no proper goals, just someone's shoes or a couple of jumpers placed goal-width apart. But who to play? None of the other primary schools had teams.

A resourceful Yorkshireman, Mr Thorpe organised fixtures against the senior girls colleges and with around fifteen to twenty fixtures a year we got more games than the football players who played other schools only on winter Friday afternoons. Many of us played footy too, so our week was full of sport. We played mid week, after school, and would travel very slowly to games in Mr Thorpe's old grey and maroon Plymouth. The girls colleges had perfect fields and we 10–12-year-old boys were well matched against 14–15-year-old girls.

Methodist Ladies College, Presbyterian Ladies College, Saint Hilda's and Perth College were our opponents. They jealously guarded their perfect grass pitches and required us to play barefoot.

Our footy boots would have damaged the pristine surfaces which were amongst the best I've ever seen anywhere in the world. This was not difficult for me as during my first years at primary school I usually went without shoes.

As our team became stronger we became competitive with the most senior teams at the girls colleges and many titanic struggles ensued. I was in the first XI from Year 3 and played for five years. Some of my fondest memories of the game go back to those times and the strict yet fair Mr Thorpe. He along with my elder brothers was most responsible for my involvement in this game. He took pains to involve all the players, often stopping the game to coach some point and then starting it by tossing the ball to a kid out on the wing to get the game flowing again. Sometimes he would use his redoubtable soccer skills to transfer play to someone who had been too long without the ball!

What did I love about the game? Its ebb and flow, its speed, the crispness of the skills, but as much as anything it was the passion of this man and later Doug McKenzie that drew me into the game. I had learned my first lesson in coaching. Be enthusiastic, make the training interesting, involve every player and you have a formula for enjoyment which will be the platform for learning and the fuel of commitment.

I also learned a lot from players at Cricketers as I progressed through the senior ranks. Bob Andrew, ten years my senior, who had also been a pupil of Mr Thorpe, was club captain at Cricketers and a significant mentor. Bob and I would both represent Australia at the Olympics in Munich. Tall and fast, Bob would always provide positive feedback to a young tyro.

Another Cricketers player John Goldie, who would coach me at Under 21 level, would pick me up from home and take me to games when I first played as a senior at club level. Enthusiastic and a hockey fanatic, John's love of the game was palpable. As a teenager I was well served by his advice and support. At secondary school our coach Ray House promoted me to the 1st XI at an early age. Our team at Christ Church Grammar would twice win the Independent Schools Championship. Ray House loved the game and his enthusiasm evident then remains to this day. At Christ Church I also came under the influence of the school's legendary physical education teacher Akos Kovacs. The stern Hungarian who had escaped communism following World War II set a standard of discipline and toughness that those growing up in the leafy western suburbs really needed. Akos told us tales of his life in Hungary and never allowed us to cut corners in the requirements of his progams of swimming, life saving and his beloved gymnastics. He emphasized that we should always aim to make useful contributions in whatever we undertook.

Outside school, Merv Adams was mysterious and exotic to the young teenager who showed promise in the game in the mid 1960s. He regaled us with stories of the Bombay Police and life in the subcontinent where he had spent his youth. India and Pakistan dominated the game in the 1950s and 1960s and Merv was a coach who introduced the flavour of subcontinental thinking into our game. Not to mention the fabulous curry puffs produced by his wife, Peg!

Merv had been a soccer player, rugby player, boxer and hockey player in his youth. Following his arrival in Australia from India after Partition, a motor vehicle accident led to a leg injury that curtailed his days as a player. The injury eventually caused Merv to have his hip fused, as was appropriate orthopaedic practice at the time. Subsequently, he became involved in coaching hockey with Old Modernians in Perth. In 1964 he took over from the redoubtable Cyril Carton to become Western Australia's senior coach.

Western Australia benefited greatly from the influence of subcontinental players after the Partition of India and Pakistan. Those were the days of the White Australia Policy, but Anglo-Indians were 'acceptable' black men and so came to Australia paying their own passage. Perth, as the cheapest Australian destination from that part of the world, benefited most and Western Australian hockey received their great knowledge and skill. The five famous Pearce brothers (Cec, Mel, Eric, Gordan and Julian) led the charge, but other greats included Kevin Carton, Don Smart, Fred Browne, Sandy Lovett, Tony Waters, Ivan Meade and Robin 'Bazza' Kirk. In the 1970s Terry Walsh was emerging as an international player. His parents came from the part of old India that is now Pakistan.

Merv had been a student at Martiniere College in Lucknow where he had been under the tutelage of Fred Browne, who would also come to live in Perth and coach Western Australia. His brother Terry was a renowned boxing promoter in India and Merv had some success himself as a bantamweight. His manner as a coach was firm but encouraging. He believed in solid work and we trained extremely hard, yet Merv could always make us laugh or lighten the most stressful session.

More than anything Merv helped us overcome the bogey of India and Pakistan. Eventually he convinced us that we could beat the subcontinental teams that so dominated the game. We needed to be very fit, we needed to work hard to nullify their brilliance, but most importantly we needed to believe in our own fast-developing skills. Merv's philosophy got us very close to India in the 1975 World Cup where we drew 1–1 with the eventual world champions. In 1976 it underpinned our Montreal campaign that saw us beat India twice (6–1 in the round game and on penalties in a repechage) and defeat Pakistan 2–1 in the semi-final. Sadly it was unexpected defeats by England in 1975 (after four penalty misses) and New Zealand in the 1976 final that robbed Merv and the team of the ultimate prize – a world or Olympic championship.

In 1979, I attended Merv Adams' memorial service at Christ Church in Claremont with my father. Stripped of the men's coaching job after the Montreal disappointment, Merv had been in Canada with the national women's team when he died of a heart attack. He was the most influential figure in my development as a player. Omnipresent at hockey fixtures, he often sat in his car and watched us train with our clubs. We would retire to the 'local' afterwards. In the early days he often wrote letters to me about my play, offering advice and making observations that penetrated my most stubborn beliefs and unearthed my hidden insecurities.

Merv added an international flavour to what Mr Thorpe and Doug McKenzie had given me. He opened up a world outside Australia that I wanted to visit. He taught us to work hard, he believed we could be world champions, he included me in state practices as a youngster before I deserved to be included and he pricked my conscience when it needed to be pricked. As I walked away from Christ Church with my father in 1979, I did not realise that within a year I would lose the man next to me also. My greatest mentor, my much admired and loved father.

My father died suddenly on a Tuesday. It was 15 January 1980. I was visiting a friend's house 10 kilometres from Sir Charles Gairdner Hospital where I had recently been a resident medical officer. I raced to the hospital and into the emergency department. Our next-door neighbour, Robert Campbell, was on duty. Rob and I had fought out hundreds of backyard tests in our school and university days. He looked worried when he emerged from the cubicle where they were attempting to resuscitate Dad. I had seen the scene many times before. A cardiac arrest is chaotic. It didn't look good.

Half an hour later Robert told Mum and the rest of us the bad news. I was numb. I felt guilty that I hadn't insisted that he seek help immediately when he 'fessed up to chest pain a few days earlier. How many times had I persuaded reluctant patients to go for further medical investigation by saying that if they were my father I would insist they did it immediately. Yet, two days earlier the best I could do was convince him to see someone on Thursday instead of playing golf.

He was 63. It was too young, and like most men with a new family I was increasingly appreciating how good a man my father was and how much I could learn from him. Just when we were getting really close he was taken away. To this day when I think of him I still feel empty with loss, cheated of his experience and wish that I had spent more time to know him better. Sudden death is perhaps better for the deceased but it is horrible for those left behind. I suspect had my father lived his three score and ten, my choices in later life may have been flavoured by his experience. He was someone whom I might have listened to.

My father was my harshest critic, but also my most loyal ally. Sometimes he told me I was arrogant in my attitude and careless with my preparation. He seldom got enthusiastic about my school results, my sporting prowess or my progress at university, but I was aware of him defending me vigorously when others were critical.

When I was fourteen, I remember my father admonishing me when I played hockey for Western Australia as an Under 16s school-boy. I had played well the day before, but overconfident and showing off I was sloppy in my warm-up and preparation. My poor performance, he opined, was a reflection of that preparation. The following quote from ice hockey great, Wayne Gretsky reminds me of my father's approach to me. The lesson about training is one Dad passed on to me at an early age.

One day, during the 1983 Stanley Cup, we'd just lost Game Three and we were down three games to none. We were practicing and afterward my dad came down to me and said, 'Why did you practice today?' 'Because we had to,' I said. 'Everybody had to.' 'Well you shouldn't have. You just wasted your time and theirs. You didn't give an effort.'

That was the last time we talked about it until later that summer. We were at my grandmother's house and she was out in the sun working in the garden, and my dad comes up to me and says, 'Look at that, seventy-nine and she's still working hard and you're twenty-three and when you're in the Stanley Cup finals, you won't even practice!'

Ever since then, the highest compliment you can pay me is to say that I work hard every day, that I never dog it.

Dad knew cricket. He played for Western Australia after the war when the team first started playing interstate games. An opening batsman noted for his resilience, he taught me to play cricket that way. I think it probably inhibited my natural development but I learned to concentrate. I learned the value of staying in the contest.

My father went to work before I got up and often came home after dark. A dentist, he worked hard. On Thursday afternoons he played golf and on Saturday or Sunday there was usually another round. That was his recreation. I wasn't aware that he had cancelled golf in the weeks before his death. It should have alerted us to the chest pains that took his life that evening. It took a lot for him to miss his beloved golf.

His unexpected death rocked me more than any event before or since. There was no goodbye, and in a year in which an Olympic dream in Moscow was shattered by political interference it was the defining event. The great disappointment of missing Moscow through the actions of wimpish hockey administrators paled into insignificance for me. Perhaps because of Dad's death I felt almost numb when that shock hit. My recovery from his death was slow and even today seems incomplete.

What did I learn from my dad? Work hard to achieve. Never take for granted anything in sport. Prepare yourself well for competition. Concentration is critical not only in slow-moving cricket but in the spontaneous physical sports also. Basics are the core of the great player's game. That is not a bad list to be gleaned from one mentor. There was no easy praise, no undeserved rewards yet I knew he cared, I knew he was in my court and I knew I could always count on him when I needed him. He was the rock in my life although I didn't really know it till he had gone. Isn't that so often the way?

During my career playing for Australia and Western Australia there were four coaches, besides Merv Adams, whose tutelage left an imprint on my approach. Arthur Sturgess, Don McWatters, Richard Aggiss and Frank Murray were all different yet in their time and in their way all played a role in my development as an athlete and, eventually as a coach.

When selected for the Munich Olympics as a young tyro in 1972, I had never met Arthur Sturgess. He had taken over as Australian coach before the Mexico Olympics after Charlie Morley was removed. Inheriting an experienced and talented team, Arthur had led them into the final. As the coach of silver medallists who lost to Pakistan in the spiteful final, he had unfinished business going into Munich.

Unfortunately the team selection was misguided and an aging team slipped to fifth place. Arthur, also the Victorian coach, was everything that Western Australia's Merv Adams was not. A slick, sophisticated advertising executive, he dressed impeccably and loved to eat out. The contrast was stark. Merv drove a dated Torana, often wore sandals and usually had on a tracksuit; never a suit. Rivalry between them was intense and our games against Victoria had a real edge.

Before Munich, our physical training was extremely strenuous and although I believe we were fit, we lacked solidity as a team. I think most agreed that the omission of Trevor Smith and Julian Pearce were glaring errors. Julian was unavailable but I believe ought have been persuaded to play. Regardless of that Arthur was analytical and diligent. He had a strategic sense of the game but perhaps lacked a feel for its beating heart. I was first introduced to the value of statistics when my game came under his microscope. I think Arthur offered much, but the errors in selection and team development hurt us.

Merv's strength was in motivation and he had a real instinct for the game. He wasn't a tactical strategist but more of a conceptual teacher. He believed we had to be given freedom to express ourselves within a broad framework. Perhaps he lacked the steel for tough decisions and in Montreal we underestimated New Zealand when it really counted. He was only national coach for a short stint but as my state coach and an influence in my youth he was a central figure in my development. For me and many like me in Western Australia in the 1960s and 1970s he was the heartbeat behind the game.

Don McWatters had captained the team in 1968 but had not played much because of an unfortunate back complaint. Some might say this was an unlucky precedent. At a time when the coaching job was still only part time, he came keen to learn and with an open mind. During his time we consolidated our belief that we could beat India and Pakistan and started to analyse and combat the powerful Europeans, principally Germany and the Netherlands. This was his greatest legacy and it was not an inconsiderable one.

Don was unlucky not to claim a major title as we would freakishly lose a semi-final to the Netherlands in Buenos Aires in the 1978 World Cup. By 1980 and Moscow our team had a winning feel. Fuelled by the disappointment of 1976 the team was mature, skilled and dynamic with the right injection of youth. Malcolm Fraser would prove to be our stopping point then. McWatters did not continue after the Moscow boycott, yet his influence led us into a period in which we became a consistent force rather than an occasional performer.

Richard Aggiss coached Western Australia after Merv Adams, taking over in 1976 and doing the job until he took the national position in 1981. Until 1988 he was Australian coach. A tall powerful fullback, 'Dodger', as he was known, inherited good teams which he was able to keep ticking over – not an easy task. In the early days he was a persuasive motivator, forceful and direct in his communication. He correctly chose the best players and fitted a structure around them rather than trying to change players to suit a way of playing.

Between 1982 and 1986 I believe Australia had the best team in the world. During that time we won every major competition except the Los Angeles Olympics. In the 1982 World Cup we lost a semi-final on penalties and then, notwithstanding Los Angeles, were dominant until our World Cup win in 1986. The first and only Australian men's team to win a World Cup, we were emphatically the best outfit there, often winning by large margins. There was a view that it could carry through to Seoul. Unfortunately the team unravelled in the months before the Seoul Olympics and perhaps all the contingencies weren't covered.

Going into Los Angeles, Richard Aggiss decided to use a rushing goalkeeper to block corner shots. This was innovative and had it been held back would have surprised opponents there. The tactic we developed was picked up by other teams and used against our own corner conversions. We were not sufficiently skilled or prepared to overcome our own tactic when it was used against us. Bitterly disappointed with our failure, I learned a lesson about timing. But perhaps my major criticism of Richard is that he left me alone too much. I would have enjoyed more direction as a player during that time. Often the most senior players want to be coached too. Knowing what I know now I would have sought more help myself. Communication must be two-way and I was not forthright in seeking assistance.

Frank Murray took over from Richard in 1989 and his record is the best of any men's coach in Australia. During his time the team was a medallist in every major competition. After the silver medal in Barcelona the team was unbalanced by some inflated egos who seemed to never really do justice to their potential.

I was not part of the Australian team at that time, but I can comment usefully on my experience of Murray as a club and state coach. Analytical and resourceful, Frank, who coached me between 1980 and 1986, offered me more than any of the other coaches involved at that time. Frank held strong views and argued strenuously for them. I believe his conviction in making his point often put others off, but he knew hockey well and his passion for the game was something I greatly admired.

When Chris Spice left the Hockeyroos in 1997, Frank applied for the job as one of my assistants. He was keen to be involved. I suspect that teaching mathematics had lost its gloss! While he was a little more defensive than I remembered, I was keen to use his expertise.

I knew Frank was diligent and knowledgeable and thought his certainty would balance with my other assistant Bob Haigh's more expansive ways and my own approach which lay somewhere in between.

It worked but by no means perfectly. I suspect it was harder to be an assistant than Frank expected. However, his contribution to the Hockeyroos' successes was significant. At training he was someone who understood the standard we wanted and could teach and emphasise what was important. On match day he was ideal in the stands for he saw the game clinically and yet at that distance his excitement did not distract the players as it could do on the bench. If I had my time again I would still choose Frank and Bob as my two assistants. Together they are the two people whose knowledge I value the most on hockey matters. Their contributions I always respected, even if I did not always agree with them.

PART TWO

6

So You Want
to be a Coach

What qualities do you need to be a successful coach? When I asked my players to name the qualities they thought were central to the job, the conclusions they reached very much matched my own. The qualities I describe here are the ones to which I aspired. If you want to be a coach these qualities can be ingredients that form part of a successful approach.

Coaching, as I have discovered, can be a very satisfying and rewarding experience. For me it was something I came to after a variety of life experiences, all of which helped to fashion my method. But essentially hockey was something I knew well, something that I was passionate about and something that I thought I could teach. I knew it, I loved it and I wanted to teach it.

I am often asked why the Hockeyroos were so successful. My answer is simple. They were successful because they were skilled superior athletes, well prepared, and they played together as a team. Coaching is not rocket science, but it requires knowledge of the game, a vision about where you are headed and ideas about how to get there, an intuitive, sometimes instinctive, feel for athletes and a capacity to interest and inspire. Honesty and consistency ought to pervade all you do.

What I feel I can most take credit for in developing the Hockeyroos through the 1990s was the ethic of training in the group. While we had as many as thirty hours per week in team activities (see Appendix 7), three times a week we trained at match tempo. Our training was designed to be physically, mentally and tactically more complex and difficult than match play. If there is one thing that underpins consistent achievement in sport it is consistent high-quality training. There is nothing more important. The habits of training become the habits of the match and under pressure good habits work for you.

A useful exercise for any coach is to ask the players what they believe are the elements that make up the ideal coach. For the coach the answers can be quite disturbing and challenging. It is worthwhile, however, because it concentrates the coach's mind on how best to reach the group of athletes. I found it equally useful to ask my players what sort of ideal player they would like to have playing next to them. This can reveal a great deal about the athletes, but equally it ought to remind the players of their obligations to one another and the team.

I conducted such enquiries a few times during my coaching tenure with the Hockeyroos. The results, regardless of the player groups, were revealing and remarkably consistent. The qualities of the ideal coach could be distilled into five main points: a coach should be knowledgeable, diligent and willing to learn, prepared to listen and flexible, consistent and, finally, must be honest. In many ways these five points are a very good template for any aspiring coach, leader or teacher.

1 A COACH SHOULD BE KNOWLEDGEABLE

Players want a coach who knows the caper. Most can bluff their way through something for a short time but pretty quickly players realise what the coach has to offer. Every coach differs in their technical, tactical, physiological and psychological competencies. Deficiencies in any area can be overcome by using experts to assist and provide input, but without a broad grasp of every aspect of the task the coach will flounder and struggle to maintain group confidence and respect. For those without access to experts, the library will become your best friend. I have always believed you can do anything and know anything if you can read.

But knowing what is required is not enough. The coach must stand for and require quality. This is critical in creating an environment of consistent quality and reproducible performances.

When I came to the job with the Hockeyroos I came with confidence in my background in hockey, but without any experience of coaching a national team. I had not even been an assistant coach to a national team, but, as a player, I had been close to a national team for many years. Seldom is anyone promoted into a position having experience of the job. You are assessed as having the requisite skills or capacities, and then with trust and an attitude of wanting to learn you work out how best to do it.

I remember in the 1983 federal election campaign one of the criticisms that was thrown at aspiring prime minister, Bob Hawke, was that he was insufficiently experienced as a parliamentarian. The assertion was patently absurd. There is no way to really assess one's readiness for such a job. While parliamentary familiarity could help, Hawke's long career in public life clearly justified his candidacy. Such criticism in any sphere usually represents a desperate attempt to discredit, rather than a meaningful objection. My appointment as Hockeyroos coach was criticised for the same reasons. I was an outsider.

Coming from outside can be either a great advantage or a disadvantage depending on the attitude of the applicant. If change is required often someone from inside may be reluctant. However someone from inside may also have seen the problems and be able to quickly get on with changing it! The outsider is often not constrained by the old ways or practices and loyalties. However for an outsider it can take some time to assess the dynamics of the place and assess what is required. In the end the appointment should be contingent on the applicant's capacity to either maintain the status quo or effect change. My brief was to effect change!

I understand that when I first applied for the job with women's hockey there was considerable discussion about my coaching credentials and experience. The vice-president of Women's Hockey Australia, Shirley Davies, was on the selection panel along with Joyce Brown, Australia's outstanding netball coach. Shirley recently told me that Joyce confidently endorsed my candidacy but added a caveat, 'If you want to go to the moon he can take you there but it will be a very bumpy ride.'

Is it presumptuous to coach a code in which you don't have hands on experience? My response would be that there are areas of specific technical and tactical knowledge that are not beyond learning. Only once one is in a position to grasp those technical and tactical aspects should the judgment be made as to whether it is feasible to coach a code in which you have little background. Experience in other codes and other countries would suggest it is possible. Certainly in the United States expert coaches are rarely former players as seems to be the norm in many Australian sporting codes.

My position for 2001 at the Fremantle Dockers is *not* as coach of the team. Rather, I am an adviser on high-performance teams and how they operate. I have wide experience in that area and hope some of my ideas and views will be relevant. For me the exercise will be one of learning about the technical and tactical aspects of the job in a different sport. I expect to learn at least as much as I share with Fremantle! I took the job because Fremantle is the worst performing team in the league, having never made the finals. This is a position in which I hope I can learn a great deal. I do not expect that it will be easy or quick to change that environment.

At the moment, I do not have an interest in coaching another code and I fear it might be too late to do so, yet I believe that such a task would not be beyond me. In the meantime, before my next big challenge, I continue to learn.

2 A COACH SHOULD BE DILIGENT AND WILLING TO LEARN

You have to watch the tapes, scout the opposition, be organised and prepared for training, for meetings, for matches and social commitments. No coach can expect their players to display these characteristics without exemplifying them by their own behaviour. The coach must try to be as knowledgeable as possible. They should question the specialists, read the research, observe opponents, watch and learn from different games and different coaches, thereby continually adding to the experiences of the group.

Rod Macqueen, the coach of the Wallabies, the Australian rugby union team, has as one of his favourite dictums a piece from the Chinese warlord Sun Tzu: 'Knowing yourself and knowing your opposition, in every battle you will be victorious . . .'

Some of the best opportunities for learning occur at coaching conferences and workshops at which coaches from various disciplines are present. Often reluctant to share information within their codes, coaches are usually willing to share their expertise across codes. Similarly at sports nights and presentation evenings and at informal dinners most of the best coaches seem to be looking for an edge.

David Parkin, Dennis Pagan and Kevin Sheedy from Australian football, Wayne Bennett from rugby league, Rale Rasic from soccer, John Buchanan from cricket, Charlie Walsh from cycling and Don Talbot from swimming are some of those with whom I have been able to share experiences, ideas and thoughts. This is always valuable.

During 1999, we organised the Hockeyroos into a number of managing committees. While committees are not always the best way to achieve outcomes efficiently, the idea was that in each of the committee areas the players would be responsible for input and ideas that could increase the team's knowledge or assist in improving our program.

One of the committees was the Lateral Inputs Committee. Its responsibility was to help us learn from other sports. Newspaper and magazine articles, television programs and videos from other sports were used to promote discussion and stimulate interest in other ways of doing things. This committee helped organise guest speakers and outings to sporting events. While the athletes were training in Perth we attended AFL football matches, NBL basketball games and NSL soccer fixtures.

These outings led to much discussion, both at the matches and in later sessions. The value was variable. Some athletes were not interested in some events, but almost always lively debate ensued and progress was made in analysis and appreciation of the general principles that can work in all sports.

While technology has greatly improved our ability to view the action in our games via video, it does have its limitations. Others can edit and do so much of the hack work for the coach. However, regardless of how technically competent one's program becomes, there is still a requirement for the coach to view the game. Only then can the coach really monitor what is relevant and what isn't. Nobody else can do this with the same degree of discernment. Likewise reviewing games with assistant coaches always leads to worthwhile discussion and progress.

There is no substitute for watching the full game live, in my view. It is only after the coach has done this that video should be used to review the game. Any team of athletes wants to feel that their coach is up to date with current trends and ideas as well as being on top of every incident on the field. There are no short cuts for this!

I always endeavoured to include relevant and recent information in my messages to the team. I remember well in 1994 at the World Cup in Dublin after our first match loss to Russia telling our distressed group that such shock losses often occurred. Indeed Italy were due to play Brazil that week in the 1994 Soccer World Cup final having lost their first match in the preliminary rounds. Italy overcame that early setback and progressed unbeaten through the tournament to the final. Relevant and recent parallels always proved useful.

3 A COACH SHOULD LISTEN AND BE FLEXIBLE

Players must be able to express their views. A coach without the capacity to listen will find the job tough. Equally, however, this does not mean any suggestion gains acceptance. There must be compelling arguments before a player's view changes a coach's approach. Listen first and then debate the merit of the suggestion is a good rule. The athletes, in the end, are the instruments through which strategy is enacted. If they don't 'own' the strategy then enacting it will be difficult!

The team's program, training and tactics, indeed every aspect of the team environment, must be able to be adjusted to handle the unforeseen or unpredictable. During a match a failing strategy often requires revision. Be ready to react and willing to use your judgment, but be wary of overreaction. Sometimes it is better to do nothing rather than overreact. Restraint can be a great virtue in coaching, but even more important is a strategy and approach which is primarily focused on 'us' and not 'them'.

Anyone who thinks they know me will tell you that I always think I am right! I am an opinionated know-all, stubborn and argumentative. I think they are only partially right for those who know me best know that while I will contest strenuously ideas and views I disagree with, I am also always listening. I think I am a user of good ideas and I am absolutely convinced that the more people in the group contributing, the more likely we are to get to the best way of doing things.

Perhaps one of the earliest and best lessons I learned from the Hockeyroos sports psychologist, Corinne Reid, was that sometimes I should listen more and say less when athletes were bravely expressing their views. I'm sure I was still sometimes guilty of talking players down, but I hope I improved. Of course, with fellow staff members discussions often became heated, but never vitriolic. The airing of passionately held ideas was almost always positive in the end. The training program, tactics and all that go with them are best owned by the whole group. Many discussions must take place before you can settle on what is best for the team.

The competitive environment almost always requires an ability to handle unexpected problems or events. Sometimes the best laid plans can quickly fail. It is always necessary to have contingency plans or to be able to ad lib when required.

Whenever a new strategy or idea is contemplated it is very useful to consider the possible pitfalls as well as the advantages. Discussion within the group of both pluses and minuses is very helpful in smoothing out the wrinkles that invariably occur when embarking on new territory.

Early on in the program we decided that in order to prove to ourselves that we could be flexible we would deliberately change our playing structure during a match. Such predetermined actions enforced a belief that we could do it and demystified the prospect of changes in style and position for individuals. Although many of the things we tried were never used in the major competitions, they all served to develop our confidence that we could handle whatever came our way.

4 A COACH SHOULD BE CONSISTENT

Coaches principally do three things in their interaction with athletes: reprimand, redirect and reward. These interactions best occur at the point of error or success and as far as possible the coach should be consistent. Experience indicates that athletes focus mainly on a coach's negative messages. From time to time objective measurement by an outsider of interactions helps evaluate our progress in this area.

During the 1994 season, the team feedback was that the coaches, myself and my assistant, Chris Spice, were too directive in our comments from the bench. A number of players said they were often distracted by directive comments such as 'Pass right' or 'Run it', while they were playing. This was particularly so if they were playing close to the bench.

If there was a sizeable crowd, the remarks would not be of such consequence as they often would not be heard, however, those on the bench waiting to enter the game were also affected. At the time we were on tour in Europe and mindful of the criticism, Chris and I endeavoured to curtail our directives from the bench.

Unfortunately as the tour moved from the continent to England the criticism remained. Corinne Reid undertook to monitor our remarks. After one match played at Lilleshall before a small crowd, some of the players again expressed the criticism. When we discussed the match Corinne came forward with some fascinating figures.

During the game Chris and I had made over two hundred and fifty positive comments, thirty neutral directives and fifteen negative remarks. Many of the negative comments were simple 'Oh no!'s or remonstrations with the umpire. This was not a profile of directive or negative interaction, yet the recollection of the players was very different to the reality.

The point I am trying to make is that those in the thick of the contest or indeed under stress in competition or at training tend to hold on to the negatives more than is useful. Often following a meeting with a player one hears feedback which contradicts one's sense of the tone of the meeting altogether. Sometimes there is real value in two coaches meeting with the player or even getting another player along to balance the message.

In February 2000 Rod Macqueen, the very successful Wallaby coach, called me to say he would be in Perth and expressed a desire to attend one of our training sessions. He duly arrived and spent the afternoon watching us train. That evening over a meal I asked him for his impressions as we shared some ideas as coaches often do. He said he had heard I was a hard bastard and that what had surprised him most was how encouraging and positive we coaches had been during the session. I'm sure the players would not have agreed as it had been a pretty tough session in the heat of February!

What is important though is that we coaches must uphold

standards and require them of the athletes. Sloppiness and short cuts must be identified and redirected or reprimanded. An important caveat here is that I believe there is no place for abusing players in any way. The message can be made without ever needing to denigrate or humiliate players. Those players who do not want to be there or who continually transgress will be removed over time by their own actions and behaviours. Equally, however, praise and encouragement are absolutely essential when earned and appropriate. Every player, even the greatest champion, responds to positive encouragement and feedback. This can be the fuel of better and greater effort every time.

5 A COACH SHOULD BE HONEST

Honesty is perhaps the most critical commodity a coach must have. Players dislike criticism and many are defensive or in denial. Their family and friends and the media are seldom objective, honest or even expert in their assessments. The coach must not fall into this trap. Objective and expert, the coach is there to provide the platform on which changes in quality and quantity are measured. Many coaches make the mistake of wanting to be liked by the athletes.

The coach worth their salt will develop in the team an appreciation of objectivity and truth that transcends ego and personal frustration. Then they will have a team that is fixed on the process of what is happening and not on what others may think is happening or what the media might say about them.

When I took over the Hockeyroos in 1993 there was an expectation that at the end of each year the coach would write a report to the selectors about each of the members of the national squad. I initially felt obliged to continue this tradition. It did serve a useful purpose as the selectors did not see all the matches or all the training and practice sessions. Given this, the reports served as a useful starting point in discussions and provided the selectors with essential background information.

It seemed to me, however, that there could be another, more useful, purpose. My report to the selectors would go to the players also and serve as a catalyst for discussion on their game. The response to this was interesting and proved beneficial. In a variety of ways over a period of time the players raised their reports with me. Over time they began to know that I would tell them what I truly thought. If he or she is open and honest yet constructive and outlines a way ahead, the coach can seldom go wrong. One gets into trouble when one does not have a candid dialogue with players. After a while my reports were written directly to the players and I sent a copy to the selectors!

In 2000, as we progressed through the Olympic-year program, some Hockeyroos were not playing to their potential. Both Katie Allen and Juliet Haslam were left out of the team for the Champions Trophy tournament in Amsterdam. Most players viewed selection in the team of eighteen to go to Europe as a sign they were still in the running to be selected for the Olympics. Only sixteen players would go to Sydney. However I told both Katie and Juliet that although they were not in my team for Europe there would be further opportunities for them to press their claims. Both responded with quality performances and in the end won their places in the Sydney team. The disappointment of being omitted from the Champions Trophy team perhaps provided the impetus for them to redouble their efforts.

I am reminded of the apposite saying of Norman Vincent Peale, the pastor who in 1952 wrote the bestseller *The Power of Positive Thinking*: 'Most people would rather be ruined by praise than saved by criticism.' These words succinctly outline one of the dilemmas of the modern sportsperson. The coach, I believe, has little choice and is almost invariably served well by candour.

Occasionally, of course, one is allowed a little freedom. For example, when commenting on a new hairstyle or choice of clothing one must be careful. 'Interesting choice,' is a better option than the complete candour of, 'God! You look weird!' Equally one may decline to comment or perhaps exaggerate praise when that may be important to lift an athlete.

Finally allow me to make one more remark concerning the attitude of good teams. I have often heard people suggest that great and dominant teams are arrogant and almost supercilious in their demeanour, and dismissive and disrespectful of their opponents. Boxing, athletics and swimming provide individual examples of such attitudes on a regular basis and often we see the sentiment betrayed in the pronouncements of lesser teams with short-term successes. And I suspect sometimes athletes use the word 'arrogant' incorrectly, not knowing its exact meaning, when they are looking to describe their optimism, confidence or aggression.

Seldom does one hear such sentiments emanate from quality teams like the Wallabies or, at a club level, Essendon. These teams respect the game, their opponents and the vagaries of competition. They can be confident, assured, aggressive, competitive and optimistic, but they are never arrogant.

Indeed it is my view that the greatest quality of the Hockeyroos was their humility. For it is this quality that underpins a willingness to learn and improve. With it goes apprehension about performance which in the best athletes is often the fuel for diligent training and a disciplined lifestyle.

Those who get success too easily or are paid excessive amounts before they have earned it are in danger. The best always remember how they got there rather than get carried away in the razzamatazz.

The coach who can engender an approach that values learning and stresses continual development will be on the way to creating a group in which humility is one of the core values. It is a critical core value in my view.

7

Never Defend a Lead

Leading can be as difficult as being behind. The error that competitors make in both of these situations is to think about the outcome rather than paying attention to what they must do for the rest of the game to secure the desired result. Attention to outcome over process can be fatal. This is a message that any novice student in sports psychology will learn at their first lecture. Yet many participants continually make this mistake to their detriment.

To the media, administrators, sponsors and the general public, the focus is always on winner and loser. This way of thinking becomes seductive and difficult to resist. It is a measure of the best athletes and the best teams that they are able to keep their heads and resist the temptations of the 'outcome obsession'.

The mental strength or discipline that is entailed in staying on task can be learned and embellished once the players are aware of the problem. By reminding them, asking them to relive past experiences and challenging them with new experiences this can occur.

At almost every training session of the Hockeyroos we played small games that required the players to compete with fatigue impacting on their performance. Often one team had a more difficult task, for example, two goals to defend or fewer players, yet they were expected to learn to continue with the task regardless of the distractions.

Whenever possible we played in tournaments where invariably one comes to the 'must win' matches. Whenever teams visited Australia we tried to incorporate into the tours a three- or four-way tournament with a final. Experience of 'must win' matches is invaluable.

We set aside times to discuss situations in which we had played 'must win' games both with success and failure. Videos of such performances can serve to remind us of our feelings and demeanour. We also often watched 'must win' games from other sports and tried to apply the experiences to our situation by empathising with the participants.

During 2000, as Sydney loomed closer, I remember one such session. We were watching a tape of the European Soccer Championship final between Italy and France. With only a minute to go the commentators had anointed the Italians as victors. Enter Francesco Totti. He had been a significant contributor, yet with only seconds left he chose to saunter back to position as his team-mate played the ball through to him.

Totti was offside. The resulting kick by the French goalkeeper Fabien Barthez fell to a Frenchman who scored to tie the match and send it into overtime. France subsequently won the game in extra time. Perhaps not even noticed by most spectators, Totti's moment of sloth proved crucial. For had he not been offside the kick-in taken by Barthez would have occurred thirty metres deeper in French territory and the outcome may well have been different.

The Hockeyroos coined the phrase 'doing a Totti' as we entered the final phase of our preparation for Sydney. It served as a useful reminder for many when they found themselves drifting in similar situations. Totti's effort to get onside ought to have been just as great whatever the situation and whatever his state of fatigue. That was the standard we were looking for. What had he been thinking with only seconds to go in the match?

So we come to the maxim 'Never defend a lead'. I am wary of coaches who talk about closing up a match or changing one's approach in response to the scoreboard. Such measures often back-fire and can be more trouble than they are worth. Critically they focus attention on the score and outcome in a way that undoes any task-orientation that has been established.

Accordingly, the whole emphasis of our way of playing was on being proactive rather than reactive. We aimed to aggressively defend and force errors and to play with a tempo and tone that dominated our opponents. The game plan was simple and uncomplicated. We would play relentlessly all of the time. If we were able to maintain momentum and tempo we would break our opponents down and eventually fracture their belief and their game. If indeed they were able to resist and overcome us then we knew we had played a worthy opponent who was better that day.

How often do we see a team try to defend a lead and come unstuck? Last season soccer team Perth Glory forfeited a 3–0 half-time score in the National Soccer League final to lose on penalties. Australian soccer similarly succumbed to Iraq in the vital World Cup qualifier in 1997. The Adelaide Crows won an AFL premiership when more than once they looked to be down and out in the final series. There are endless examples. Did the teams that led in these cases become anxious about the result and lose sight of their task. I suspect that these sorts of explanations are appropriate. Perhaps they got ahead of themselves and started to think about the celebration before the win was achieved.

What happens to teams is that they become very determined about defending in such circumstances but forget about attack. They lose form and structure and suffer diminished endeavour when they get the ball and so it keeps coming back at them and pressure mounts. Eventually if their grip starts to slip they can lose form totally and disintegrate.

Our strategy was to play our undifferentiated game all the time regardless of the situation. If we were down, we would be aggressively seeking to score. If we were up, then another goal would further crush our opponents and put them out of the game. Our strategy always revolved around a parsimonious defence, and by playing and defending in the other team's half we were doing what came naturally.

I hated the tactic of closing the game down and wasting time in the corner of the field. Done too soon or too often it was distasteful and against the spirit of the game. Likewise I always felt that if we got near the scoring zone we should always try to score rather than play 'smart' possession around the perimeter. Such tactics in my view are undesirable and ought to be outlawed.

My reason for this way of playing was to give certainty and task-definition to the players. Not only was our method enterprising and good for the game, it served the purpose of being appropriate whether we were behind or in front. We trained and played that way all the time; it was our trademark. We aimed to get a lead then we aimed to increase it; we would never defend a lead.

Every team has to work out its own way of playing. The coach and players must devise a strategy or game plan that they believe can work for them that best utilises their resources and appropriately competes with the opposition.

I always found it very useful observing and reading about the way our opponents approached the game. I noticed that there were fundamental differences in the way teams played from country to country. Essentially, there were European, Asian, African and American approaches to contend with. Each in its own way reflected part of the culture and experience of those nations.

Our most significant American opponent during the past decade has been Argentina. While USA and Canada were often contenders they did not have the quality of Argentina whose hockey play was very similar in style to the way they approached their national obsession – soccer. Enigmatic, emotional and highly skilled, yet at times lazy, they play at a slow tempo.

Their game is essentially a counter-attacking one in which the mistakes of opponents in midfield or attack produce many of their best opportunities. During the time I coached, Argentina had a few outstanding players who technically were the equal of any in the world. Karina Masotta and Luciana Aymar were very fast and skilful, able to beat opponents effortlessly one on one and then able to involve team-mates in making goal chances or scoring themselves.

In Vanina Oneto, a player lacking that crucial element of pace, they had a very good finisher and corner winner. Her strength on the ball and desperation in the scoring circle were her compensation for lack of speed. Cecilia Rognoni was fiery and tough, yet a skilled tackler and intercepter and possessed superb passing. As a penalty corner hitter she perhaps lacked consistency, but given more work in this area she could be anything! Magadalena Aicega in deep defence was quick, composed and had great judgment in her tackling and intercepting.

Argentina twice played us in major competition finals, the World Cup in 1994 and the Sydney Olympics. Each time, I believed, they had the capacity to beat us if we were not vigilant.

Their counter-attacking style always became more convincing as time passed in a game and there was no score on the board. In 1994 we did not break the deadlock until well into the second half even though until then they had rarely threatened our goal. In Sydney, I think they were a little too pleased to have made the final and had we taken our chances we should have settled the encounter earlier.

I always wondered how difficult they might be if they played a little more aggressively and offensively. It would be interesting to try to change their style, but I suspect the methods and habits of thousands of club matches (not to mention tens of thousands of soccer matches) infect the psyche of all involved. There is no doubt that Argentina are capable of breaking teams open; they beat New Zealand 7–1 to qualify for the final in Sydney. It is rare, however, that they take that chance.

Hockey is a game where a watertight defence and outstanding

goalkeeping can bring about success and Spain's gold medal in 1992 was a case in point. No doubt a supportive home crowd played their part, but the spirit and discipline of the players underlined what can be done with limited resources. The team contained some very good players but did not have the ability to win by playing offensively. By using their counter-attacking game and ensuring safety at the back, they achieved a remarkable gold medal win. I suspect a few breaks and being underestimated by opponents helped.

Like Spain, the Germans play a game that is organised, disciplined and based on possession and counter-attack. My impression is that the Germans take the view that the game starts with the points being shared and the score 0–0. Their aim is to not forfeit their point and to try to pinch their opponent's point when they overcommit themselves. This is best done by having as much possession as possible and only attacking or penetrating when it is most advantageous. It is a no-risk strategy and the rigid disciplines in defence entail one on one marking with very little flexibility. Listening to coaches during matches and reading various interviews have helped confirm this impression.

Germany's successful coach Paul Lissek made these comments when quizzed in an internet interview about his defensive methods in 1998. 'There is no point in going forward and scoring three goals but end up losing 4–3. I believe the defence has to be reinforced and attack begins from deep cover. Therefore speed is the crucial element. You have to make your counter-attacks fast and catch your opponents on the break every time you get a chance.'

Similarly, the Perth Glory's successful German coach, Bernd Stange, betrays his origins in his media comments regarding the Perth team's performances. In the early part of 2000 he said in the *West Australian*, 'I gave the players strict orders to defend as a unit which meant even our forwards coming back to help out – and they did it really well. I told them to be patient and wait for chances with counter-attacks. They came and we had many possibilities to score again and were unlucky not to do so.'

Certainly, their method has brought the Germans a lot of success and in soccer until recently they were always a contender. Hockey and soccer are games in which scoring is intrinsically difficult. In hockey the limited scoring area, small goal, defence from all players and a goalkeeper with special powers all play a part in making scoring difficult. In soccer the large ball that's easily blocked, walls of players defending, and a goalkeeper with special powers as well as numbers in defence can make scoring extremely hard.

Given the low-scoring nature of hockey it is not surprising that the careful Germans adopt a low-risk strategy, but I cannot help but wonder if they are not selling themselves short as during my time they produced some of the most skilled and brilliant players in the game. Stefan Blöcher was one of the most outstanding athletes I have seen. Huge in stature, fast and skilful on both sides, he was a consistent goal scorer. His injury in the semi-final in Seoul and subsequent absence in the final perhaps cost Germany an Olympic gold medal.

The German women only once made the victory dais in major competitions during my time with the Hockeyroos, yet they were always difficult to play against and probably under-performed given their level of talent. Britta Becker, Heike Lätsch and Natasha Keller were all world class, but perhaps each lacked vital elements in their games. I always felt the Germans were victims of their own caution and somewhat uncertain about themselves when playing us.

In both 1996 and 2000 they started well and seemed on course to become Olympic medallists only to lose their way. I was often of the view that they appeared too wedded to the score and not analytical enough about what had actually happened in their games. They occasionally appeared to underestimate the lesser teams and thus were surprised and beaten by teams like China that were below them in ranking and standard.

The Dutch lacked nothing in confidence and belief, yet at times their bravado appeared ill-placed. I well remember the crowd and players celebrating jubilantly after their 5–1 semi-final win against

Germany in Utrecht in 1998. To the Queen standard 'We are the Champions' they swaggered around the pitch as though their job was completed. This performance did much to steel a determined group of Hockeyroos sitting in the stands for their encounter with the Dutch in the final.

For the Hockeyroos, there were few more gratifying sounds than the final whistle two days later. We had beaten the Dutch team convincingly in spite of a very noisy parochial crowd and an unfortunate goal conceded in the first thirty seconds of the match.

I had not even taken my seat on the bench when a couple of minor errors snowballed into a goal front melee that yielded a scrambling messy goal. The football stadium in Utrecht was overflowing with orange-clad supporters in raptures about their team's beginning. Perhaps they anticipated they would overrun Australia as they had done with Germany a day or so earlier. Given the pulsating and hostile environment our performance that day was truly exceptional.

It can be an advantage to be down sometimes as it can give real definition and purpose to the team. I believe such was the case that day when the Netherlands scored fortuitously in the first minute. Almost immediately the players went about recovering the situation and we occupied ourselves making scoring chances – the thing we were best at.

In 1999 I cut the following quote out of the newspaper. I believe it reflected how I had felt that day: 'There's something about certain football teams that elevates them beyond the rest and they never give in. They were 1–0 down and there was not a person in Old Trafford who panicked. The crowd was quiet, the players got on with it and I waited.' That was a proud Manchester United manager Alex Ferguson, speaking after his side clinched the English Premier League with a 2–1 win over Tottenham.

By Sydney many were predicting that the Netherlands were better than us and would win Olympic gold, but our whitewash of them was not so surprising. It was my view that in Utrecht they had their best chance to beat us, and their best team. No new players had emerged in the two years since Utrecht to surprise us, and Jeanette Lewin, one of their best, had retired. Given the return to the Hockeyroos of Jenny Morris and the emergence of Angie Skirving and Rachel Imison, the balance was heading in the other direction.

While the Dutch were more likely to hurt us and more adventurous in attack, their pattern entailed many elements of the Germans' play. Strength was crucial in protecting the ball, delivering hard passes and physically imposing themselves in our space. Their excellent corner conversions were the linchpin of their game. A long list of powerful hitters and flickers have dominated the Dutch men's game and also usually have been evident in the women's game.

The British game has always been built on defence. The players are fit, fast and robust, yet without the finesse and polish of continental Europeans, much in the manner that British soccer lacks the finesse of the continental game. Rugby offers a parallel: the British are defensive kickers, the French and Oceanic teams run the ball more and play a more expansive game.

The British women's game has been well endowed with numbers and a school-based development program yet the senior teams have never made it to the top of the podium in major competition. While the British complain that they must compete as England, Scotland and Wales, it has always seemed to me that this entails as much advantage as disadvantage. Certainly many more players are able to be exposed to the international game. In Australia we would be pleased to be able to field a couple of teams in international competitions! It certainly doesn't hurt to develop depth.

At a distance it seems clear that India and Pakistan need some organisation, discipline and tactical support to utilise what is still the most gifted player group in the world. As long as their pride continues to overwhelm their willingness to learn and be contemporary, they will not realise their potential.

India and Pakistan's success, or lack of it, may be crucial to hockey's long-term survival in those countries. Without successful teams a billion people will no longer crowd around television sets to cheer on their heroes. Many have already switched their allegiance to cricket as subcontinental performances at international hockey competitions have declined.

Yet the players of the subcontinent are exquisite to watch. Their quickness, fluency, superb skills at passing, changing direction, and deception are unparalleled. I believe strongly that with a solid structure and organised approach they could once again be pre-eminent. My fear is that time could run out for the game in the subcontinent.

I do believe that a Eurocentric International Hockey Federation has subtly caused a diminishing of India's and Pakistan's chances of succeeding internationally. The removal of the offside rule, ostensibly a move to make the game more attacking, has had the reverse effect and diminished subcontinental chances of penetrating strong defences. Urgent reconsideration of such shifts on the field are required. Equally the continued emphasis on a power game has not enhanced India's and Pakistan's chances. However most to blame is their unwillingness to seek help from outside. One could say that in hockey pride does come before a fall!

The South Africans only emerged early in the last decade after years of isolation. Their game has a characteristic strength and physical side that is seen in their rugby and cricket. In both men and women's hockey they can be very good. Initially they were very keen to savour the international game and they always proved competitive if a little unpolished. The failure of the South African Olympic Committee to support their men's hockey team to compete in Sydney was very unfortunate. Their record suggests they would have acquitted themselves well.

The game has much potential to grow in Africa. In the 1960s and 1970s Kenya's Asian population helped to produce very good teams and more recently Egypt have been competitive. In 1980 Zimbabwe won a surprising gold in women's hockey in the boycotted Moscow Olympics. The future of the game in South Africa will, I believe, hinge on involving a wider base of athletes from all groups and overcoming the tensions inherent in such moves.

Given our proximity it is surprising that there is not more similarity between ourselves and the New Zealanders. Their game is much more dour and defensive than ours, and while the right-sided excesses of the past have declined, at times old habits are recognisable in their play. They could improve their results by playing more aggressively.

Unfortunately their 1976 men's team triumph has not been followed by any significant growth in the game. They often have skilled players but seem to lack depth and consistency. In the men's game they have struggled to stay in the top ten in recent times. Their small player pool is probably to blame, but I suspect they have the ability to be a force again.

In the women's game the story has been better and in recent years they have been a top six team. Perhaps in Sydney they made the mistake of believing too much of their own publicity rather than paying attention to what was happening. In the end a sixth place was flattering for them, and although they may have had misfortune against Spain that was not the case against Germany or China. In both cases they were very fortunate to take points against teams that dominated possession and scoring chances.

Their team had pace and skill, but by being too defensive, they could never sustain any attacking pressure. Had they asked for more from their wing defenders they may have surprised themselves. Likewise in Anna Lawrence they had a skilled and dangerous forward, yet she spent too much time in her own half. I suspect they were victims of their own caution and reluctance to take chances. They played this way throughout the Olympics and had nearly the most shots recorded against them of any team. I wonder if they did not bring that upon themselves.

So we move on to Australia. Australian teams do have a distinctive style, but it is not, as most overseas players seem to believe, homogeneous. The great advantage of our geography is that in each of the population centres there is the capacity for innovation and experimentation.

It was never my intention that all women's hockey in Australia should be played the same way. I believe we can best encourage diversity and difference by allowing coaches of state and city teams to do things their way. The mix of experiences and methods in structure, training and competing will build resilience and flexibility. In any area of modern life these qualities are essential.

There are, I believe, core characteristics of Australians in sport, and hockey serves as a good indicator. Generally we are aggressive and win-orientated. Europeans see our game as technically inefficient and physically demanding. I prefer to view this as a commitment to working hard to make things happen rather than slowly choking the opposition or waiting for mistakes. In hockey Australia has generally been one of the highest scoring teams in both the men's and women's game. We generally avoid one on one marking and defensive tactics. Our solution to the defence dilemma is aggression in tackling and error forcing.

Compared with many countries Australians play with enthusiasm and passion, take risks and try to win. In the past (and even today) we have perhaps underestimated the value of teamwork, organisation and discipline. These last three things I worked very hard to include in the Hockeyroos' game.

Finally, and I think crucially, we have always been good learners. Perhaps this reflects the cultural cringe of earlier times. I prefer to think it is merely an appreciation of what is good and a desire to emulate it. Throughout the 1960s and 1970s we learned much from the dominant Asians and the good European teams. Invariably we worked at putting what we saw overseas into our game.

Hockey from India and Pakistan first came to our shores via migration after Partition, but we continued to learn throughout the second half of the last century via our overseas representatives. Indoor hockey from Germany, the power methods of the Dutch and the finesse and quickness of subcontinental players have all contributed to our hybrid style.

Given a core method which often mimics the culture and ethos of a nation, each team has the spin and influence of the coach which refines these national traits. Australian men's teams have not strayed too far from a traditional structure. The women, over the last eight years, created a whole new way of formatting their team. Neither way is necessarily better, for in the end the individual quality of players counts. However, sometimes a sea change in approach can ignite the individuals in a way which enhances their whole attitude to the game. Indeed the challenge of swinging back to a more traditional way of playing might now be the best catalyst for improvement for Australia's women. I will watch the direction taken by our teams with interest.

I have endeavoured to give a thumbnail sketch of some of the hockey world's main contenders. I believe that too many of them are too keen to defend a lead rather than seek to extend a lead. There is, of course, a time and place for everything but my contention is that the former approach is often preferred even though the latter has much more utility. Although at times it may entail more risk, certainly for me it is the preferred option. As a way of teaching it gives a freedom and excitement to the task which facilitates development and interest. The additional bonus is a game which is more exciting for spectators.

8

Flair – an Overrated Commodity

Too many boys just want to start
If not they don't want any part
And then at times some have a flair
That makes one wonder if they care
> 'They Call Me Coach', John Wooden

It almost seems an Australian credo to admire the brilliant and spectacular rather than the solid, unobtrusive, simple and effective approach. We'd rather look good failing. Being slipshod is overlooked if we play with panache. Thorough and clinical are boring! My view is that if we considered the matter soberly we'd choose methodical efficiency over flashy inconsistency. Then why the penchant for the flair? Am I off target? Whenever our players were asked to characterise their style and describe what is good about their way of playing, the 'f' word was raised and revered. Whatever the sport, whatever the context, athletes, commentators, fans and many coaches love flair.

Perhaps it is the allure of getting something for nothing that is attractive. 'I did well in the exams but I didn't study.' 'It's just natural ability.' These are the attitudes that abound in our schools, and our workplaces, yet mostly life and sport are not like that. All the elite performers in sport have natural ability and it is usually the utilisation of that ability to the fullest that distinguishes the truly outstanding performers. A lottery winner is lucky, but there is no luck in being skilled at a difficult task. Luck does not get you there. Luck might see you born with fast-twitch muscle fibres, but training hones the craft and skill of a champion.

Like coach John Wooden in his rhyme about UCLA's prospects back in 1964, I think flair is overrated. Wooden was the 'winningest' coach in the highly competitive college basketball circuit in the United States, a legend in his own lifetime. Kareem Abdul-Jabbar was the most famous player of the hundreds who passed through his ranks to play professionally in the National Basketball Association. He said of Wooden:

> John Wooden believed in supreme conditioning and unwavering fundamentals, not only knowing which plays to run and how to run them but being capable of calling up the physical and emotional stamina at the precise time you need it to win . . . He preferred thorough preparation over the need to rise to an occasion. Let others try to rise to a level we had already attained; we would be there to begin with.

'Flairy' is often lairy and, like Wooden, it often makes me wonder if athletes care enough about getting it right. The 'look away' pass that misses the mark usually could have been given more effectively without the 'look away'. But flair can be defined in a number of ways. In the sense that it encapsulates our talent or feel for any particular activity, it's fine. However, it is more often used to describe the spectacular, unusual or downright outrageous pieces of a performance or game, or indeed the stylishness of a performer whether they are effective or not.

My thesis is that brilliant play is usually just superior, practised skill, well executed, rather than some extravagant spontaneous streak of genius. Brilliant, exact skill I encourage and expect. Unfortunately many top athletes make the mistake of chasing the extravagant and spectacular to the detriment of their core game. The athlete who does so, and it is a very common occurrence, is often distracted, erratic and inefficient.

Nobody could put flair in its real place better than Alex Ferguson in his description of soccer star Eric Cantona, the brilliant Frenchman who so influenced the game of Manchester United for nearly a decade.

> I was struck at once by his insistence on making the easy pass whenever possible, a characteristic that showed itself as a great strength of his game in his time with us. Nobody had more imagination when it came to spotting the opportunity for an improbable and devastating pass, or more technical dexterity in threading the ball through crowding defenders. But, like all truly exceptional creative players, Cantona did something extravagant only when it was necessary.

He went on to describe Cantona's practice ethic which he first observed at Manchester United.

> He applied himself flawlessly but it was the end of our session that really impressed me. As his team-mates were vanishing from the pitch at the Cliff, he approached me and asked if he could have the assistance of two players. 'What for?' I asked. 'To practice' he replied.' . . . Many people have justifiably acclaimed Cantona as a catalyst who had a crucial impact on our successes while he was with the club but nothing he did in matches meant more than the way he opened my eyes to the indispensability of practice. Practice makes players.

Alyson Annan is a brilliant and gifted athlete. She, like Cantona, has that ability to visualise and execute the improbable and devastating pass. As long as I live I will remember her doing so in Mar del Plata against Germany in 1995. Chris Spice, my assistant, and I looked at one another incredulously when Alyson smashed a ball from the left defensive corner of the field. There were passes in mid-field just twenty or thirty metres away. Was she just cracking the ball away from the danger zone? Only Alyson saw Michelle Andrews lurking dangerously close to the German goal seventy metres away. The resulting goal was in the mind of no one else at the ground until Alyson conceived of it and delivered her killer pass.

Unfortunately, Alyson does not yet have the other great quality of Cantona – the practice ethic. Her previously crisp and faultless basics have suffered in recent times as a result. In 2000 she applied herself better and regained some lost ground, but even the very best cannot afford to be shoddy trainers. I hope in the future that she will give her basics more attention for her technique is sound, only the regular polishing of those basics has slipped.

Statistics from the Olympics in Sydney show Alyson scored four goals from thirty-seven shots. In Atlanta, where I thought her game was of better quality because her practice and preparation had been less careless, the score was eight goals from just over twenty shots.

Some Hockeyroos whose practice ethic was outstanding were Rechelle Hawkes, Kate Starre, Juliet Haslam, Liane Tooth, Jenny Morris, Lisa Carruthers, Renita Garard and Louise Dobson and, of the more recent players, Melanie Twitt and Carmel Souter. More often than not these athletes needed to be dragged off the pitch at the end of a session. They set an example for team-mates which was far more influential than any exhortation from coaches. These players came to training to learn and they infected the whole team with their enthusiasm. As a result they and their team-mates were more able to do seemingly impossible and fantastic things in prac-tice and in games.

Whenever we see the freakish skills of Gary Ablett or Peter Daicos allowing them to score from an impossible position; whenever Mark Waugh catches effortlessly in slips or Ricky Ponting throws down the wicket from side-on; whenever Tiger Woods makes an improbable shot or we remember the scoring of Michael Jordan we are contemplating superior practised skill. In each case skill has been honed by practice in preparation for the opportunity to be expressed in competition. By practising and perfecting 'the impossible' athletes make these things happen.

It was observed that Johan Cruyff always seemed to have time on the field. When asked why he was not a player with lots of tricks or an elaborate method, one of the century's greatest soccer players responded, 'I never practise tricks. I play very simple. That's what it is all about. Playing simple football is the hardest thing. That's the problem for all trainers . . .'

When I was growing up and watching Australian football there were three outstanding Western Australians who exemplified the quality of champions. The stories of John Todd, Barry Cable and Graham Farmer all speak of a practice ethic that underpinned their brilliance. That brilliance was the expression of superior practised skill refined in varied circumstances, but with perfection the aim. With all his experience of the Australian game and its very best players, Kevin Sheedy, Essendon's legendary long-serving coach, still sings the praises of Cable's professionalism, his preparation and his training ethic. He has seen few who could match it.

As an aspiring young opening batsman in the late 1960s I had the experience of playing against Dennis Lillee. I first faced him in a one-day club match at the WACA ground in 1969 on the west wicket. I was still a schoolboy and playing for West Perth cricket club. Club captain Rod Marsh alerted me to the dynamism of Lillee. As I prepared to bat he generously encouraged me by saying he thought Lillee was exceptionally fast and he was glad it was me and not him who was opening! The raw and then erratic Lillee was bowling at fearsome pace in a way that sent more than one shiver up my spine. Needless to say my adventure at the crease was brief!

Three years later when I first toured with the Western Australian cricket team I roomed with Dennis. A tyro opener and the emerging superstar of world cricket, we had a lot of fun. Dennis liked to play pranks off the field but through it all his competitive determination and technical skill were exceptional. The bank officer from Perth would become the world's best fast bowler during the next decade and secure his future at a time when only the very best could do so through playing cricket.

Lillee was the best bowler I have seen in contemporary cricket. I would not venture to comment about former times. Notwithstanding his unfortunate back injury, Lillee would take a record number of wickets at the best strike rate of any comparable bowler. If his wickets taken during the time of World Series Cricket were included, as they ought to be, he would have an even more distinguished record.

Naturally gifted as all champions must be, Lillee's consistency as a wicket taker was underpinned by a work ethic at training and a practised technique which in his time set him apart from other fast bowlers. He worked much harder than anyone else.

At the nets he worked on his accuracy and the variety that made him so potent. Of course besides his skill as a bowler, Lillee had the other indispensable quality of great champions – a competitive bent that was unyielding. However, the cornerstone of his success was brilliant reproducible skill. Without that all the bravado in the world would not have achieved such long-term consistency. Only that level of skill could back up the fearsome stare that unnerved many and undid the careers of competent test players.

My belief has always been that the best athletes have the best and most reliable basics. This is the foundation on which a player's game is built and to ignore it is to flirt with form, that nebulous condition which for many athletes constitutes a great part of self-image.

When I look back on my career as an athlete I know there were many more gifted players than me, yet I believe there were few who prepared and practised as assiduously in every part of their game. Sometimes, just sometimes, I surprised myself with what I could do. Those were moments of sheer exhilaration but they occurred as often at practice as in matches. In many ways they were the drug to which the perfectionist became addicted and by practising the most difficult skills I became accustomed to performing them. There was no special magic quality, just superior practised skill.

There are, of course, great variations in ability between athletes, and some who train and prepare poorly are able to do brilliant things on the field. Some would argue that the existence of these athletes refutes my contention about superior practised skill. My response is that such gifted individuals could be even better if they practised properly, and that seldom can these athletes sustain their level of competence as a true champion does. Often their performances are flighty and fickle; this is the mark of an underachiever. These are not the athletes that earn my admiration. They frustrate the coach and supporter. They tantalise and disappoint spectators and team-mates, but most of all they disappoint themselves.

In playgrounds in Australia every day we see and hear the rhetoric which supports flashy performers. Natural ability is too often worshipped as an end in itself and to achieve without trying hard is considered superior to studying or practising diligently. These attitudes which permeate our society militate against good practice whether the endeavour be sporting, academic, social, artistic or corporate. Like physical beauty, natural ability is a gift of God, not a badge of achievement.

Of course there are some athletes with brilliant practised skill who are not able to do justice to their potential. George Best was a maestro with the round ball, yet his flawed personality and excessive lifestyle caused him to underachieve. Kim Hughes was as brilliant a talent as has been seen in Australian cricket in the last three decades yet he averaged 37 in 70 tests for Australia. Admittedly Hughes played against the mighty West Indies at their peak, but he had the potential to play more than 100 tests and average 50 or more in my view. Greg Norman has only two major titles to his name. Given his potential that record does not reflect what he was capable of doing in golf. Twins Mark and Steve Waugh are closer in natural gifts than their records would suggest. Every sport has its list of underachievers whose records do not do justice to their God-given gifts.

So brilliant skill, however practised, is not enough. The imponderable quality of mental strength or resilience is also required. Norman, I understand, was a hard worker. Hughes and Best did not become so brilliant without a lot of practice, but something kept them from realising their potential. The truly great champions last longer and do more than these sportsmen achieved given their talent and opportunities.

Why do sportspeople underachieve? I can only conjecture about Best, but it seems his fame and habits off the field distracted him. Kim Hughes, whom I saw at close range from the time he was sixteen, was always easily distracted. His fame and brilliance, friction with World Series Cricket and his stint of captaincy were all factors that distracted him. He never had the cold stare and composure of Greg Chappell, he was too easily diverted from his task.

In golf I have long held the view that appearance money is a cancer that gnaws away at competitiveness. Once a player receives more for turning up than the winner can earn, the edge must be lost from their competitive instinct. They become an entertainer rather than a competitor. Surely professional golf ought to be about turning up to play for the money. Once players are paid before they hit a ball it will show in competition and performance.

My thesis is that superior practised skill is really what we call flair. It is on the training track that the great craftsmen and women of sport are developed, but no doubt there are still those who are sceptical. Let me allow a great champion to convince you.

One of the best ever female tennis players, Martina Navratilova, sums it up:

You can be out there in the middle of a tough match pleading to yourself, 'Concentrate! Concentrate!' and it won't happen for you. Concentration is much more elusive than that.

The concentration you need has to come to you way before your match. Concentration is born on the practice court, alone with your ground strokes, your foot speed and everything else. You must mentally treat your practice sessions as matches, concentrating on every ball you hit. You must be keen, alert, and enthused, and as you cover all your shots, thinking about just one thing at a time, you are making the mental process more and more automatic. This is what a true tennis craftsman achieves. A better quality practice creates a better quality match.

Like all great champions, Navratilova's excellence was born in perfect practice, diligently pursued, and then expressed in the pressure of a match. We've already seen in Chapter 5 how Wayne Gretsky, the world's greatest ice hockey player, also came to place immense importance on proper practice.

I always saw it as my duty to try and help athletes to realise their potential. With many I feel my input played a role in doing so, yet there were always those who seemed to be out of reach. As a coach one of the great challenges is to find the key to unlock the occult talent of some athletes. However, you can only help those who want help – those who are looking for improvement and are willing to change and work at it. From my experience all the best players in a wide range of sports come into this category. There are those with enigmatic and brilliant skills but they would not meet my criteria of greatness, for without continual polishing and perfecting at practice they did not last or were never consistent.

9

Athletes are People too

Every athlete in a team has characteristics that distinguish them from one another. Every athlete best receives the messages of a coach in different ways. Every athlete sees the world differently and is motivated by a range of factors that vary for each of them. So how can the coach reach them all? How do you manage these disparate individuals?

A coach makes a mistake if he thinks the group will be homogeneous in their behaviours or contributions. You cannot treat all players the same way. You can best reach players through individual interactions and exchanges.

Players may be influenced by their peers, their spouse, their family and friends, the media and fans. Sometimes it seems, given this gallery of influences, that the coach is just another voice in the crowd. In order to be influential, the coach has to mark out their territory. Respect and authority must be earned. This demands time: time to listen, time to consult, time for everyone in the team. In modern sporting teams one person cannot do justice to this task.

Assistant coaches, paramedical and medical staff, psychologists and other advisers all play a part in supporting athletes.

There are myriad factors that can impact on preparation and performance. They are the same factors that influence individuals in any job or position. They are the factors that disrupt families and relationships. They are the same things that distract us from functioning optimally in everyday life. The best coaches know what these things are for all their players and staff and recognise their impact on athletes and colleagues.

Relationship issues of all kinds can affect athletes just as career and financial issues, drugs and pop culture pressures can overload the already stressful environment of competitive sport. Too often athletes try to ignore many of these issues in a mad rush to devote all their energy to their sport. The one-dimensional outcome of such an approach can seriously retard the athlete's future growth and development as a well-rounded individual. Coaches should endeavour whenever possible to develop and encourage the whole person. The long-term rewards are obvious, but in the short term you can often find yourself with a better balanced and more productive performer.

Many of our most brilliant and talented athletes are by their very nature and upbringing narrowly focused and one-dimensional. A coach cannot change an athlete's background, but perhaps can provide another perspective or an environment in which more can be discovered or learned. The opportunities offered by sport often open up a world that could never have been imagined for athletes from Maryborough, Shepparton, Toowoomba, Newcastle or even the capital cities of Australia. In the Hockeyroos we always endeavoured to make their experiences more than just hockey.

In a way that most Australians never experience we travelled in every continent and had contact with people from all around the world. These were great opportunities to grow and learn about the world beyond our backyard. Many of the Hockeyroos used these opportunities wisely and one of the great pleasures of the job was to see the players mature and broaden their outlook as the years passed.

During my time with the Hockeyroos we dealt with a range of issues of the type which bedevil every group of individuals who want to perform at their best. Qualities such as generosity and tolerance come into focus when the task is to work co-operatively in a team. The team's best interest always has to be in each athlete's field of vision. Many times individuals are caught in the gap between personal performance and team outcomes. A benefit of participating in team sports is the way in which we learn to balance the cohering but sometimes conflicting interests of self and team.

In 1999, we introduced Angie Skirving to our program. As an eighteen-year-old just out of school the intensity of the program meant that for Angie it was to be a very demanding period. She went from school to a full training load with senior players. This is the sort of transition that is made by hundreds of aspiring athletes in the AFL and other football codes. It occurs when elite athletes go to the Australian Institute of Sport or to state academies or even move from the country to a capital city. As if the training loads are not enough, the dislocation from family and the pressures of living away from home compound the stress. We knew Angie was struggling with the intensity. We knew she was struggling with the workload. We knew she missed home and friends but we could also see her maturing and growing. Her workload was lightened. She often got days off and she was encouraged through form lapses and low days. The staff did this and generously many of her team-mates were there to support her too. Angie wasn't treated exactly the same as everyone else. As much as possible we helped her and when in 2000 she was ready for the full workload the team and Angie received their reward.

In November 2000, Angie wrote me a wonderful letter which, in part, read 'Thank you so much for all the opportunities you gave me and for believing in me . . . I used to be so scared of you . . . tears used to well up in my eyes whenever you yelled something at me during training. I think it took me about a year and a half to learn you were only trying to help me become the best player I could be.'

Yes, we showed faith in Angie and tried to manage the stresses that she faced, but in the end it was Angie who won a place for herself. Her team-mates were rewarded for their generosity towards her by having a new, productive and brilliant young player in their team. For the staff the satisfaction was in refreshing the team and facilitating the development of a fine young woman and brilliant athlete.

During 2000 a handful of our players found themselves subject to severe stresses unrelated to the performance pressures of hockey. Severely ill parents or partners, relationship traumas, family bereavements, separation from loved ones or spouses were some of the issues that they faced. In every case the prescription for dealing with the situation was different. No doubt some felt that we were not sympathetic to their plight. Some might think we played favourites or may believe that the rules were not the same for every-one. My response would be that I never promised the same treatment for everyone. What I tried to do was deal with each situation on its merits.

This can only occur if there is trust – trust in the judgments and consistency of the staff and in the honesty of the players. In the end some players got time off to deal with issues. Some missed parts of the program; sometimes we accepted diminished performance for a period. The bottom line was that while we were empathetic to the stresses along the way, our goal and theirs was the same: to have the best prepared team in Sydney, a team that would be ready to perform.

But this was not the whole story. I hoped that the players would be prepared for a life after Sydney. To do well in Sydney we had to organise and develop our abilities and skills. We had accepted that challenge and we were not willing or able to postpone it. We intended to get it right together. I thought that such an endeavour would be a great lesson in life and one which would give the players confidence to tackle any of the issues they might later face. It could be a template for a life lived fully. The environment of the team does not allow one to duck or hide. You are measured and assessed and honest self-appraisal is required. I hoped that all involved with the Hockeyroos would see and learn the value of aiming for something and giving it your all regardless of the outcome.

One's soft underbelly is exposed on the sporting arena. It is not possible to hide flaws and weaknesses. They are exposed and exploited. The best athletes are interested in self-discovery and analyse their abilities. They correct their faults, work on the weaknesses and develop and expand their strengths.

How many of us procrastinate and play hide-and-seek with reality in our everyday lives? We are often able to skate through relationships, work or study without fully developing our abilities or honestly appraising our actions. Those who seek excellence in anything cannot afford such an approach. Those who seek to be excellent at sport without learning this lesson will be exposed.

Shakespeare put it well in *Hamlet*. He usually seemed to be able to see through human frailty. He wrote, 'This above all: to thine own self be true. And it must follow as the night the day/Thou canst not then be false to any man . . .' Let me illustrate with an example that may seem controversial yet is real and as overlooked in sport as it is in many areas of our lives. It is the unnecessarily vexed issue of homosexuality.

I often had homosexual team-mates. At club, state and national level there were homosexual players in the teams I played for and against. Some of us were aware of our team-mates' sexuality, some suspected it and others were blissfully ignorant.

Homosexuality is an issue that in men's sport remains taboo. Everyone appears to be in denial. There are 650 elite footballers in the Australian Football League yet ask any club coach, president or player and you would not find many admissions that homosexuality exists in the AFL. Yet it is more than half a century since Kinsey published his landmark study of male sexual behaviour. He asserted approximately 10 per cent of the male population was homosexual or at least not purely heterosexual. He also asserted that the percentage of the population that is gay is probably reflected in every subset of society. Sporting teams are unlikely to be so dramatically different from society in general that they are full of gay athletes or devoid of them.

Why is it important? Why indeed do I mention it? I do so because I believe the best performance comes from athletes who are honest with themselves – honest about their strengths and weaknesses as athletes and honest about all other factors that influence their performance and that make up their life.

One's sporting life usually stretches from the teenage years to the mid thirties. Those late teen years are difficult for many reasons, not the least being one's emerging sexuality and uncertain and new relationship experiences. Add to that confusion about career paths, study pressures, a burgeoning drug and pop culture and hormonal fluctuations and this is a difficult time for any teenager.

The intense pressures of high-performance sport can magnify all of these factors. With a very few exceptions men's sport and the 'mates' culture surrounding it do not handle these matters honestly. I am not suggesting that homosexual athletes should 'out' themselves. Those who are gay have calculated, I believe, that the stress of such an admission would be greater than the covert pretence. What I am saying is that athletes in such situations usually do not produce their best.

In women's sport the story is different.

There is usually more honesty about matters of sexuality amongst women in teams. However, if the issue is not recognised and able to be openly discussed, it will have the potential to disturb team harmony and performance. My strong impression of the Dutch women's hockey teams of 1994 and 2000 was that this issue was part of the cause of disruption and disaffection to the extent that those teams under-performed on the field. Indeed in 1994 the Dutch coach, Bert Wentick, came to speak with me about his concerns. The only advice I could offer was that this issue was best addressed openly rather than remaining covert.

Holland is a country full of contradictions. In the late 1980s I spent a week in Amsterdam studying the approach to the treatment of drug addiction. The openness and sophistication of their programs was an eye-opener. Certainly they embraced harm minimisation more strongly than we did, and still do. As part of my research I travelled on the 'addicts bus' which doles out treatments on the streets and offers needle exchange.

Some, of course, would argue that the ready availability of marijuana is a catalyst for their hard drug problems. I suspect that the issue is much more complicated than that. Certainly the position of Amsterdam and Rotterdam as huge trading centres makes for easy access to prohibited substances.

The open and explicit sex industry and the generally relaxed atmosphere on the streets gives an impression that does not seem to be matched in hockey circles. Hockey spectators dress very well, coaches wear ties and jackets and the atmosphere is elitist. In Holland hockey is a game of the upper class and I suspect that is why in a country of such openness those in hockey have a conservative outlook. Perhaps that is why the issue of sexuality appeared to cause some of the difficulty for those underperforming teams in 1994 and 2000.

To the great credit of the Hockeyroos this issue was open and out there and while we had hiccups it was never divisive or out of control. At any one time in our squad of twenty to thirty athletes we had a handful of players who were openly gay. The vast majority were not so disposed and there were a few who were clearly struggling to clarify their preference.

Those who were gay weren't 'recruiting' the younger players, weren't hostile to the heterosexuals, weren't more difficult to handle or disruptive. Indeed their openness often set a tone for the group that was admirable and positive. Their honesty, which I doubt is ever easy, required real conviction and courage.

On the day of the Olympic final, as I did each day of the

competition, I wrote a thought for the day on the team noticeboard. I usually tried to choose a message relevant to the stage of the tournament, our next opponent or the mood of the group. On 29 September 2000, the message came from a little book called *Words On Courage* that Corinne Reid our sports psychologist had given me in the days before. The piece, early in the small book, encapsulates why I thought these gay athletes added so much to the tenor of our group. On that day, when the athletes had to be strong, the quote I chose was 'Where is the University of Courage? . . . The University of Courage is to do what you believe in!'

On the day of the Olympic final one has to be brave. Such matches are not won by timid hearts. Indeed, it is a fatal mistake to be conservative on such a day. For the team, with our style, this was a day when we had to go out and take the game by the scruff of the neck. To do this we had to be brave, true to ourselves, and what we believed in.

During my eight years as coach there were three or four occasions when team members had relationships with one another. In every case they understood the parameters of the relationship within a team environment. Mostly these relationships did not endure, just as relationships of heterosexual players ebbed and flowed. This experience was no different to that which I had seen occur with team-mates in men's teams. However, one was overt and one was covert! This is a big difference and in my view it can count in performance.

The same realistic approach is valid for another social taboo that affects sport. The issues in sport mimic society; they are not separate from it. Drugs abound in sport just as they do in society. People use them to feel better, to find release and to escape. They use them because it is exciting and forbidden, because it changes their reality and because drugs are there. Whether it is tobacco, alcohol, ecstasy or amphetamines, marijuana, narcotics or cocaine it is part of modern life, just as it was part of life a century ago and in ancient times. Athletes take drugs for the same reasons and some also take them for performance enhancement.

We ought not to get too precious about this matter. We need solutions that work, guidelines to direct athletes and laws which reflect reality. Those who seek advantage in performance through drugs are cheats and should not be allowed to compete again. While all agree that performance enhancers should have no place in sport, many professional sports teams wrestle with the problem of social drug use. Sanctions like fines, advice and assistance seem appropriate first measures. Recidivism should probably lead to sacking or suspension just as it would in any job.

Drugs like marijuana used consistently appear to inhibit volition, and alcohol and tobacco clearly are not performance enhancing. Users, while not cheating, have no place in a team for they diminish the team and let down their team-mates. Sportspeople are not the best or worst of society – they are a group which crosses the full spectrum. Athletes are people too.

10

Always Look Behind
the Result

After the victory in Atlanta I made the comment that I thought we had lost enough times to make our opponents think they could beat us. Korea knew they were close to us, Argentina had beaten us twice in 1994 and we struggled against them in 1995. Spain beat us in 1995 and Great Britain, Germany and Holland all drew with us in the Olympic lead-up.

I think had we been more outstanding then our opponents might have worked even harder in 1996. I suspect that they all thought they were a little closer to us than they were and that on the day they might be able to upset us. I always thought we played with a fair bit in reserve. Confidentially, I wrote to the board of Australian Women's Hockey on June 18 1996, four weeks before the Olympics.

> It has always been my belief that given the present rules and low-scoring nature of our game that it was necessary to be 15 per cent better than the opposition to be assured of victory in a tournament like the Olympics. At the start of the year I thought we were perhaps 10 per cent ahead. I hope we have clawed another 5 per cent!

Among the coaches and management, there was a view that we should try to completely dominate the game by always playing our best combination. Although I liked the idea I thought that we got the balance about right. While we never didn't try to win any particular game we often were experimental in our selection of personnel or tactics. Accordingly the win–loss record shows some interesting trends.

	Played	Won %	Lost %	Drawn %	Goals for and against
World Cups/					
Olympic Games	30	26 (86.7)	1 (3.3)	3 (10)	102/24
Champions					
Trophies	30	23 (76.6)	3 (10)	4 (13.3)	85/25
All other matches	193	149 (77.2)	26 (13.5)	18 (9.3)	627/190

This table demonstrates the differential between our performances in all other matches and our performances at Champions Trophies and World Cups and Olympic Games. While the Champions Trophy tournament was important to us and it brought six of the best teams together every year, we often used it to experiment with tactics, players and strategy. In lesser tournaments, tours and against teams visiting Australia we were even more adventurous.

Accordingly, our record in all other matches and in the Champions Trophy is significantly different to our record at the major competitions that we were keenest to win. Our winning percentage in the toughest competitions – the World Cups and the Olympics – against the best opponents, all also wanting to win, was better than for all our other matches over that time.

While individual results can be deceptive the cumulative result over a large number of games is worthy of analysis. Indeed when one considers that we played many matches against 'lesser' teams then if our approach was to win with our best team all the time our record in games other than major championships should be better than against our toughest opponents at major competitions.

When assessing win–loss records one should be wary of a record obtained against lesser opponents. If you are aiming to be the best then it is necessary to challenge the best teams. We rarely played against some of the weaker nations as we were concerned that it would not be beneficial to our quest to keep challenging our standards. Preserving a good record for the books was never a concern.

We had a number of unbeaten sequences during my eight years. The greatest started in Atlanta in September 1995 and finished in New Delhi in December 1996. During that time we were unbeaten for 41 consecutive matches which included the 1996 Olympics and 1995 Champions Trophy. Eventually at the end of 1996 we succumbed to India in the Indira Gandhi Gold Cup tournament in Delhi. With only a handful of Atlanta Olympians playing at the end of a long hard year and in the most hostile of lands we were outplayed 3–0 to end our run. To the team's great credit, five days later we thrashed Korea in the final 6–2 in a dramatic turnaround after the loss to India and a subsequent loss to Korea in the last round match.

Hockey is a game in which the score regularly doesn't reflect the relative merit of a team's play. The team making the most chances and playing offensively can be defeated by dour resistance and a few moments of inspiration in attack, or even by a foolish error by a defender. Some people say that's the way the game is. Like soccer, its beauty and mystery is wrapped up in the serendipity of such events. While accepting that I think it is only part of the story.

For a coach to rely on chance and the rare piece of brilliance or an opposition error will only produce erratic and inconsistent performances. To have higher expectations a coach must build a team that consistently outscores opponents and is parsimonious in defence. This is not done by having a good striker or two, a good midfield or a good defence. It is done by having all those things plus a range of alternatives for each line. The aim is to have a consolidated flexible team that has quality in every department of the game.

In order to build such a team the coach must be willing to look behind the result every time the team plays to analyse what actually happened and how well the team performed regardless of the sometimes fickle pattern of goal scoring that is the sole focus of the media, other pundits and often, unfortunately, the players.

In 1995 we lost only one game. That loss was in the pre-Olympic tournament to Spain and without it our unbeaten streak would have been much longer and more impressive. However that loss was not even close to the worst game we played that year. There were a couple of matches when we were outplayed, but came away with a draw or win. On the day in August that we lost to Spain we had nearly thirty goal shots to their two! Some brilliant Spanish goalkeeping, some poor Australian goal shooting and two appalling lapses in our defence cost us the game, 1–2. Five days later when the teams met again in the final we created fewer chances and won 4–0. The lesson is clear – coaches must always look behind the result.

Analysis of performance is crucial to the team and coach. Both parties must soberly assess performance and progress. A focus merely on the score can pitch a team into depression or reinforce self-delusion. Neither of these outcomes is useful or desirable.

Let me give you two recent examples that were part of our lead-up to the Olympics in Sydney. In May 2000 we played two matches against Great Britain in Glasgow. We played poorly and lost both matches 1–3 and 2–3. Thus we were outscored six goals to three. However, goal shots told another story – thirty-three to eleven in our favour – and the penalty corners were nine to five in our favour. There was, however, one other incredible statistic. Great Britain scored four of their five corners, an amazing 80 per cent efficiency rate.

Notwithstanding some poor defending and our lack of finish and crispness, the picture was not one of our team being outplayed. Indeed I made the point at the time that if Great Britain could score 80 per cent of their corners at the Olympics they would surely be medallists. In Sydney they only achieved 17.6 per cent conversion and accordingly finished well outside the medals in eighth place. Achieving 17.6 was still a good conversion rate but far short of their extraordinary 80 per cent in Glasgow.

Another example of how results can deceive comes from our record against the Netherlands leading into the Sydney Olympics. If you look at Australia's record against the Netherlands overall and indeed during the two years prior to the Olympics, it would seem that the Dutch were our toughest opponents. However the results do not necessarily reflect what was happening. Hence, my belief, outlined in Chapter 7 that as the Olympics approached we were drawing further away from the Dutch who had peaked in 1998 at Utrecht.

	Played	Won	Lost	Drew	For	Against
Australia vs Netherlands 1993–2000 All matches	28	15	6	7	63	38
Australia vs Netherlands Dec 1998–2000 to Sydney	8	1	4	3	14	19

In the eight games played after the World Cup in 1998 and up to the Olympics in September 2000 we never played our strongest team. Indeed in five of the matches (three lost and two drawn) we had fewer than half of our best team playing. This was because we were experimenting with tactics or our system or trying to develop new players with a view to improving our team for Sydney. In those eight games we only had one win – that was in Brisbane in the final of the Champions Trophy in 1999. Again, players who would perform in Sydney such as Jenny Morris, Kate Starre, Katie Allen and Angie Skirving were not playing that day.

Equally in the Champions Trophy in Amsterdam three months

before Sydney, Rechelle Hawkes, Juliet Haslam and Katie Allen did not play when we lost to the Dutch 1–2. Given that the Netherlands team during that time was quite static, I was not overly concerned by the results. I believed that with our full complement on board we could break their team open. We only needed to hold our nerve.

To measure our circle penetrations and goal shots was another way to look behind the result. In the end my concern was always about the number and quality of goal shots both for and against. If you look behind the match results, the statistics reveal an interesting picture.

			Shots F/A	Differential Shots F–A
1998	World Cup Final	Score 3–2	15 / 7	+ 8
June 1999	Champions Trophy Final	Score 3–2	22 / 4	+ 18
August 1999	Four Nations Final	Score 3–4 (extra time)	18 / 13	+ 5
2000	Champions Trophy (round match)	Score 1–2	22 / 7	+ 15
2000	Medal Pool Sydney Olympics	Score 5–0	25 / 7	+ 18

Except for the game played in early August 1999 the differential of shots for and against is high and increasing after the World Cup final. At Milton Keynes that day our team was only at half strength, yet led till late in the match, losing only in extra time. Though some of the other results went against us I knew that we were doing better than in 1998 when I thought the Netherlands team was at its best.

From a distance it appeared that the Netherlands became comfortable and stabilised their team much too early, the justification being some results which were not realistically assessed. Their team was treading water for much of 1999 and 2000, while we were actively looking to improve. Argentina, which would eventually make the Olympic final, were introducing new young talent but there was no evidence of the Dutch doing that. They had a winning team and were not going to change it.

This approach, of never changing a winning team, has to be one of the great fallacies of sport. In many ways sport is a very conservative part of society. It is strewn with mythology and clichés. They are regurgitated incessantly and their validity only is a function of frequency rather than objectivity.

Of course you should change your team if it could be improved regardless of the result of the last matches. The team that won last week, won last season's premiership, or has been on a winning streak can always be improved. Really good teams are constantly searching for improvement and unchanged winning teams are often heading for disaster. A team in which the players feel they 'own' a place is in the process of destroying itself from within. Coaches and players who start to believe the rhetoric of such teams make a fatal mistake.

It is not so long ago that this rationale was used by journalists about the national cricket team. No doubt it was also a view held within the team. It was widely agreed that Stuart MacGill was a hothead who wouldn't cut it at test level. Only Shane Warne's injury provided the proof of the fallacy. Steve Waugh would not be able to lead like Mark 'Tubby' Taylor. Adam Gilchrist was a backstop, not a wicket keeper. Only Ian Healy could handle Shane Warne and there wasn't that much difference in their batting. Justin Langer and Matthew Hayden weren't up to it. Eventually, given an opportunity, they have all shown otherwise.

There are always young players who can do the job. The measure of an athlete can only be performance and coaches must constantly search for ways to improve, ways to give their team an edge. What makes teams great is consistent, sustained performances and tuning and changing are important for teams to become 'chronic' achievers.

What about another popular myth about being 'in the zone' or having 'hot hands'? What's the explanation of this phenomenon? Is there a connection between body and brain that allows for exceptional performances sometimes?

Stephen Jay Gould is a palaeontologist with a fascination for sports, baseball in particular, and some knowledge of statistics. In his absorbing book *Life's Grandeur* he debunks the concept of hot hands.

Gould argues convincingly that athletes do not have sequences of consecutive scoring any more frequently than can be predicted using their average shooting percentage. Using data collected from basketball researchers showed that the probability of a player scoring a second goal did not increase following an initial successful shot beyond what would be expected by chance and the average shooting percentage of the player.

For example if you toss a coin you could expect to get four heads in a row once every sixteen sequences of four tosses. Similarly, a player with an average shooting percentage of 50 per cent would throw four baskets in a row once in every sixteen sequences of four throws. They would also miss four in a row once in every sixteen sequences of four throws.

A player with an average scoring percentage of 66 per cent would get four baskets in a row sixteen times out of eighty-one sequences of four throws. That is close to one in every five sequences and much more frequent than a player with a 50 per cent scoring average.

Players might feel 'hot' or 'in the groove' when they have a game that falls into the high-scoring range of chance but this doesn't happen more frequently than probability says it should given the athlete's ability.

However Gould agrees that some performances are exceptional and fall outside the range of events that can be explained by statistics or predicted given past performances. Joe DiMaggio's 56-game hitting streak is so many standard deviations outside the mean that it should not have happened at all. Bob Beamon's leap of 29 feet 2½ inches in 1968 at the Mexico Olympics was a similar freak event, it was not surpassed until Mike Powell jumped 29 feet 4½ inches in the World Championships in 1991, nearly 23 years later, although one-off freak performances are not so surprising. They can be understood, whereas to hit in 56 baseball games consecutively is incredible.

So nice try, but 'hot hands' don't really exist. Athletes who improve their shooting accuracy have more sequences of brilliance than other athletes, and the answer isn't some special mental state. It is practice and quality! It might sound dull, but sports performances are about playing the percentages. In every instant of the game we play the percentages. A batsman in cricket is put out of his comfort zone when the bowling is to his less preferred side. That minimises scoring and maximises the chances of a dismissal. By developing an all-round game with strength everywhere a batsman can overcome such a deficiency.

The cat and mouse of game strategy and competition is built on statistics and percentages. This applies in every game whatever the level of competence and skill. Building your strengths, improving your weaknesses, searching for opposition weakness, denying their strengths, exploiting their deficiencies. This is competitive sport.

11

The Problem
of Selection

Whether it is choosing who'll play every weekend for your club team, finalising the squad for the AFL draft or choosing the Olympic team after a rigorous process over many months, selection time is a difficult time. No longer can you wait and see how a player will go in the next match or practice session. You are required to make a decision and those decisions are rarely easy or clear. Always there will be a few athletes who just make it and invariably a couple who are very unlucky.

It was June 1996, and we sat in the car park and tried to finalise our already lengthy considerations. We had hoped that a change of scenery would enable us to crystallise our thoughts. We watched a late arrival at the hotel attempt to negotiate the narrow driveway. Perhaps tiredness or alcohol was impeding his driving skill. We needed no such impediments to make our task difficult. Sitting on the low concrete barriers outside the front steps of the Hotel Schipol the problem was no clearer, but at least we were out of our stuffy room.

The Hotel Schipol is situated a short distance from Amsterdam's airport on a very busy motorway among vast flat fields separated by ubiquitous channels of water. It appears to be the middle of nowhere. As we'd returned to this hotel in the afternoon, the task had loomed ahead of us and I had not looked forward to it with any relish. Earlier in the day we had played the Netherlands in a very tough encounter at Amstelveen, a leafy suburb of Amsterdam. The enthusiastic crowd had been pleased with the 1–1 draw against Australia. For me the score meant little.

We were at the end of a very busy European tour. In twelve days we had played seven matches. Undefeated and with two draws, the results were satisfactory but we had come away to select the Olympic team. The matches had provided us with our final chance to consider the possibilities before deciding who would go to Atlanta.

The evening of 9 June was the date designated to make the final choices. Sandy Pisani was the selector travelling with us and that evening Sandy, Chris Spice and I would sit down after dinner to try and settle on the final team. The plan was that we would ring through to Women's Hockey with the team so that the wheels could be set in motion for an announcement early the following week.

The next morning, the team would return to Australia and the announcement would follow the day after their return. The players would have a week in which to absorb the news before returning to Perth for training. Sandy was chairperson of the selection panel and was in constant communication with Jeanette Slade in Australia. Sandy, Jeanette and myself were the official panel, but Chris would sit in with Sandy and me that night ten thousand kilometres from home.

It was not possible to delay our decision until we returned to Australia as I was heading off to London in order to watch a tournament featuring Spain, Great Britain, Germany and the Netherlands. It was important to see Spain as they would be our first opponents in five weeks time and they were the only team we had not already played that year.

My experiences of selection panels in women's hockey were universally good. I cannot remember an occasion when we did not eventually agree on a combination. It was a credit to the capacity of the individual selectors to think through the requirements and assess the players. Often there was lengthy discussion but we always seemed to sort it out. I think our remarkable concord was assisted by the thoroughness of the process which included regular discussion, reassessment and evaluation. Often done informally, this allowed for a good starting position when we sat down to settle matters.

The evening of 9 June was warm and balmy. I know this because by 1 am on 10 June, Chris, Sandy and I were still sitting outside the hotel. The wide and busy motorway throbbed all night but fortunately was about two hundred metres from the hotel entrance. We had decided to go outside to get fresh air and a drink from the nearby 24-hour petrol station that provided a service for motorists and snacks for hotel patrons.

We were in selection block! The bulk of the team had been settled and, as is always the case, the last couple were extremely close. You try to apply the objective criteria rigidly, you apply others more subjectively, you do it on instinct, you look at it every which way and you come up with a different combination each time. It seemed the only method we did not resort to was tossing a coin!

The climate in Atlanta was a factor that weighed heavily on my mind. Temperatures in excess of 30°C and high humidity would require a strategy and preparation unlike anything previously attempted. Whereas in men's hockey playing in the tropics had been common, the women had little experience of this. I favoured selecting skilled midfielders and playing more of them in such conditions. Flexible midfielders offered more than static specialists at both ends of the ground.

The difficult selections had included choosing between Liane Tooth or Katie Allen, Louise Dobson or Alison Peek or Karen Smith, Danni Roche or Claire Mitchell-Taverner and Clover Maitland or

Justine Sowry. Having settled all those we were down to deciding between Nikki Mott or Jackie Pereira. Tooth's extra speed, form and experience had been undeniable, Dobson offered speed and could hit corners, Roche had great form and Maitland had done nothing wrong, but Mott and Pereira were different styles of player for the same position. This was the most difficult type of decision.

So there we sat like three exhausted and misplaced students after a night out. We drank our Pepsis and tried to find other ways to look at our dilemma. Sandy rang Jeanette to consult, we tossed her thoughts around and still seemed to go nowhere.

That day we had left Katrina Powell out of the match. She had already convinced us of her merit. She had been concerned but I had told her with a poker face that being left out could be good or bad and she would have to wait for the team to be announced like everyone else. Neither Mott nor Pereira were spectacular that day but both had shown pretty good form all tour. Whoever would be left out would be very unlucky.

It wasn't until about 2 or 3 am that we settled on Jackie Pereira. In the end we went for the proven goal scorer and tough competitor over the brilliant dribbler who won penalty corners but seldom scored herself. While I thought that Jackie would be good I wondered if Nikki Mott might be able to really hurt teams when they tired in the Atlanta sun. She could turn opponents inside out, but had never been as consistent as one would have liked. On tour she had played brilliantly in Germany but was still a junior. I was not sure she was ready. By the time the Sydney Olympics came round Nikki had added a fearsome corner shot to her repertoire, but back then neither of the two had much to offer on corners. However Jackie, forever the goal sneak, could rebound very well, often picking up an opportunist goal off the goalkeeper's pads.

Next day the team left Amsterdam for home and I went on to London. It is not a pleasant experience knowing which players would later be elated and which would be crushed as you chat with them on the bus or at the airport. I hated having that knowledge.

I was pleased to be in a London taxi. I would see a show that night. *Les Miserables* seemed appropriate!

When I got to my hotel room I wrote to each of those players who had missed out. Nikki was only twenty and she would make it later, but I could not get her out of my mind those next few days. She had come so close to being selected. She had been in form and would have done well, I was sure of that. The same applied to Katie Allen. She had played well. Unfortunately for her, someone else had played slightly better. Alison Peek, Claire Mitchell-Taverner and Justine Sowry must have half expected to miss out as they had not toured Europe. Their best chance had been a form slump by someone on tour. Karen Smith, a seventeen-year-old, had shown a lot of talent and promise, but unfortunately had been stricken with appendicitis five days earlier. Unable to play the last three matches and facing a few weeks of recovery, she was not quite ready for selection. All the players not chosen would be disappointed. The depth of that disappointment in some cases would come out repeatedly during the next four years.

The process of selecting that team for the Atlanta Olympics in 1996 is one of the most traumatic experiences that I have been through. I felt especially for Nikki Mott and Katie Allen. Nikki appeared to take the news well, while Katie was obviously hurt. Both in their own ways would recover. They would pursue their dream with the hope of doing better next time. In elite sport you have to present yourself to be a contender and that sometimes leads to great disappointment.

It was not ideal that I was in London when the selections were announced, but as the players were all over the country there would not be much one could do for them anyway. It was important to see Spain so I headed for Milton Keynes. A planned city an hour out of London, Milton Keynes is the home to headquarters of English hockey. A sterile place, it reminded me of Canberra and my parliamentary days when I had to run when the division bells rang. I was better off in my new job despite the selection trauma.

There is no easy way to tell someone that they have not made the team. In my days as a cricketer for Western Australia, I remember well the tension of opening the morning newspaper to find out if I had been chosen to play. As a peripheral member of the team in the first few years I certainly had my ups and downs at the hands of the selectors.

In 1970, I was bitterly disappointed to miss out on the Western Australian senior hockey team for the national championships in Perth. At the time I believed my omission meant the end of any ambition I might have had to play for Australia in the Munich Olympics in 1972.

Perhaps I was fortunate to have had two sports and a career going at the same time. Somehow the disappointments in one area seemed often to be balanced by a win elsewhere, or a challenge in another field. Yet, I think, for the athletes who aspire to be in the Olympic team and who devote months and years to that end, Olympic selection is the great quest. So it was for the Hockeyroos during my time with the team between 1993 and 2000. What occurred in the Netherlands in early June 1996 was the final stanza of a selection process that had grown during the previous three years.

The other major selections were for the World Cups in 1994 and 1998, and the Olympics in 2000. The Champions Trophy tournaments were significant events in 1993, 1995, 1997 and 1999 but they did not assume the same importance as the World Cups and Olympics, both only held every four years. In 2000 the International Hockey Federation, in its wisdom, decided that the Champions Trophy, which pitted the world's six best against each other in one tournament, would be held annually rather than biannually. I believed the previous pattern was more desirable, especially as the new structure would require us to play the Champions Trophy three months before the Olympics. That did not seem ideal!

My attitude to the various competitions developed during my first couple of years in the job. Initially, we took the approach that as many players as possible ought to be exposed to international matches. This was achieved by selecting as many as possible who appeared likely to make the top team and playing every team member in every game. With sixteen playing every game instead of eleven, twelve or thirteen, the number of players exposed to the international game grew quite rapidly.

In 1993, we took what looked to be close to our best group to the Champions Trophy in Amsterdam. Throughout early 1994 we toured South Africa, India and Argentina with a variety of players from the squad. Many players who may not have been entirely ready for the senior team played during this time. It was my view that only by playing them could we realistically assess them. This meant our record of wins and losses might not be so good, but our aim was always to have the best group available and ready to play in Atlanta.

The World Cup in Dublin in 1994 would provide a good starting point for our assault on Atlanta. Those who played were all considered as possibilities for Atlanta. The experience of a World Cup tournament would be invaluable to the newer players. The major tournaments like the World Cup bring together all the best teams, and the experience of playing in front of large crowds away from home can never be underestimated. The bonus was that a World Cup win ensured Olympic participation. It would remove the distraction of Olympic qualifying and enable us to plan long term.

As it turned out, we struggled early in Dublin and after three games had lost to Russia and drawn with Spain. Facing the possibility of finishing outside the semi-finals we needed wins in our last two matches to confirm a semi-final spot. Players do not often get to play under such pressures. The World Cup in 1994 taught us much about where we were and who we wanted to be.

As the program developed I came to the view that to maximise our chances in Atlanta, we needed a block of centralised training to achieve the required fitness levels, skills and cohesiveness for such conditions. While athletes were located all around the country it was difficult to ensure standards of fitness and oversee technical and tactical preparation.

Perhaps our toughest test in the lead-up to Atlanta came at the Champions Trophy in Mar del Plata in September 1995. Mar del

Plata is the Argentinian equivalent of the Gold Coast in Queensland, about an hour's flight south of Buenos Aires. A beach resort on the Atlantic and crowded in the summer, it was extremely windy and at times quite cold in September. It had been the site of a recent Pan American Games and so a number of quality sporting facilities had been established there. Argentina, having developed a very good women's team, were amongst the favourites to win. In the Dublin World Cup in 1994 we had played them in a tough final and they meant business playing at home a little more than a year later.

In September Mar del Plata was not in full swing so all the teams were staying at the Grand Hotel Provincial on Boulevard Maritimo on the windswept Atlantic beach. The huge Peronesque building had a magnificent marble entry hall with frescos and brilliant murals on a domed ceiling. The stairs arced up to an enormous lobby with pillars framing a huge mahogany reception desk. Light streamed in through elaborate leadlights. Unfortunately, it was there that the luxury ceased. While you could rollerblade down the wide marbled corridors, the room fittings, service, plumbing and food were also from the time of Peron!

So we came to this windswept time-warped place, still in hibernation as winter was closing, to play at the end of a very busy year. We had started training in February, played in Hobart and Adelaide in March and April, toured Europe in May and June, and then been to Canada and Atlanta in July and August. On the way to Argentina we stopped in Sydney for three tests against Great Britain and by the time we had settled in Mar del Plata we had lost count of our frequent flyer points.

What we learned in Mar del Plata was that Korea were very good. We had not seen them all year. Our last encounter with them had been in July 1994, when we'd had to beat them in the final round match of the World Cup in order to make the semi-finals. In September 1995 they were a completely different proposition. Still quick, strong, organised and skilled, they now had a couple of potent goal scorers and their penalty corners were threatening. This was an all-round team without an obvious weakness and they overran all other teams to qualify for the final.

In our round match we trailed 0–2 at half-time, but thanks to some of our best ever form, plus some luck, recovered to win 4–2 with the fourth goal coming in the last minute. I felt however, that the huge effort coming at the end of a tough season just about used up all our energy and emotional resources. We went into the final favoured and undefeated after struggling with Argentina in the last match. I was not confident, we were looking tired and Korea now knew they were close to us.

At least we started well and for twenty minutes we were dominant. We scored at the end of the first half but soon our game deteriorated. For the rest of the match we were outplayed and eventually we were scored against. Throughout the second half we were under siege and although we had a few good moments we only scraped out of the game with 1–1 at full-time. On penalties we won 4–3. This time Justine Sowry did well. Karen Marsden had withdrawn through injury before the tournament and Justine shaded Clover Maitland as a penalty saver.

The result goes down as a victory to us, but I went away from the tournament convinced that to win in Atlanta we would have to overcome Korea. Germany, Holland, Argentina, Great Britain, USA and Spain all presented threats, but in my heart of hearts I knew Korea was easily the best of them.

Their athleticism was special, their work ethic and discipline unquestioned, and they also had a body of very skilled players who could penetrate and hurt us. Eun-Jung Chang, Eun-Jung Cho, Chang-Sook Kwon, Ji-Young Lee and Hyun-Jung Woo were all potential match-winners. Chang with Alyson Annan, would be the leading goal scorer in Atlanta and Cho the leading penalty corner scorer. However, just as important was their newfound belief in themselves. Although they were obviously disappointed after the final I was sure that they knew how close our two teams were.

I resolved to make sure that we kept our focus on this team. At the end of 1995, they gave further evidence of their quality when they romped through the Olympic qualifying tournament in Cape Town. We made sure that we would play them in the lead up to Atlanta to further measure their progress. As it was we met them twice in Atlanta. In our round match we came from behind to tie the game with 17 seconds remaining and in the final only broke loose in the second half. Without closely monitoring Korea's progress I suspect we could have easily underestimated them in Atlanta.

After Atlanta I realised how different a competition at home would be. I knew we would need plenty of resilience. The distractions and expectations could be overwhelming. Not only would we have to get the hockey issues right, we would need the toughest athletes mentally to function in that environment.

During 2000 we gradually sorted out what we were looking for in terms of individual players in selecting our team. In May we took away a Champions Trophy team that we thought could win, but more importantly it was a team that would help us find out who wanted Olympic selection most. Some of those left behind were still in contention; we knew what they could do. I was unsure about some who flew to Glasgow with us.

Our form dip to lose twice to Great Britain and to not make the final in Amsterdam was not entirely unexpected and it served to ensure that the group kept events in perspective. Our expectations wouldn't get away from us and our doubts were refreshed. Three months out from the Olympics it was not such a bad outcome.

A series of matches in early July saw us lose to New Zealand, yet emphatic wins at the end of the week over Germany and New Zealand were reassuring. As we entered the final selection lap we played against China, a team underestimated by almost everyone. I had seen them play very well in the qualifier in March and not wanting to be overexposed to Korea who we had already played against in four matches over Easter in Perth, I chose to play China instead. Although we won all four matches none were easy.

Most observers were surprised when China made the medal rounds in Sydney. Given their form in late July I rated them as likely to cause an upset. By beating both the Netherlands and Germany they earned their fifth place. It was a difficult week when we played those last matches against them. With nineteen players left in our group we knew that three would miss out. Another selection dilemma lay ahead.

I checked out of the hotel alone. The Chinese team were preparing to go home and the Australian players were already scattering across the country. I had been ready to spend the night in Sydney but selection had been settled in about three to four hours. An all-night stint was not required and I could catch the last flight to Perth and get myself an extra day at home.

After the last of our four matches against China during the last week of July 2000 we were ready to select the team for Sydney. While there was some concern that it was very late, and indeed the Australian Olympic Committee had tried to push the selection date forward, we had prevailed. Interestingly, some involved in the softball program later told me they thought they had selected their team much too early in April. I'm glad we didn't succumb to the pressure. There were those in the team who would have liked selection earlier, but such pressures are usually more about being reassured and comfortable and not about optimal preparation.

During the year the players had been asked twice to select their best team. It was interesting to notice how their selections changed and to compare their instincts and judgments with those of the coaches and selectors. At their first attempt they'd had two differences from my preferred team and at least two differences from the teams chosen by the other coaches, Bob Haigh and Frank Murray. Indeed none of us selected the same team. Later in the year we repeated the exercise with similarly diverging results.

The official selection group was larger this time, but still it was not necessary to get down to voting for individuals. Because we had worked through the issues over the previous months and reduced the group to nineteen for the matches against China, we were dealing with a manageable number of permutations.

Sandy Pisani was still chairperson. She had been joined by Jackie Potter from New South Wales, Kerry Wharton from Queensland and another South Australian, Jane Lamprey. During the previous couple of years all of them had seen us play in various locations overseas and had observed most of the activity in Australia. These four were responsible for selecting junior teams as well as being involved with the senior team. The dual responsibilities allowed them to be aware of exactly the requirements of the game at its elite level. Certainly this would be helpful in assessing the juniors. Too often junior squad selectors don't understand the elite requirements.

We had met from time to time during the previous six months and had selected the Champions Trophy team in a telephone link-up. Now I joined the others in Sandy's hotel room in Parramatta, where the final judgments would be made. Again I was unpleasantly aware that our decisions would impact greatly on the players. It was a responsibility that everyone took very seriously.

This time we settled on the first fourteen players quite quickly, but the last two were again devilishly difficult. Only after some very determined review and comparison did we get closer to a decision. It was not simply a case of comparing individuals with one another. We had to consider how each combination of players would function. Often one offered strength somewhere but a potential deficiency elsewhere.

There were two crucial issues. First, the injury to Shelley Andrews which had ruled her out of contention left us with only three strikers. We had to decide if they were the best three or whether we ought to move a midfielder forward. Both Claire Mitchell-Taverner and Alyson Annan could do it, but that would impact adversely on the midfield. Opinion differed on this matter but I was keen to have the three specialists as I knew an injury would leave us very vulnerable if we only took two specialist strikers. Julie Towers therefore

Before the first game at the Sydney Olympics – 'Listen to me, remember our plans and every little incident counts.'

Out to dinner, 2001. Carmen is relaxed as always and even I am smiling, the Olympics are well and truly over.

Libby and Jonathon flank their friend Pete McKerracher after the win on 29 September 2000. Gerry Garard, husband of Hockeyroo Renita, is in the background.

Oscar at about seven months old in the garden.

A family shot taken in 1963. Left to right: elder brother John, myself (the youngest), Mum, sister Judy, Dad and brother David.

My first ever team at Dalkeith Primary School, 1960.
At eight years of age I am in the front row on the far left.

My first coach, Wilfred Thorpe. He involved all of us in the game and we had great fun.

A political candidate in 1982, with Kate, aged three. Notice my hair!

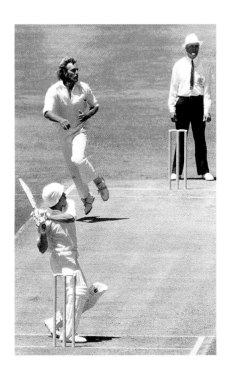

Gillette Cup Semifinal, playing against Queensland at the WACA in 1976. Hitting Dennis Schuller for 4: a rare occurrence. I top scored with 25 in the 'Miracle Match'. We were bowled out for 77 but then dismissed Queensland for 62.

BELOW: Another close call; batting for Western Australia at the GABBA against Queensland in 1978. I batted most of the day for 93!

Merv Adams, the man who helped us believe
we could beat India and Pakistan in the 1970s.
Perhaps the most influential figure in my
sporting development.

In Perth in 1979, versus Netherlands; breaking away from some close marking by the
Dutch. [Photograph: Geoff Fisher, Fisher Studio]

Standing next to the President of Pakistan General Mohammad Zia-Ul Haq. Australia's first win in the Champion's Trophy, 1983.

Karachi, 1982, shaking hands with Pakistan Captain Munawaruz Zaman before the match, with a full house in the background.

OPPOSITE: After winning the Peugeot Trophy in a four-nation tournament in Amsterdam, 1981.

The Champion's Trophy, which we won in 1983, was very heavy – little wonder, it was made of pure silver. This was our first win in the coveted tournament.

Australia's only World Championship victory in London, 1986. I'm on the right with my hand on the trophy, a bearded Colin Batch is on the left.

Seoul, 1988. I was a proud flag bearer at the Olympic Opening Ceremony.

Chatting with Opposition leader Bill Hayden at a fundraising dinner in Perth in 1982.

Prime Minister Bob Hawke, Jonathon (aged three) and myself during the 1987 election campaign.

The young medico atop a cluttered desk, 1982.

The opening of the Redcliffe Bridge with Premier Peter Dowding, April 1988. He got to cut the ribbon!

BELOW: With my assistant coach Chris Spice (left) in 1994. We shared a coaching award – coaches must work as a team.

Nova Peris with Libby at Perth airport after our triumphant return from Atlanta in 1996.
Nova was a great competitor during her time with the Hockeyroos.

The players and staff on the dais after our win in Sydney. My strongest emotion was one of relief.

After the match in Atlanta. Satisfied members of the off-field team. Left to right: Meg McIntyre (physiotherapist), Wendy Pritchard (manager), Ross Smith (physiotherapist), Brian Glencross in cap (high-performance manager) and Kathleen Partridge (goalkeeping coach).

Hockeyroos enjoying a victory lap in Sydney after the final.

Nine Hockeyroos with Wendy Pritchard (manager) on the far left, Corinne Reid (psychologist) and Trish Heberle (video coach) next to her, outside our home in the village before the Opening Ceremony, 15 September 2000.

Press shot in the lead up to the 2000 Olympics. Father and daughters Kate and Libby.
[Photograph: WA Newspapers]

Happy Hockeyroos after the final in Sydney 2000. Katrina Powell is missing from the photo.

had a spot. Indeed once we had determined to go with three specialists up front the midfield was quickly settled. Mitchell-Taverner, Annan, Renita Garard and Rechelle Hawkes would play there and a desperately unfortunate Karen Smith missed out. Claire Mitchell-Taverner would play exceptionally in the Olympic Final. Her two best games for her country would be in her two biggest games, the World Cup Final in 1998 and in the Sydney Final.

The other very difficult issue was to decide on the corner battery. Having agreed we needed Katie Allen's toughness in defence, we could not have the luxury of two hitters without losing flexibility elsewhere. Representing 40 to 50 per cent of scoring corners, would be crucial. Jenny Morris was our best hitter and Bianca Langham and Louise Dobson were not far behind. Morris, back from injury, looked to be getting better as the months passed. The other two waxed and waned a little but were credible alternatives with some form.

My concern was about having back-up. In Alyson Annan and Nikki Mott we had two good flickers who could hit at a pinch. Was that enough? Could we do without Dobson and Langham? A review of our games throughout the season showed that we were more successful flicking than hitting and so I thought we might be able to go without a back-up hitter. It was a risk, but calculated, and worth it I thought.

That judgment allowed us to take the more versatile Juliet Haslam who could play in defence, midfield and at a pinch as a striker (which is where she had played in 1992). Additionally Haslam had attacking and defensive skills on corners. She was also brave and liked to score – she would do so in the final.

Karen Smith, Louise Dobson and Bianca Langham were very good players unlucky to miss out. If required I was confident about all of them, and indeed when Jenny Morris looked doubtful with a muscle strain a week out from Sydney, one of them was nearly called up. Each of them bounced back in the weeks after selection to display their readiness to be still considered if required.

Louise Dobson gave everything and I know was greatly disappointed. There was little more she could have done. Her effervescence in the midfield nearly got her there. Karen Smith had been close in 1996 and had missed out again. Still only twenty-one, her stick work and work rate had improved dramatically. She was very, very unlucky. She still has a distinguished career ahead of her. Bianca Langham was an option in a variety of positions, but when we decided against taking a second corner hitter, her chances diminished. Katie Allen had more resilience and Bianca's form throughout 2000 had not been emphatic. At the beginning of the year all three coaches had chosen Bianca in their teams. No doubt she is one who would have been keen on the earliest possible selection had she known that!

On the long drive from the Parramatta hotel to the airport I tried to imagine how each player would react. Those selected are never the immediate problem. Those who would miss out would be crestfallen. On the flight I wrote to each of them. I think it helps but nothing can really make that horrible realisation seem okay. Only time helps and we had to be back together in a week.

The selection was no easier than in 1996. All three who missed the final cut were worthy of places. I felt especially for Karen, Bianca and Louise. During the final training phase there were periods where their disappointment would overwhelm them. My first meetings with each of them were difficult. Tearful and emotionally wounded to their great credit each of them was very brave for the period.

Those selected are delighted for themselves but often deeply sympathetic to friends and team-mates who have been omitted. This ambivalence can make the whole group fragile and on edge. As coaches it is a time when you have players distracted by selection issues yet you require all of them to continue focusing and finalising details for Sydney. Those who are reserves must know the plays yet always feel like extras no matter how things are organised.

12

Criteria for Selection

In 1996 we spent some time considering and recording a selection method and selection criteria that would be as transparent and objective as possible. The players deserved to know what sorts of things counted. The selection process up until then had reflected a growing implicit set of criteria. The requirement of Olympic accountability made us keener to have clear guidelines.

The criteria reflected my experience of many years playing and coaching before 1993, and my three years with the Hockeyroos as well as considerations specific to Atlanta in particular (weather, competition format and principal opponents). They proved to be an important and effective checklist when assessing players and balancing the team that would represent Australia in the most intensive competitive environment.

Knowing how we in Australia prepare for the Olympics and having closely watched our opponents prepare, it is clear that this event, held every four years, is the one which every team wants most. As I've already suggested, many coaches make the mistake of settling on their team too early in the piece, whereas I believe continued challenge and stimulation right up to the event leaves players in the best frame of mind to perform.

The criteria represent an appropriate formula for a team selection close to the event. This avoids the problem of athletes peaking too early or relaxing after selection and it also ensures sufficient time to get used to the idea of being in the team. Selecting too late can be as detrimental as selecting too early. Each coach may see the situation differently, but I suspect few would not agree that there is an optimal time for most teams to be selected. The difficult bit with teams is that some individuals within the team will not always be enamoured with the process or timing whatever or whenever it is!

I should point out that these criteria cannot totally objectify the selection process for teams. In the end choosing players in a sport like hockey – a complex, integrated team activity – will always be heavily subjective as those aspects we measure objectively, like aerobic capacity, only tell a small part of the tale. While swimming, athletics and cycling can measure performances more objectively, it is not possible in our sport.

Here then are the selection criteria we devised for the Hockeyroos. They are also broadly relevant in sports with a long season and week to week commitments such as Australian football and club rugby.

1 PHYSICAL QUALITIES

Speed, in particular, is of paramount interest to me here. It cannot be everything but it sure helps. It can enable you to break open a defence and it can help you cover up errors. It causes opponents to play conservatively and opposing coaches to adjust strategy. It allows players to take greater risks when measuring their margin for error. Of course its absence ought not automatically exclude a player. Players without this precious commodity very often develop other aspects of their game to compensate: they read the play better, they develop exquisite and special skills, they learn a way of playing that can counter faster opponents, they learn to operate in 'traffic'. There are so many examples. Carlton's Greg Williams, twice a Brownlow medallist, lacked speed, but knew where to find the ball. He had very quick hands, knew how to deliver the ball and was a courageous competitor.

Her speed initially earned Nova Peris a look-in with the Hockeyroos; it made Alyson Annan special and it enabled Lisa Carruthers to change from attacker to defender. But two players lacking in this commodity and without a compensating aerobic capacity made Hockeyroo Olympic teams because of their other attributes.

Renita Garard (nee Farrell) lacked speed but built up her game in other areas. Her ball control and basics were exceptional, she read the play early, worked on becoming essential in our set plays and she set a standard in training and off-field discipline that could not be discounted. Katie Allen did not have the quickness or agility that defenders usually need, yet became a rock on which a defence could be built. What she did have in spades was courage. While most women's sports do not require physical courage, hockey is exceptional in this respect. Katie is the sort of athlete who would put her body on the line in any situation to stop an opponent scoring. Her basics were sound, her trapping exceptional and her ability to plug a hole with crucial tackles around our defence circle was first rate. These two players were the only field players selected without the speed and agility that are usually essential ingredients of our game.

Whatever the sport, speed is a commodity that is essential. The ability to bowl fast enabled the West Indies to dominate world cricket for more than a decade. The soccer coaches at the Australian Institute of Sport in Canberra recognise agility and speed off the mark as the most important determinants of a lad's likelihood to succeed. Australian footballers today play at a speed that would dazzle the greats of the 1970s let alone the 1950s. Softball is dominated by fast pitching. The list goes on and on. Speed of movement and action is a winning quality.

In hockey aerobic capacity is essential in almost every position except deep defender (Katie Allen's position) and goalkeeper. While our strikers are seen as explosive players usually they cannot fulfil their defensive roles or continue to make dynamic movements without this capacity.

Given the size of the pitch and the speed of the ball, there are very few occasions when players are not in a play-making position on the field. In 1996 in Atlanta, the correlation between the capacity to endure in the heat and the player's aerobic capacity to endure was well understood. Everyone's aerobic capacity had to be maximised to ensure that we could maintain our tempo in every game of the tournament.

Kate Starre, who had been a fullback and forward in previous times, was one of our best athletes in this respect. Her tremendous work rate was underpinned by exceptional aerobic fitness and a great desire to be in the action. Kate was never one to be on the periphery. Her capacity to get in the play to defend and also go forward was crucial to our team. In Atlanta and Sydney she played as a defensive midfielder, yet in both tournaments scored or set up crucial goals by venturing forward appropriately.

When one looks at Australian football, the game of a Robert Harvey, Shane Crawford, Shane Woewodin or Peter Bell is underpinned by their terrific aerobic capacity. I still remember the work of Nobby Stiles and Alan Ball in 1966 when England became world soccer champions. These players were the engine room of the team. Every team needs such nomadic players. They tie the spaces together, connecting team-mates with one another, and run across lines to outnumber opponents and penetrate defences.

In Sydney the Hockeyroos engine room was powered principally by Kate Starre, Rechelle Hawkes and Claire Mitchell-Taverner. Two who did not make it to Sydney were Karen Smith and Louise Dobson. Had the weather been hotter, one of these two may have been closer to selection as we may have required more aerobic capacity.

The other essential physical quality is strength. Strength generally underpins explosive power and is translated into hitting speed, acceleration, agility and ability to maintain balance when bumped or interfered with. Nikki Hudson (nee Mott), Alyson Annan, Katrina Powell and Jenny Morris between them scored eighteen of our twenty-five goals in Sydney and they are all strong and powerful athletes. For goalkeeping also it is a critical ingredient emphasised to the extent that little aerobic training is done by the goalkeepers. Of course in the various football codes strength and power are crucial components for any aspiring performer as body contact is a significant part of the contest.

These physical qualities are essential, but rarely the defining characteristics in selection. So we move on to the other criteria.

2 CURRENT FORM

Nothing is more important than this. It is rare that a player in the midst of an appalling season will have a form reversal in the heat of the toughest contest. The player with moderate form may transform their performance and those who are enigmatic tend to remain so with many fluctuations in form. Of course there may be mitigating circumstances which when considered can be relevant. Injury and illness can affect performance and cause temporary form losses. In such cases the nature of the problem and duration of its effect bear consideration.

Form slumps of short duration are common and a few poor matches are understandable. Quality players will turn this around. However, sustained poor form in an athlete without a solid record of form or a history of being able to 'change up' should ring alarm bells. In every major campaign of the Hockeyroos there have been one or two athletes who have suffered a form slump. Sometimes it appears that as they realise what is happening their anxiety about selection militates against them turning their form around. While the importance of form is difficult to quantify, this should be the quality that receives heaviest weighting. Often the out of form player will be good at training or while playing at a lower tempo, but seem to just be off the pace at the higher tempo of competition or against the best quality opposition.

Stories of the out of form champion doing it on the day in my experience are the exception rather than the rule. The Australian cricket team in India in March 2001 did not replace Ricky Ponting in the third test of the series. They made a judgment that he might turn his poor form around. My view, at the time, was that he was unlikely to recover given the cauldron of the competition into which he would be thrown. The availability of a well-performed replacement made the decision more perplexing. Probably Ponting was saved by his good form in a practice match two weeks earlier, yet the signs in the second test were clear – he was off the pace. His failure in the third test confirmed this. Usually such slumps in quality players are not terminal. However some immediate relief followed by a period of consolidated work and reflection can help.

3 PAST RECORD

A record of previous good performances in major competitions or in situations where athletes have been under pressure, for example, in club or state finals, should be taken into account. A player's form and demeanour when playing for a poor team should also be considered. Most athletes can perform well in a winning combination but to perform well in a losing team is often a sign of real quality.

A past record, however, must be measured against current form. Certainly the aging athlete just hanging on might want the selectors to consider their past record, but this must be done with caution. Too often aging athletes have the benefit of 'sympathy' selection – such decisions can rebound in the selectors' faces.

In assessing the record of seasoned athletes one often has to contrast it with the blank slate of the improving tyro without experience in major competition. The calculation of merit in such cases requires fine judgment. One of my strongest views is that we ignore youth at our peril when selecting.

In calculating the merits of selecting on past record each situation will differ and needs to be individually assessed. Wayne Bennett's inspired choice of Allan Langer to play for Queensland in the final State of Origin game in 2001 did not only reflect an appreciation of Langer's fantastic record in major competitions. Langer's form (albeit in a lesser competition) was good, he was injury free and he was motivated by a great will to climb one final hurdle.

This 'one game' scenario is unique but putting all these factors together you have a powerful force. Yet the most powerful force of all can be the belief of a coach in the athlete and in this case the confidence shown by Bennett in the brave and motivated Langer was a further irresistible element. Alfie's final state of origin rugby game was to prove a brilliant success. For Rechelle Hawkes Sydney's final would provide a similarly spectacular finale.

Perhaps the most difficult judgment that coaches have to make is assessing the right time for an athlete to leave or be replaced. Rarely do athletes get it right for themselves, going too early sometimes, but too late more often! I suspect that I stayed too long when I competed in Seoul. I know that I could have played on in my cricket career had I not had other things to do.

4 SPECIAL QUALITIES

Some athletes have qualities that are hard to quantify or categorise, yet they are indispensable. In soccer and hockey, the goal scorer is often a quirky character, unorthodox, usually with an explosive quality and frequently with a certain single-mindedness.

Jackie Pereira was an exceptional goal scorer in women's hockey. The first to score one hundred goals for Australia, her trademark was the diving deflection, made while sliding across the turf. The great qualities of Jackie were her exceptional agility and acceleration and her timing and courage. Not the most skilled ball handler, she knew how to score. In 1996 we took her to Atlanta. The selection was close between Jackie and the rapidly improving twenty-year-old Nikki Mott. In the end it was Jackie's goal-scoring record that swayed the selection. While being a solid contributor throughout and playing a very good final, Jackie didn't score in the tournament but the threat of her scoring was ever present.

During her last years at the top Jackie managed to adapt her game better than I had expected as she came to grips with an approach that required the goal scoring to be shared rather than focused on one or two attackers. To her credit Jackie was able to retain her quality and so became a twin gold medallist in Atlanta.

Katrina Powell and Shelley Andrews are two very different players and personalities, yet they both had that special knack. Consistent scorers all around the world, these two were always alert for a chance. Off balance, diving, rebounding or slogging it from the top, these two both steadily scored a goal every second game over the years. Such players are indispensable.

Good as these three were, none could match Alyson Annan, the best goal getter in the women's game. She has the advantage of being a corner taker and a field goal scorer. Alyson averages nearly a goal a game these days. The secret is her quickness of action and execution. Usually well balanced, often anticipating play in an uncanny way, Alyson, if she continues as she is, will be the first women's player in the world to score two hundred international goals.

In the men's game Ron Riley, Terry Walsh and Mark Hagar all were greatly gifted. I suspect Riley who played in the 1960s and 1970s, with today's opportunities would have been sensational. His speed, balance, timing and single-mindedness were special.

In every sport the goal scorers are revered. At times I believe the focus on them is not deserved and downright ignorant. Indeed to focus on one or two goal scorers can make any team very vulnerable. A team is best served by having a number of scoring options. One of the most difficult teams to counter is the team in which everyone is looking to score.

One of the greats of soccer that I remember was Gerd Müller. The nuggety centre-forward hardly touched the ball in some matches, but was often on hand to slot away the half chance. It was just such a goal in the 1974 World Cup final in Munich that broke the deadlock for Germany. Müller wasn't particularly quick, wasn't tall, wasn't a wizard on the dribble, but he knew where to be and how to punish. It is a skill to be able to do that. It is developed and honed by practice so it becomes instinctive.

When asked what went through his mind as the ball was at his feet that day, Müller commented that he just acted instinctively – there was no thought process. Thinking, I suspect, is for defenders and midfielders. It is not the stuff of goal scorers – they act best on their instincts and reflexes.

Most of those who succeed in being a goal scorer seem to have always concentrated on that aspect of their game. Perhaps they didn't have the attributes (for example, aerobic capacity) which would have assisted them elsewhere, or maybe astute coaches recognised early their penchant for scoring and reinforced it.

As an athlete I always wanted to be in the play. Waiting for the ball to come to me was never interesting, but the buzz of scoring was exciting. In a special way scoring was the best feeling. Scoring a goal had the capacity to change the complexion of your day. I actively encouraged all my midfielders to be goal takers.

I am not aware of any studies to quantify the effect of scoring, but time and again I have seen players lifted and enthused dramatically by scoring a goal. I firmly believe that the scoring (even if it entails only the conversion of a penalty earned by another) lifts a player's performance by as much as 20 per cent. The effect is sometimes transitory, usually lasts for the rest of the game and sometimes is sufficient to induce a shift in form over longer periods.

Conversely, the 'missed sitter' or failed conversion has the potential to trigger a doubt crisis in the vulnerable player. For one whose game is built on scoring or being the finisher, then the potential for such lability is ever present. Goals can become their lifeblood and *raison d'être.* I tried to avoid this situation in my teams by expanding the number of goal scoring options and routes and encouraging everyone to become a goal scorer. Best not to have all your eggs in one basket!

So what other special qualities might attract one to a player? In 1980 I played with a Dutch club, Laren, in a weekend tournament. At the time I was considering playing a season there. I was interested in their way of playing. Our opponents that weekend included teams from Spain, England and Germany. The German team Limburg HC included the brilliant Stefan Blöcher who was capable of winning the game by himself with his speed and skill. During the game our team employed a marking defender to destroy Blöcher's effectiveness. Besides Blöcher, the rest of the players were evenly matched and the game was a close affair until Limburg scored just before time.

My assessment of the tactic was that it worked pretty well. Indeed we nearly got a draw and could have stolen a win if we had taken one of our chances. A team that was probably 10 to 20 per cent better nearly stumbled against us. One of our lesser players nearly succeeded in nullifying our opponent's champion player for the whole match.

Australian hockey players are generally sceptical of such tactics, certainly in the 1970s most of us were. However, given the right circumstances and the right conditions these are legitimate and effective means of operating. Australian football is a game in which such tactics are commonly employed to telling effect. If the match-up is right, one's opponents can be seriously damaged by a good 'tagger'. My word of caution would be that such a way of playing ought to be discouraged in young players as it can limit the aspirations and the horizons of the developing athlete.

I spent much of my playing career having to contend with such tactics myself. I think there is nothing which brings home to you more the need for teamwork than that type of play. Without combined and well-organised efforts, spoiling tactics can significantly debilitate a team's playmakers and method. The mentality and physical skill required to fulfil such a role are not obvious in all players. A capacity to nullify and mark opponents is another example of the special qualities which one may look for in making a selection.

5 SET PLAY SKILLS

Hockey is a game in which scoring opportunities can be almost completely eliminated if your defence operates effectively. In Sydney we only had one field goal scored against our defence in eight matches. That goal was a consolation goal in the final match. In hockey it is too easy to defend. Accordingly it is sometimes only through set plays – essentially the penalty corners – that scoring is possible against a tight defence.

Because of this we placed a great deal of emphasis on this aspect of our play. Every player was encouraged to perfect the skills required for penalty corners. While we had a template of corner routines, there were as many as fifty variations of the core moves and many of these were rarely used for fear of overexposure. It was sometimes necessary to invent new variations during a tournament to use against a particular opponent. This was frequently attempted in minor tournaments to convince the players that it was possible. However the core of our preparation occurred in training. The momentum of practice would increase as we approached major competitions. Earlier on, our time would be spent perfecting the basic pieces of the puzzle.

Essentially what was required was a fast, accurate push-out, effective and consistent stopping and powerful and accurate goal shots or passes for deflections into goal. Our Olympic team contained not one player who did not have a special skill or ability to contribute to this aspect of our game in attack or defence.

A critic might look at our Olympic corner conversion rate and say we were not the most efficient corner converter or defender in the tournament (efficiency being measured as number scored divided by number earned.) That is so, but it does not allow for the fact that we did not use our most potent corners in any game until it was absolutely necessary. I am not sure this is true of the other teams. More telling, perhaps, is that in the Olympic final in Atlanta we scored 50 per cent and in Sydney we scored 50 per cent of our first four corners. That is a very good conversion rate. Most teams would be delighted with 20 to 30 per cent.

Every player in our squad understood that these specific set play skills were critical to their selection chances. Over my time as coach, these skills quite often tipped the scales in selection consideration.

Every game has its set plays or dead ball situations as they are called in soccer. In the AFL, stoppages, out of bounds situations and point kick-ins are the focus of considerable emphasis these days. A relatively recent phenomenon is the use of designated kickers for shots outside 50 metres. With increasing numbers in defence the capacity for players to score with long kicks parallels the importance of the three point shooter in basketball.

6 FLEXIBILITY AND VERSATILITY

Whatever the game the tendency towards greater versatility in players has been evident over the last decades. This, of course, is a trend not only seen in sport, it is evident in the workplace where multiskilling and retraining for different types of work are common practice.

In cricket for much of this century it was expected that tailenders would slog or merely go through the motions of run scoring. The utility of these players being competent and determined batsmen in a game which requires every player to bat seems self-evident. At a time when gentlemen played the game and fielding was mainly carried out with the feet it may have been okay! It is just poor practice now.

Similarly the skills and athleticism of fielders have been improved exponentially by one-day cricket, a game in which all-rounders are the rule. I don't expect that Australia will ever have another keeper who is not an accomplished batsman. The standard set by Adam Gilchrist will be the measure of future keeping aspirants. Rod Marsh, Alan Knott, Jeffrey Dujon and Ian Healy all were part of this evolution.

In Australian football, the ability to play all over the field is essential to Kevin Sheedy's method, and players must be capable on both sides of their body and be athletically competitive unless possessing some special capacity. The one-dimensional dinosaurs are being phased out as if some metaphorical ice age was washing over the game.

For the Hockeyroos, the message was a clear one. They should look at versatility as an asset that could make them indispensable to the team. Players had to be used to playing both left and right side, and should develop attacking and defensive skills. During play they should expect continuous interchange according to the match situation.

While the fluency desired was not always forthcoming, the expectation was understood by the players. In the end I believe they were challenged by this expectation and their enjoyment of the game was enhanced. The spin-off in performance was that players expanded their range of skills and thus their capacity to be involved in and impact upon the game. Opponents found it difficult to clearly define our way of playing, and when injuries or unavailability meant that we were without some players we had ready-made alternatives.

In Atlanta such versatility became very important. After the second match, Jackie Pereira developed an infection in her already sutured knee. Spiking a temperature, she was unable to play in our second and third games against Argentina and Germany and our midfielders had to fulfil her attacking role.

Against Argentina a 7–1 blow-out took the pressure off, but the game against Germany was very tight and closely contested. Played in the heat of the day it would severely tax us. Our only goal was scored at close range by an adventurous Danni Roche who was filling Jackie's shoes as striker. Danni had been playing at defensive midfield in the tournament but her original selection had been confirmed by her willingness to get forward. In our preparation her goal-scoring bent had been evident and there was no doubt it influenced her selection. It was something that I was very pleased about that day!

There remain two areas that complete the selection criteria. They are perhaps the most nebulous but also in many cases the most critical differentiating qualities between athletes. They are team orientation and mental strength.

7 TEAM ORIENTATION

Team orientation refers to how a player fits within the group. Is their influence on and off the field beneficial and positive? Are they, in spite of personal disappointments or issues, able to contribute usefully? I do not know of any objective measure that enables one to determine such issues. It is not clear how one best makes such judgments, but at different times and for different reasons they must be made.

While feedback from players is an important part of the selectors' considerations, one must trust one's own assessment. Players have favourites much more than coaches do. Their club or state teammates, those of similar age or background, and sometimes those who threaten their position may not be accurately assessed.

It was always an interesting exercise to ask the athletes to select their team. The tendency to be sympathetic to friends and like-thinking players did not greatly affect core player selections, but certainly appeared to operate on the final few places. Such exercises build an appreciation of the complexity of the selection task, and if done well provide valuable feedback to staff as well as an important insight for players into the stress of selecting.

Complex integrated team activities such as hockey, Australian football, soccer, rugby, netball and basketball require co-operative, co-ordinated actions, both continuous and spontaneous. An athlete whose primary goal is not the success of the team will usually not improve the team's performance. Athletes are occasionally self-centred to the detriment of the team, but rarely is it a consistent pattern of behaviour. What is common, however, is that the athlete is distracted by outside influences such as the media, family, friends, personal issues and lifestyle issues which can absorb and overwhelm them. These influences can cause athletes to lose awareness of the team dynamic that contributes to performance. Being able to co-operate and work together is critical to team sport.

Some athletes see their sport as a release from the humdrum of everyday life and as such it provides an environment in which reality is left behind. The game becomes the focus of all their attention. Such athletes, in my experience, are the most reliable and consistent. Their total absorption in the game is a commitment to the co-operative endeavour of their team. I like to think I came into this category.

8 MENTAL STRENGTH

How do you define this quality? Mental strength encompasses a range of attributes which go to an athlete's ability to reproduce their skills in the cauldron of competition. Having a cool head, dealing with adversity and organising and disciplining yourself to be properly prepared all fall within the category of mental strength.

As Corinne Reid put it so well in a note to me during 2000, 'We need firefighters'. She meant that people with passion and determination tested by difficult and challenging environments and sets of experiences are most likely to get it right under the stress of competition.

As a coach one walks a tightrope between training and testing with adversity, teaching skill and tactics and providing support and showing faith in athletes. Every athlete has doubts and uncertainties and all sometimes find themselves in situations that they cannot handle. The experience of being out of one's depth is crucial for the development of coping strategies and the belief that problems are not insurmountable.

Accordingly, when I talk about mental strength I am really referring to resilience. This one word best encapsulates what I want in a player – one who springs back from shock or depression or upset and keeps going.

I want athletes who can overcome adversity, be it defeat in a contest, injury, non-selection, poor form, personal problems, bad press or team-mates who let them down. I want athletes who have the courage to express their own opinions and argue the case for what they believe, but at the same time will be willing to put the team's good ahead of their personal wishes or ambitions. Those too wrapped up in their own performance are sometimes prone to over-react when things don't work out, and find themselves sent off or disciplined. I want an athlete who can manage their frustrations for their own good and that of the team. Finally I want an athlete who will push themselves in preparing to compete. An athlete who understands that it is their demeanour and discipline that can infect the whole team in a positive way.

An athlete who had all these qualities would be exceptional. It is rare to find one such player. Yet the criteria outlined here ought to be the template to which every athlete aspires. These behaviours can be learned and developed and coaches must learn to look for them, require them and reward them. In the end, of course, you would always select an athlete with a swag of these qualities.

13

Beware Aspiring Captains

It was nice to be chosen as captain. It gave me a boost. It often happened to me but even from a young age I think I knew that the most important thing for the captain to do was play well himself. The example one sets is one of the best ways in which the team's performance can be elevated by the captain.

Once I started to think seriously about such things, and that was not until I was in my twenties and playing first class cricket and international hockey, it seemed pretty obvious that playing came first and captaincy second. I was puzzled by the English cricket team model that selected the average player Mike Brearley as the captain and then picked the team around him. It seemed to me an absurd method and one that only made sense if there was a very serious shortage of talented players who could be selected for their cricket skills first.

There were two circumstances that led me towards my view that captaincy was not some sort of special talent and that it was not true that some were born to lead and others to follow.

I played cricket for Western Australia in the 1970s, as part of a talented and resourceful team. During the period in which I played we won the Sheffield Shield (now the Pura Cup) on four occasions. At different times John Inverarity and Rod Marsh were in charge, and while they differed in style and temperament, the team largely went along okay. While some decisions were not transparent, most were. Often they resulted from discussion and debate as the game unfolded. Certainly on the field the interplay was lively and it appeared clear that a number of different views contributed to better decision-making and more creativity than only one source of input.

Also, in a game such as cricket it often occurs that ideas or actions initiated by individuals provide the pathway or direction needed at any time. The captain may not bowl or field the ball, the captain may not even be out in the middle batting, but the players doing so can make good judgments and decisions and assess things too. In the end every team functions best with a critical mass of leaders, who, by their actions, decisions and judgments, ensure quality performance. It was thus in the Western Australian team. Rod Marsh, Dennis Lillee, Ross Edwards, Bob Massie, Graeme Watson, Graeme Wood, Bruce Laird, Terry Alderman, Kim Hughes, Bruce Yardley, Tony Mann and John Inverarity all played for Australia and by their demeanour and the quality of their actions were leaders. Only a couple had the title 'captain'.

In 1974, aged twenty-two, I was appointed captain of the Western Australian senior hockey team. We were to contest the National Championships in Adelaide. The team, in spite of having a new flavour to it with the addition of brilliant young players in Terry Walsh, David Bell and Craig Boyce, contained many senior Australian players and the former Australian and Western Australian captains Brian Glencross and Richard Aggiss.

My appointment was surprising to me and quite a shock to the establishment. I believe it occurred because Western Australia had performed very poorly the previous year when they failed to make the finals in Hobart. They had taken an older team and change was now in the air. However, for me, being in the position of leadership while the former leaders remained was difficult.

I was lucky Glencross and Aggiss were supportive team players who contributed as they would have done regardless of their official status. I got on with the job of playing well and we got through, but it became clear to me that a good team is a co-operative unit best served by the contributions of a critical mass of players who display, exhibit and support the common goals of the group. No one person can embody this, no one person should be expected to do so. In hockey, unlike cricket, there is not time to discuss matters on the field; you have to get on with it. In the helter-skelter of competition a captain does well if he or she does their job well as a player.

I find it interesting that players aspire to be captain. Although I often had the job it was never something I aspired to. I don't think my ego worked that way. To me, the game and its intricacies were always the great interest. I was keen to be successful and accordingly played with the team in mind, but none of that was tied up with a view on the primacy of captaincy.

It seemed to me that to embellish the team's performance, I needed to prepare well and play well. What happened off the field could influence team dynamics and so was important, and as captain I also had a role as a conduit between management and staff. But that was all.

There are many reasons why one wouldn't want the captaincy. First, the ceremonial duties can be a burden and distraction. Secondly, the focus of attention can be stressful and intrusive, and often an unforgiving media are looking for reasons for success or failure. I still remember a very lonely drive to the TV studio in Los Angeles following our semi-final loss to Pakistan in 1984. As team captain I had to front up to an interview for Australian television a few hours after the game. It was one of the unhappiest days of my sporting life and the last thing I wanted to do. Thirdly, there are duties on field that can interfere with performance, such as the need to deal with umpires, or, in cricket, the need to make tactical decisions.

Many who aspire to captaincy and indeed often solicit the job are by their nature and actions the wrong people. In professional sport, they may become more marketable or receive more money. Not a good reason! Some may like the idea of captaincy and the prestige that goes with it. Not a good reason! Some may truly believe that they are leaders and others ought to follow. Not a good reason! Others see it as a way to curry favour or get closer to management and the decision-making. Again, not a good reason! Beware aspiring captains.

When I began with the Hockeyroos in 1993, Sharon Buchanan was the captain. She had led the team in 1992 and was an outstanding player, but was coming to the end of her playing days. She had been responsible for me applying for the job and indeed sat on the panel that determined my appointment. At the time of the interviews I had presumed she was not continuing as a player. I do not think current players should adjudicate on coaching appointments.

I had only been in the job a few months and Sharon had led the team in our early games when we came to consider the appointment of a captain for the major competition of 1993. Sharon was obvious, but I felt that Rechelle Hawkes, a younger player, also brilliant, might be a catalyst for renewal. Hawkes would still be around for Atlanta whereas that was uncertain in Sharon's case.

It was a gamble, albeit only a small one as I didn't view captaincy as a critical issue. Of course, it may have been so to some of the players, but that was something we would need to sort out. The selection of Hawkes said three things. The message I wanted to send her was that I believed it was time she did more; she was a brilliant player but not yet dominant enough and sometimes inclined to be on the periphery. To the team the selection said we will change things and embrace youth. To Sharon, accompanied by appropriate counselling, it said she was released to concentrate on playing well. It also sent the message that I didn't think she'd be in Atlanta in 1996 and I wanted to see someone else in the position. Of course if Sharon did well released from the captaincy it would be her best chance of continuing with the Hockeyroos.

I thought that Sharon would be struggling to play in Atlanta, but that given her keenness in 1994 would be a part of our World Cup team that year. After playing well in 1993 she retired – against my advice. I was disappointed. I thought she was a year early, but always such decisions are subjective. When she left she was on top and playing well in a winning team!

In spite of preserving the status quo in terms of having a captain, albeit a new one, in that first year, I was far from happy with the position. My view, well established by 1994 since first conceiving it in the 1970s, was that captaincy was an anachronistic concept. It was a leftover from bygone times when all of the games we now play in this twenty-first century were established. The nineteenth-century notion of captaincy came from a time when society, business and the family were hierarchical and paternalistic. Someone in control or in charge told you what to do, how and when to do it, and you followed instructions implicitly. Things don't actually operate best that way in most areas, and indeed attitudes have changed.

Sport, however, is a bastion of conservatism and captaincy is a concept that maintains a position of almost mystical importance for most people involved whether playing, coaching or in administration. Discussions in the media, in boardrooms, in selection panels often revolve around the captaincy and its impact on some aspect of the game. Such discussions are usually banal and rarely touch on the real areas of responsibility of athletes and coaches which are to perform and enrich their sports through fair competition in a spirit that seeks to be excellent.

During the next couple of years I was keen to discover a better way of encouraging leadership in every player. I wanted all of them to be switched on to the game in the same way as one would expect from a captain. Every player ought to behave like a captain both on and off the field. That would be the aim.

Up until 1996 we expanded the leadership group so that a good cross-section of the team was involved. At major competitions we usually had four of the sixteen in the leadership group. This satisfied the International Hockey Federation requirement that someone on the field be designated as captain, as often the captains or vice-captains would be off the pitch being interchanged. Never or rarely were all four off together!

My experience told me that leadership was exhibited in a number of ways by different personalities. Most athletes exhibited these behaviours sometimes, but most had failings or were also deficient in some areas. Some of these qualities stemmed from personality or character, but many were teachable and could be learned and carried out with practice. This could occur in the same way one taught hockey skills. We set out to build a group who valued these things.

Some athletes display leadership by their attitude and demeanour at training. By their approach they can lift the quality of a session by infecting their team-mates with enthusiasm. Some by their inspirational on-field exploits lift their team-mates. Others are socially gregarious and by being inclusive of others can play an important role in enhancing the harmony of the group. Others are good listeners and more considerate of others' thoughts and ideas and thus improve the tolerance of the group. Some are willing to speak their minds and disagree with prevailing wisdoms and so bring an honesty to team discussions. Others will accept criticism without reacting defensively. This improves team learning and openness.

Fundamental to teams functioning well are a shared set of goals and beliefs which underpin the demeanour and behaviour of the group. There will always be differences, however, in interpretation of what is required or meant by any set of beliefs. This is very much like relationships – values and requirements must be clear and adhered to if a relationship is to work. In the end teams only function well when the group members accept that the group must come first, and so sometimes personal wishes, views or aspirations must be put aside. This is easier said than done.

Behaviours which can conflict with a group ethos and which can fragment harmony and respect are myriad. Lack of punctuality, poor training habits (being lazy, sloppy or careless), and complaining about training or commitments with the team all obviously come into this category. With relationships the same sorts of behaviours can cause downfall.

There are also less obvious ways of undermining group cohesiveness. The 'shop steward' who is always 'representing' the team and its interests is often someone who is pushing their own interests – beware! Those who are anxious about their form, selection, their career ending, contract negotiations or are distracted by outside interests all have potential to divert team focus and direction.

However, by widening the leadership group one minimises the possibility of individuals or one group in the team being able to dominate the group values. It also requires more athletes to consider team issues and team dynamics. This keeps the focus on the team. It requires athletes to see themselves as a team leader in their demeanour on and off the field. The best results are obtained if each individual develops themselves as a leader – that way everyone is thinking of what is best for the group.

The problem of captaincy has spilled over into another antiquated sporting custom. Fortunately during my time with the Hockeyroos, the tradition of the captain and vice-captain being selectors on tour became obsolete. All of our players played all of the time. The practice of team leaders being selectors, which I believe still occurs in the men's game, can make for very difficult decisions and circumstances in touring groups. Indeed, I think it is hard for player–selectors to be objective.

I'm not convinced that an out of form Mark Taylor was able to be objective about his test place, nor was it appropriate for a struggling Shane Warne to be selecting who should play on tour of the West Indies. While these situations may have been handled adequately, I am not convinced that using player–selectors reflects the modern reality of full-time coaches and readily available and mobile selectors. The recent decision by the Australian Cricket Board to strike out John Buchanan as a tour selector while retaining the captain and vice-captain is, in my view, bizarre and illogical, not to say archaic. It appears to be a decision born of mistrust, never a useful factor in such matters.

I well remember 1984, when as captain of the Australian men's hockey team I had to act as a selector with the coach Richard Aggiss, and the vice-captain, Jim Irvine, who had a significant Achilles tendon injury in the lead-up to the Los Angeles Olympic Games. Jim, a friend and my room-mate, was struggling to get fit for the Games. I did not believe he would make it but was keen for him to be given every chance to prove himself.

As long as the team had a back-up player available, we would be okay. After touring the Netherlands and playing in Vancouver, we arrived in Los Angeles and Jim was still problematic. John Bestall was flown into LA to provide back-up but my strong view expressed to the coach and manager was that Jim wasn't fit and wouldn't make it in time for the Games. Achilles tendon injuries are notoriously difficult and Jim, even with a significant heel lift to lessen the load, was struggling to walk without difficulty.

I found myself trying to be supportive of my friend and room-mate while trying to be objective as to his fitness. I saw up close the tension and stress on Jim. I saw it in myself and I presume the management felt it too. The final decision was to be made after a vigorous training workout a couple of days before the Games began. Unfortunately, I injured one of my intercostal muscles while practising penalty shots early in the session and was not there when the tests on Jim were carried out. I had already expressed my strong view that Jim wasn't sound. I was gobsmacked when I heard that he had passed the test. At the time, preoccupied with my own inconvenient but relatively insignificant injury, I let it go, but it would come back to haunt us during the competition.

I don't know exactly what advice the management received about Jim's condition but I think we made a mistake. As a selector on tour my capacity to adjudicate on the day the decision was made was interfered with by my own injury and thus my absence from the practice field for Jim's test. But more importantly there was sustained tension caused by both myself and Jim being selectors.

Jim would only play in fits and starts during the tournament. Fortunately, his place was capably filled by the versatile Michael Nobbs. Michael played very well every time he was required and by the time we came to the finals I was confident that he should play.

Then unfortunately events conspired against us. David Bell, our experienced and world-class right half, strained his hamstring. It was only a minor problem but as we were approaching the semi-final against Pakistan we had to decide what to do. Only two substitutes were allowed at that time and to play a doubtful player was risky. There was no way to test David's hamstring without risking an early recurrence of the injury. He had rested in our last round game. Jim was 80 per cent fit, but with him at least we knew what we were getting. His was a chronic injury and unlikely to deteriorate during the game.

If neither Jim nor David played we would have a completely new right-side defence for the critical semi-final. In the end, in the name of experience, we took Jim into the game and didn't risk David. Grant Boyce played right half and was serviceable but Jim was not sharp. He had not been throughout the competition and against some very quick Pakistanis it hurt us. We lost a pulsating encounter 1–0. Pakistan scored on a breakaway in the first half and defended valiantly as we fought to equalise on a hot, energy-sapping summer day. The goal, like all such pivotal goals, could have been averted by any one of a number of interventions. One of those might have been Jim making an interception as he ran in cover. Fully fit and sharp he may have made it.

There is no control condition in sport. You don't know if the outcome might have been different if you had made another choice. What I do know is that we made a mistake going into the Games with Irvine and it probably hurt us at a crucial time. Perhaps the decision was sentimental, perhaps it was just a punt gone wrong, perhaps it was poor judgment by the experts who advised us or perhaps the coaches just got it wrong about the extent to which Jim would be affected.

It is a lesson I learned and a mistake that I hope I will not make as a coach. In 1994, I decided that Liane Tooth was not physically sound the day before we went to Dublin for the World Cup. I was determined to give such a loyal and long-serving player every chance. I remember at the time some thought I was too hard on Tooth as I insisted she complete a demanding sprint regime that day. She failed and twenty-year-old Katie Allen got her chance. In the end when our other fullback, Tammy Ghisalberti, stumbled in the competition, Allen played a pivotal role in our victory.

Suffice to say the player–selector formula is one I do not endorse. Such situations test beyond reasonable levels one's objectivity and can also distract from one's performance of either duty – playing or selecting.

I don't doubt that our fascination with captains will continue for a while longer. Sport has never been a very progressive social force. In recent years as many as four Socceroos put their names forward aspiring to the job of captain. The West Coast Eagles leadership speculation seemed to fill newspaper articles on a weekly basis before the season began.

However, there are signs of change. Increasingly, leadership groups are expanding and the leadership role of every player in the team is being examined and outlined. Soon many teams will embrace a new leadership paradigm – that of a leaderful team. I will observe that with interest!

14

A Leaderful Team

In 1996, we planned to select our team for the Atlanta Olympics in early June after our European tour through Britain, Germany and the Netherlands. This would leave us approximately six weeks for fine-tuning before the Games commenced in mid July. In November 1995 the players and support staff agreed that this program would allow us to pick a form team which would give us our best chance to play well in Atlanta.

There were a number of players in our squad who were striving to claim a place in the team. Every match we played, and there were about twenty, was going to be a chance to press for an Olympic berth. In the past, Olympic teams had been selected much earlier than this. I was concerned that early selection did not allow for the best preparation. Players tended to relax once selected and fitness would be crucial in Atlanta. The competitiveness of the whole group played a role in lifting standards and ensured those standards were maintained.

Equally, even after selection the reserve players would be required to continue training. There were two purposes here. First, they might be required to perform in case of injury, illness or accident. Secondly, the Olympics, while important, represented only one milestone for a player in a career. Many had more improving to do and being with the squad was part of their continuing education. The shorter this period the easier it would be. Players had expressed concern that there should be sufficient time to develop combinations. Would six weeks be long enough, they wondered. It was my view that it was and anyway we were already working on total flexibility because of our team interchange policy. Much of that flexibility and much of the combination work was already happening and would continue right through to Atlanta.

The pros and cons were debated and the matter settled even though some harboured doubts. I was not surprised, therefore, when in late March 1996 a delegation of players came to me suggesting that we select the team earlier. The argument about combinations was again raised. I suspected it also had something to do with confirming travel arrangements for families and friends and avoiding a prolonged period of insecurity about selection.

The group of players who claimed to represent the whole team wanted selection brought forward a month or more and certainly before our European tour. The players said they had consulted widely and the rest of the squad felt the same. My instinct was to say no immediately, but I decided to take the discussion to the whole group. I felt that it would be harder to select a form team earlier than planned, and I was concerned about how we would keep those who would miss out training and preparing for a longer time. Also, I was not convinced that everyone in the group felt as the group of senior players had indicated. I wanted to see if there really was a consensus on this.

After discussing the issues at a meeting the players had a secret ballot on whether or not to bring selection forward. The result was edifying! Only eight out of twenty-four voted to bring the selection forward. The majority felt there was much left to do to show their best. Sixteen opted to preserve the schedule as determined in 1995. Clearly they wanted more time to press for a team spot. There was more to do.

This little story was for me a graphic example of how small factions within a team can change or divert attention from the shared goals and identity of the group. The elite group of seniors had their own reasons for wanting early selection. Some may have genuinely wanted more time to polish combinations. Many had family and friends travelling to Atlanta and had practical decisions to make. Some expected to go and would have liked to have that confirmed so they could feel comfortable. I don't think there was much of this on a conscious level nor do I think such actions are malicious or calculating. I think, however, that regardless of motive, leaders can undermine group goals and group maintenance because they sometimes exert their personal superiority at the expense of the group's shared identity.

After the experience in 1996 when thankfully the team made a correct decision to stick to our program I was even more keen to share the leadership as widely as possible. A new leadership paradigm was required – I wanted a leaderful team.

At the beginning of 1997, I was keen to go further in changing the leadership format. I was concerned that Rechelle Hawkes was seen as the captain regardless of the reality that others shared the role and I was certain that for her good and that of the team it would be a good idea to change that situation.

The issue would become one of timing and method. Rechelle had the quality to play through to Sydney. She would be thirty-three then and perhaps finding her training and competitiveness on the wane. My experience had been that the removal of the leadership responsibilities could release pressure and precipitate a type of renewal. I felt that might work for her.

This fitted nicely with an approach which would involve as many as possible in the leadership of the team. We had determined that such an approach would best allow individuals to express themselves in the team's performances and within the team environment on and off the field.

'Social loafing' was discussed openly. This attitude or behaviour which says, 'Someone else will do it,' 'It's someone else's problem' or, 'They can fix it,' was to be shunned. We discussed the fact that social loafing occurred as groups grew larger or when leaders were appointed. Group members tended to become less 'curious' and less interested in contributing in such groups. This was one of the things that led to my view that by involving all the squad in leadership and requiring it of every athlete, we would get more consistent contributions from all. Equally this approach would release the pressure from the designated leaders as duties would be shared more evenly.

During 1997 and 1998, we tinkered with the leadership structure and included some new faces, but late in 1998 I thought it was time to go further. We had already established an ethos of interchange and appointed co-captains and vice-captains. The new approach would not be such a great step given that during 1998 we'd already had six different captains and vice-captains in Rechelle Hawkes, Juliet Haslam, Renita Garard, Nikki Mott, Kate Starre and Alyson Annan.

At the beginning of 1999, we started to prepare the ground for change. The topic had been discussed previously informally and the concept of an expanded leadership group had been readily accepted and had worked well. I believed it was time to take the next step and before we began training in February I had lunch with Rechelle Hawkes to outline my plans. Although we had shared the leadership throughout the previous four years, Rechelle was the media's choice as captain and the best known player. She had the media and public profile as leader of the team.

In my time with the Hockeyroos and given my knowledge of the game Rechelle Hawkes, in my opinion, was pound for pound the best female player in the world through the 1990s. While Annan is more brilliant and could eventually claim this accolade in her time, Hawkes had built a terrific all-round game. She was not the quickest; didn't have the best stick skills; and wasn't a great goal scorer, but she did all those things well. She probably was one of the best trappers of the ball, her change of direction was brilliant and her passing was penetrating and deft. She could tackle, she was aerobically outstanding and she read the game instinctively.

All of those things make up a technically gifted player, but on top of that Rechelle set an example in training and diligence that greatly influenced others. I can remember only a handful of matches in my eight years when she played poorly or let us down. More important perhaps were her performances in crucial games. She often made vital contributions in critical situations. None perhaps more typical than the penalty stroke she earned in Sydney against the Netherlands seconds before half-time. When many were walking towards the change rooms for the half-time break, she received brilliantly from a Lisa Carruthers pass and with skill and purpose penetrated into the scoring circle to be fouled as she positioned to shoot. That incident broke open a tight match and exemplifies the quality of Rechelle's play. Three Olympic gold medals in fact says it all.

I had chosen Rechelle as captain in 1993 because she was a skilled player with a wonderful training ethic. She was not the most outgoing member of the team but was well liked and always a team player. She occasionally drifted to the periphery of a game and I felt that she could have been more forthright with her opinions in meetings, but on the whole she was close to maximising her leadership potential.

My concern was that I wanted that from every member of the group. I believed only by giving effect to my approach could this be achieved. I believed that by not designating a leader we would require every player to look at their approach in a new way. Of course I expected to still get the same quality of leadership from Hawkes. But this was to be an invitation for others to widen their horizons.

Rechelle was receptive but probably not convinced. No doubt she enjoyed some degree of prestige from the captaincy, but I think two things allowed her to see the value in my proposal. At thirty-one she realised that to keep her own game in order less responsibility would be a relief. She was never a self-promoter; her renown had come almost entirely as a result of the quality of her performance.

Secondly, it was not as though she was being replaced. She would share the duties with fifteen others and I'm sure she knew that many other team members had much to offer. Having Rechelle and others positive about the shift made the selling of the change more easy. There was, as expected, widespread media comment about the move. The streak of conservatism that runs through sport is indeed wide and deep.

Corinne Reid ran a couple of very valuable sessions with the group outlining some of the rationale behind our move. Social loafing was to be outlawed. Curiosity was encouraged and learned helplessness (sitting by and watching without ever getting involved) was discouraged. We were looking for more from everyone and we expected them all to behave as leaders.

In my briefing with the media I was careful to describe our aim as the development of a leaderful team. We believed that within the group we had a lot of athletes whose leadership was dormant. While encouraging them to be active leaders, as we had in the past, might have touched the surface, we were now requiring them to do more. At different times they would all be cast in the role on match day and we would expect leadership off the field from all of them.

The best teams have a critical mass of leaders and at any one time a bunch of them must demonstrate it. It is not good enough to wait for someone else to do something. By giving practical and complete effect to this view by having no designated captain, I believed we would get more out of some players whose leadership skills lay quiescent. I still expected the others to deliver, but hopefully we would widen the base of leadership in the team.

Of course the media made a meal of this approach. 'Leading the Leaderless Team' appeared in the *Australian* on 1 March 1999. The article's byline was certainly inflammatory: 'One of Australia's greatest former team captains, Hockeyroos boss Ric Charlesworth, has suddenly sacked his own team's captains – all six of them. Chip Le Grand reports on hockey's communist coach.' The body of the article went even further. Lenin was evoked as a bogey!

I'm sure it made good copy but it was off the point. Clearly this was a concept which would take some time to sell outside the team. Fortunately the athletes were more realistic and accepting. Already we had become used to sharing the load with all sixteen athletes in any match. Already they understood that we were best served not by one leader and a bunch of followers, but by a vibrant group of players who were encouraged to show initiative. Already they were aware that this move would thwart the leadership ambitions of a few whose motives may not have been perfect.

The battle for captaincy within a club or team can be internally disruptive and destructive. The West Coast Eagles in recent times or Australia's Socceroos in 1999 are cases in point. In some ways the position is not worth the trouble and certainly this was an unintended practical benefit of our move.

While there was much criticism and speculation about this initiative there were a few pockets of support. Some were surprising and all added something to my already solid resolve. On 24 March, I received the following note from Michelle Ryan at the School of Life Sciences, Department of Psychology at the Australian National University.

> I read with interest an article in the *Australian* entitled, 'Leading the Leaderless Team'. In particular, your idea of handing leadership roles to each team member was extremely thought-provoking and I believe that such a move provides a great practical example of the leadership research we are conducting at the Australian National University. I have enclosed a copy of a recent article on leadership that I hope you find interesting.

Michelle's note reinforced my view and increased my confidence in the move. Subsequently, I have had contact with others at the

Australian National University. The research of Alexander Haslam, also from Psychology, certainly supported the model we were developing in our team.

The article Michelle Ryan sent me was written by Alexander Haslam and entitled 'Inspecting the Emperor's Clothes: Evidence that Random Selection of Leaders can Enhance Group Performance'. The abstract gives a clue to the contents of the article:

> This article tests the hypothesis that group performance might be superior when leaders are randomly rather than systematically selected . . . Results suggest that systematically selected leaders can undermine group goals and group maintenance. The possibility that this occurs because leaders assert their personal superiority at the expense of shared social identity is discussed.

Of course there were those who were waiting for the team to perform badly and who quickly seized on poor results as being indicative of a leadership decline in the Hockeyroos. Always there will be those who wish to find a simple identifiable cause, a glib rationale, for every eventuality.

Any coach worth their salt must be able to look much deeper than that. Team sports are complex, integrated, competitive, unpredictable contests. Seldom is any one factor the critical element in success or failure. Being analytical is crucial for the coach and accordingly I am attracted to the catchy adage of the American author, editor and critic H.L. Mencken: 'For every complex problem there is a simple solution and it is usually wrong!'

When in early 1999 we nearly lost a series to South Africa, losing games in Cape Town and Pretoria, I did not think it was leadership-related. When we were beaten with a golden goal in Milton Keynes by the Netherlands later in the year and when we placed third three months before Sydney, I never thought leadership was lacking because of our approach. It was and always is much more complex than that and we must learn to look behind the result for invariably a variety of factors contribute to any win or loss.

Throughout the last two years of my time with the Hockeyroos, we further developed and refined our leaderful team. Some players made progress in their personal leadership skills. All of them at some stage were 'captain' in matches.

In itself this is not necessarily a groundbreaking move, but it is an example of how some of the old conventions of sport are perhaps out of their time. Already it is increasingly common for teams to have leadership groups rather than relying on one or two individuals.

By making our stand and giving practical effect to it in all our matches in 1999 and 2000, the players became much more aware of their responsibilities to the team and I think we expanded our critical mass of leaders. That probably did make a little difference in the end.

15

After Atlanta

The hockey tournament at the Olympics can be a roller-coaster ride of ups and downs. To reach the finals in Atlanta we had to play seven matches in eleven days, and then on the thirteenth day, as the Olympics were drawing to a close, play the final. For the hockey athlete there can be no greater occasion.

In Atlanta as in Sydney the final was played on a warm evening heavy with atmosphere. There is something about night matches that seems to increase the drama. Perhaps it is because with every-one except the players in darkness the focus of attention on the pitch is so concentrated. On 1 August 1996 in the late afternoon heat we waited outside our accommodation for the little trolley carts that would take us to the bus station. Nobody spoke. By the final day our journey to Morris Brown College was very familiar. We did not get lost. There was no accident. In the early days in Atlanta both these things occurred. The bus drivers were now familiar with the route.

As I sat on the bus on the way to the ground I tried to recall a similar bus journey twenty years earlier in Montreal when we had ridden to Molson Stadium for an Olympic final against New Zealand. Our team was young and relatively inexperienced, not like the Hockeyroos of 1996. We had been so full of expectation that day but we probably were not ready for what was ahead in the way that the Hockeyroos were ready.

It was dusk as the Hockeyroos entered the stadium for our match. The bronze medal game between Great Britain and the Netherlands had gone into extra time and penalties. We waited in the change rooms. The mood was determined, there was a quiet resolve, a purposefulness which goes with the occasion.

You can only feel well prepared if you have done all the work in the months and years before. Even then everyone has doubts and they need to be conquered. The team meeting had focused on the simple central issues. No more was necessary. Any more would be superfluous and distracting. As the players lined up with Korea to walk onto the pitch they knew the ultimate exam was about to begin.

The first fifteen minutes were tight. They had one chance, a corner, caused by a nervous error. Korea's excellent routine was wayward. We pressed and made chances. Nothing till a corner earned by Juliet Haslam. Alyson Annan's shot was excellent, the routine for which we had been criticised earlier in the tournament was flawless; 1–0. For the rest of the first half we were on top. We were rarely threatened until just before half-time. Korea's second corner, and an unfortunate error by Clover after a poor shot meant 1–1 at half-time.

As we walked across the field at half-time I felt we were playing well. We were unlucky to be 1–1. We deserved a lead on our play. My half-time talk was positive. We could improve but we had played well. If we continued they would not be able to stay with us. The signs were there, but like a five setter in tennis it would be our persistence that could win the day. Trust your skills. Trust your instincts. Trust in each other.

Our second half was emphatic yet some desperate defence saw

Korea still in the game at 1–2 with ten minutes remaining. Our second goal came from a penalty stroke awarded for a breach on the goal line. It came after some sustained pressure and a number of shots had been saved by a Korean team under siege. Katrina Powell's brilliant goal settled the issue with seven minutes left. There was still tension, yet we were playing at our best. In Atlanta our final game deserved better than 3–1 but as time ran out that was irrelevant. To defeat Korea we had to be at our best and that night we did get close to it.

My principal emotion, as it was to be in Sydney was great relief. With no family or huge support group present, the celebrations were kept within the team. A few nights at Lulu's Bait Shack will always be recalled and the long flight home was just a haze. Atlanta was great but Sydney would be more special, I thought, because it would be home and the build-up of expectations, home crowd support and stress would all be magnified.

Following our success in Atlanta I had to wrestle with the problem of what to do next. The Olympic win brought with it a sense of achievement but in the following weeks I would find that I was unable to relax for too long as I contemplated my future. The Hockeyroos and the men's team were keen to appoint coaches for Sydney 2000.

The Australian men under Frank Murray had been cruelly deprived of a gold medal chance by a very controversial umpiring decision in their semi-final with Spain. Luck, however, ran with them against Germany and they won bronze. Frank would not continue – his last couple of years had been laden with controversy and the stress had been enormous.

In the same circumstances I don't think I could have continued as Frank had done. It says something for his toughness. Some would call it stubbornness. Frank left with the best record of any Australian men's coach, a record that still stands up. Frank had publicly anointed me for the men's job although I was not convinced that I wanted it.

During the previous few months I had been thinking about the future. When I took the job I had thought that four years was not long enough to really build a team. I believed six or seven was ideal. This, of course, did not fit neatly into any four-year Olympic cycle as administrators would wish. I believed there was more to do with the Hockeyroos but was concerned that nearly eight years might be too long with one team.

Additionally, Chris Spice, my assistant coach, was champing at the bit to take over and the scenario of me moving to the men's team fitted nicely with his plans. Chris and I had discussed his ambition. Earlier, in 1994, I had felt that Atlanta might be enough for me but I realised that I was enjoying coaching and still had more to do with the Hockeyroos.

Over a period of time I had come to the conclusion that I would like to stay in it a little longer. The dilemma was that another four years might be too much. Both the previous coaches in men's hockey, I suspected, had struggled the last year or so of an eight-year cycle. Frank Murray and Richard Aggiss before him had not been at their best in years seven and eight. It is hard to keep fresh and the athletes need to hear a different message or at least messages that appear different to them.

Hence soon after our return I found myself having to decide between the men's and women's programs. The choice was as clear as mud. On one hand I knew the Hockeyroos and a core of very good players remained. The junior players coming through were not as good as they had been in 1993, so there would not be such a good flow of new talent. However, many of those staying on still had room to improve and we had established some good cultural attitudes in the group. Could we go further? That would be a challenge.

Women's hockey had taken a risk with me in 1992 and I felt some loyalty to them. They frustrated me sometimes – I thought we could market and promote the team much better and we did not exert enough influence at the international level in the International Hockey Federation. I thought they could do more in these areas.

Brenda Cawood, the general manager, was a tireless worker for hockey and with Pam Tye, the president, worked hard to entice me back.

I sought a package similar to those of some of the other high-profile Australian Institute of Sport coaches, but I knew that our game was limited in what it could afford. In the end money was not a consideration as the men made the more substantial offer.

In many ways the men's job was more attractive. If I took it Chris would almost certainly get the women's job and any conflict there would be avoided. My enquiries indicated that the group of young male players emerging was very good. In 1997, under Barry Dancer's management, this group would win the Junior World Cup to confirm this potential.

The men's job had more 'up side' as they had still not made the top step of the victory dais at the Olympics and they certainly were good enough to do so. However, looking at their squad I thought there would probably need to be an 'attitude cleanout'.

There was one disturbing aspect of the men's approach. Initially they were concerned that I might want to use Frank Murray or others who did not meet with their approval. I made it clear that I ought to be able to have the assistants I desired and eventually they retreated on that. This did cause me some concern but I think their retreat was genuine.

In the end I made the decision principally for what may seem to many a strange reason. I believe the hardest thing to do in sport is to win again. Coaches seeking a second premiership often come unstuck. Consecutive Olympic wins had never been achieved in the women's game and in the men's game it was half a century since India had dominated the game to win gold at the 1952 and 1956 Games.

I would have to contend with a group of gold medallists who might know it all, and coming through was a new group that was not as talented as the previous group. Some who missed out were emotionally down and would need to rebuild their belief. The expectations would be enormous and could overwhelm us, and in Sydney the distractions would be huge. Our opponents who had perhaps been surprised by us would be ready for us in 2000.

Perhaps worst of all Chris would be greatly disappointed. He had expressed the view that he did not want to be an assistant coach for another cycle. I hoped our friendship could survive but I was not optimistic that he would stay.

When you must make a decision such as this one it is never easy or simple. Both of the options were attractive and had their advantages and disadvantages. I turned my back on the men's program knowing that there was a good group of players coming through and that the players would be highly motivated to win that elusive gold in Sydney. Additionally, I was hopeful that I might get another chance with the men's team at a later date. One of course can never know if that chance would ever come again. In the end I believed that the challenge of staying on top was the greatest challenge for a coach. I took the women's job.

Central to the dilemma I faced having made the decision was the future of the women's program. Nineteen ninety-seven had already been tagged as a Junior World Cup year with only a limited senior program. During the year we would put most emphasis on the junior team and assessing the players in that group who had senior potential. The senior group would only be able to play about twenty-five matches in the year. We would endeavour to retain the Champions Trophy in Berlin in June, but it would be difficult.

Soon after I made the decision to stay with the women I thought that I might lose the services of Chris. His immediate reaction was one of great disappointment as I knew it would be. He was ambitious to be head coach, but had been a loyal and committed assistant. Chris handled it by keeping his distance and indeed was absent from women's hockey's celebration dinner at the end of 1996.

Thankfully we remained in contact. He had been the first to know of my decision and while he was restless he agreed to stay on, but indicated that he might look elsewhere. In 1997 he would have the role of coaching the Junior World Cup team while he was assistant to the senior team. As the year progressed there was some tension as I was aware that others were courting Chris.

With increased funding courtesy of the Australian Sports Commission we could engage a third assistant coach as well as a goalkeeping coach. I felt I wanted someone who came from left field and so chose Bob Haigh, my former Australian team-mate, as an assistant. He was perhaps the person with whom I felt the most affinity in hockey and who remains one of the most interesting thinkers in the game. Kathleen Partridge was appointed as our part-time goalkeeping coach. A gold medallist from Seoul, Kathleen was a high school English teacher. During the four years I believe she played an important part in improving the quality of our goalkeeping.

Unfortunately Bob's appointment did not improve things with Chris. He felt left out of the process and while Chris and I continued to get on well I soon became aware of friction between Bob and Chris. They were different personalities, but I suspect in another environment would have got on well. To her eternal credit, Corinne Reid played a pivotal role in soothing the troubled waters of the triangle as best she could.

By mid year, after securing the Champions Trophy in Berlin in a thrilling final on a shocking pitch, it was obvious Chris would be moving. He was successfully seduced by the English to be the high-performance director for English hockey. Chris would play an administrative role utilising all the expertise that had made him an invaluable part of our program.

In hockey this was the beginning of a trend that would see four Australians move from our program to the United Kingdom by the end of the Olympic cycle. There was Chris, Barry Dancer as the English men's coach, Neil Hawgood at club level and Steve College who became the Scottish coach and assistant to the British coach.

The poaching undertaken by English hockey in the late 1990s is similar to that seen in cricket and rugby league in which Australians are very popular as coaches and players in Britain. Indeed the advent of lottery funding will no doubt bring about a renaissance in British sport if it continues and is spent wisely. The salaries are extraordinary by Australian standards yet it seems a small price for the British to pay for the accumulated expertise developed in Australia during the last two decades.

Chris has recently terminated his contract with English hockey after being head-hunted by English rugby union to establish their high-performance program. This year his salary will probably match what I earned in the last eight years as head coach in Australia. He has well and truly landed on his feet and I hope he appreciates what a favour I did him back in 1996!

In 1997 I made sure we did not give too much away. Knowing that Chris was being targeted I did not introduce anything that was new or that led towards a new direction. Players move around from time to time and while they often take valuable information with them they are not as knowledgeable as coaches. Chris, even in administration, would have an impact on the leakage of knowledge from our sport in Australia. I wanted to limit the damage, so in 1997 we did nothing radical or even very different in terms of training tactics or structure.

Following the Commonwealth Games in Kuala Lumpur in 1998, I returned home satisfied with the outcome but unsure as to how we could improve our team. Michelle Andrews's form had been good, yet I was still concerned about her soundness in the long term. She suffered from chronic knee pain and I was not confident she could get through to Sydney. That left us with only three top-class strikers, plus Kelly Free, who might make it but who was yet to confirm her quality consistently. A cruel knee injury early in 1999 would unkindly unravel her aspirations.

In midfield we were probably okay as Karen Smith, Brooke Morrison and Kris Towers all provided quality back-up, and Juliet Haslam, Kate Starre and Alison Peek could all fill gaps there.

However, our defence concerned me. Thankfully, Lisa Powell (soon to be Carruthers) was improving as a left defender. Indeed, she was relishing the challenge and she had the pace which I so keenly wanted there. However Juliet Haslam, Bianca Langham and Louise Dobson might be required elsewhere as defensive midfielders or deep defenders and so we needed more coverage in the wing defender positions. One whom I was keen on was Angie Skirving, a seventeen-year-old from Toowoomba who had done well in the national league, and looked a likely type. Tall, angular, quick and with strength and toughness, her skills were a little raw but her defensive positioning and judgment were very advanced for some-one of her age and experience. She was principally a defender and we believed her lack of fine ball skills would not preclude her from making the senior team for Sydney given steady improvement. Other prospects included junior team players Melanie Twitt and Carmel Souter. Both would get opportunities and while they were more accomplished players than Skirving in 1998, perhaps both lacked her raw talent and potential. Beyond that there were few other possibilities.

Knee injuries had not been helpful in 1997. Janita Ogilvie had been the best defender in our Junior World Cup team. Included in a number of senior internationals, she was in my view likely to be in our team in Sydney. Balanced, quick, fluent and a smart player with good all-round skills, Janita had it all. She was perhaps a casual trainer and her lifestyle reflected a certain bohemian character but she was very promising.

In South Africa before the Junior World Cup she ruptured her anterior cruciate ligament and required a reconstruction. While she stayed with our program early in 1998 her enthusiasm waned and eventually she fell out of the game. I have received a couple of letters from her since but it seems she has chosen to go another way in her life. For her sake, I hope she is happy with her pathway. If she was to decide to play again I am sure that Janita could still do very well if she put her mind to it.

I had been disappointed when Nova Peris had decided to give athletics a go after 1996. She had been a terrific competitor. Not the most fluent or skilled ball handler, Nova's pace and athleticism, her timing and determination had been outstanding. I believed that we could have done more polishing of her game and she would have been useful in midfield as well as providing assured wing defence. Before 1996 our time had been spent getting her to master the positional requirements of left defender. I thought we would be able to go a bit further with other aspects of her game.

However Nova, always her own person, was keen to represent Australia in another sport and I wished her well in her quest. It did not surprise me that she made the Commonwealth Games athletics team – she was a talented and very determined young woman. I can honestly say that nobody was more delighted than me when she won the 200 metres in Kuala Lumpur. All the girls followed the heats closely and we were at the hockey stadium when the final was run. I remember watching on a TV monitor as she stormed home.

She came to visit us that night. With our final ahead of us I was keen that Nova not stay too long as her excitement had the potential to derail some of our less experienced girls. Nova is a larger than life character and her joy and satisfaction at the result was overflowing.

She had mentioned, however, from time to time, that she missed the camaraderie of our group and that athletics could be a lonely environment. Nova had come from outside and her win in Kuala Lumpur at the expense of one of the sport's favourites, Melinda Gainsford-Taylor, did not make for a comfortable life in athletics circles.

At the time some were critical of Nova for her comments made immediately after the race. I have never heard them in context, yet I felt watching the race that Nova ought not be blamed for Gainsford-Taylor's misfortune or her emphatic post-race celebration. All she could ever do was run her best and I have always found her to be gracious and honest about her performances be they good or bad.

What made Nova such a good competitor was her ability to acknowledge where she was at and her determination to set things right.

In 1994 at the World Cup in Dublin, having lost to Russia, I remember walking across the field with a tearful Nova who could not be consoled after that first match. The next day against Argentina she was like a panther, alert and ready to play with yesterday's disappointment appropriately filed for experience. Again in 1996 in Atlanta early ordinary form was replaced by determined, resilient defence and calculated brilliant counter-attacking as the tournament went on. In the Olympic final, Nova was quite brilliant – one of our best.

It was therefore not a surprise to me when in October 1998 I received a phone call from Nova. 'Hi Nova, what can I do for you?' I half expected a request for some advice or the name or number of a contact. That was what our conversations usually entailed.

'I want to play hockey again.'

'Are you sure? Tell me why . . . What has happened?'

'I've been thinking about it for some time, especially since KL. Athletics has been great but I miss the girls. It's hard in athletics to do it all by yourself . . .'

The conversation covered the territory of her last two years and the Commonwealth Games performance. During the Games Nova had been a constant visitor to our floor and obviously enjoyed the companionship that our team environment provided. She was keen to return but I was wary that this might be a reaction to the let-down that must have followed Nova's return from the Games. People think that only the losers suffer after the high of such events. Those who are successful or win medals suffer a similar let-down to those who are not successful or who failed to reach their goal.

Nova indicated that she would be in Perth in a few weeks and we arranged to meet then. I said I would say nothing but indicated I would love to have her return provided we could work out a fair and acceptable way to reintroduce her. Her ability was unquestioned. Physically she could do it, but she would have to change her sprinter's ways and lengthen her training regime.

It was a nice surprise and her return would help ensure that we had the depth in our defence that I sought. If Nova was to return, then only our shallowness at the front stood in the way of us having all bases covered.

When I met Nova again, she was steadfast in her view. She'd thought about it and discussed it with Sean Kneebone, her (then) partner, manager and her child Jessica's father. She appeared to have gone into it deeply. I explained that we had moved on since Atlanta. Lisa Carruthers had been playing as a defender and in some respects was a better player there than Nova. However, given a year I believed she could regain a place in the team and she could add to our versatility. There were some problems fitting her into the Medal Incentive Scheme, but I thought those could be sorted out with John Coates or Herb Elliott, who directly oversaw that area for the Australian Olympic Committee. Already they had been amenable to giving us some flexibility in this program, which rewarded past medal winners and highly ranked athletes who were preparing for Sydney.

While more convinced than before, I knew Nova would be getting a tug from athletics. Certainly athletics offered better potential for a personal profile plus the special chance to represent Australia in two sports at two separate Olympics. I counselled her to be sure about what she wanted as the decision to return was a big one. This meeting took place at the Oriel cafe in Subiaco and I remember it particularly as after Nova left I had a meeting with Damian Drum, the newly appointed Dockers coach. Damian saw me with Nova and suggested something was afoot. I was circumspect, as I remember, but he recently reminded me about it when we were discussing the fickle nature of player negotiations!

Given Nova's continued enthusiasm I spoke to the selectors and John Coates about how her return might be managed. As I was yet to be convinced that Nova's decision was final, I indicated to her that we would be announcing our squad after returning from Argentina in mid December. I wanted to be sure of her for both our sakes.

With John Coates, the details were settled regarding her medal incentive status and the selectors agreed that we could include her in our squad. I heard from the local hockey people in Perth that Nova had been in contact with them about club arrangements and John Coates confirmed his discussions with Nova in a letter.

I also took the opportunity to discuss her possible return with Lisa Carruthers who was playing in Nova's old position. I knew that the players would be discussing it, as rumours have a way of gathering momentum. I indicated that Nova had no guarantee of returning to her position and would have to be considered for selection like every other squad member. The players, I think, took the view they'd wait and see. If she could add something to the team then that would be good.

Just before our return from Argentina, where we had taken a very young group of prospective players and a few senior players who had missed the Commonwealth Games, stories appeared in the press that Nova would return to hockey. Imagine my surprise when the day before the squad announcement we received news to the contrary.

At the last minute the lure of another sport and the unique possibility that went with it changed Nova's mind. Sean informed me and was apologetic – Nova, I suspect, was a little too embarrassed to front me immediately. When we spoke a week or two later there was only a little disappointment from me. It would have been a good challenge for her to return and her enthusiasm would have been good for the group. However, I had always had doubts and athletes are always changing their minds. Such decisions are always difficult.

Indeed, none of the athletes are there for any other reason bar their own volition, and to compete at Olympic level in a team you have to really want to be there. There were, during this time, at least five athletes in our sights whom we thought could improve our squad in Sydney. They were Jenny Morris, Nova Peris, Angie Skirving, Kelly Free and Janita Ogilvie. Morris, recovering from her second knee reconstruction, would eventually get there and assert her class. Nova chose another sport and Janita unfortunately suffered the injury that was just enough to knock her off the pathway to elite performance. Kelly Free cruelly would suffer a similar fate. Skirving would surprise a few as she worked towards a goal that in 1998 seemed out of reach. Unfortunately Michelle Andrews would succumb to her knee injuries and would not be able to complete the journey. Michelle was a proven performer and her availability would have given us coverage at the front. However, as we moved into 2000 it became clear Michelle would not be able to get through the season. Bitterly disappointed, Michelle pulled out when she could not compete in our mid season camp in Sydney.

It is never possible to cover every base as thoroughly as you would like. There are always unforeseen events which disrupt the best laid plans. Injuries, illness, personal crises, changing priorities and shifts in athletes' levels of motivation can change your plans. As we moved closer to the games in Sydney at different times all of these things would affect our preparations.

Recently in the AFL there has been much concern over the high rate of anterior cruciate injuries in footballers. Indeed four West Coast Eagles players have suffered this fate this year. This injury, however, is much more common in women. Three of the five players mentioned above would suffer this injury in the lead up to Sydney. In Atlanta in 1996 four of our sixteen team members had had reconstructions. That represents 25 per cent. The football numbers appear minor against that figure.

16

Chronic Achievement

... it is not the beginning or the continuing but the carrying on until it is utterly finished that yieldeth the true glory.

From a prayer by Sir Francis Drake before Cadiz, 19 April 1587

In November 1999 I presented this quote to the Hockeyroos as we were in camp at Couran Cove in Queensland preparing for what would prove to be our most difficult year together. We had come to the final phase of a difficult four years but only victory in Sydney would satisfy our high ambitions. Ron Clarke's resort on North Stradbroke Island was an ideal setting to prepare for our greatest challenge ten months away in Sydney.

When I decided to continue with the Hockeyroos I asked myself how could we best face a further period of three to four years with an already successful team and opponents hungry for revenge. In 1997 while the focus was on the junior team, we spent time facing up to the obstacles ahead. We tried to anticipate the things that would stand in our way as we headed into a further four-year period during which we would try to repeat our victories of 1994 at the World Cup and 1996 at the Olympics in Atlanta.

In late 1996, I canvassed some of these obstacles when I spoke at the National Coaching Conference in Brisbane. In that presentation I identified the need to introduce new players and challenge the old. I expounded the need to be innovative and not merely use the previous formula. I identified money, fame, the media and Sydney hype as obstacles. I considered complacency and apathy and discussed a range of challenges from new rules to new technology. Clearly it was crucial that we follow a new path rather than the one trodden on the way to Atlanta.

In almost every sport the most difficult task is to try and repeat a success. That is why the Oarsome Foursome and Kieren Perkins have gained such respect in Australia. They achieved what sporting people knew was very difficult. They were able to repeat a success four years later.

In Australian football repeating a premiership win the next season is a rare and special achievement which is only seen about once or twice a decade. The sustained dominance of the West Indies in the 1980s was an example from cricket and the Chicago Bulls in basketball and Manchester United in soccer are other teams which have dominated their sports in this way. In my view such dominance is the true measure of a great team.

When I began with the Hockeyroos in 1993 I always believed that we could win at the World Cup and the Olympics. I believed the players had the quality to be world champions. It wasn't until later that I started to think we might be able to build a team that would dominate our sport. I knew that such achievements were rare and I knew what some of the pitfalls were. Only by dealing with these pitfalls could we successfully continue after our fabulous first four years.

Corinne Reid, our psychologist, who had worked very effectively with the program from 1994 to 1996 had agreed to remain. As someone from outside the sport and without any background in hockey, she had an important role to play in helping establish our direction.

Her capacity to draw the 'hockey people' back from the minutiae of sport-specific issues to look at the larger picture was significant. The program would have to be more inclusive and less directive if we were to maintain interest and involvement. It fitted with my broad philosophical position that required players to take more initiative on the field. However Corinne emphasised the need to underpin this by increasing the player input to the program off the field and gradually devolving 'ownership' to the player group. For example our weekly program in 2000 was an amalgam of player and coach input. My experience was that as 'hockey people' coaches can become too caught up in the detail of the program and lose perspective as to where they are going in a larger framework.

Leading up to 1996 I had said to the players that I hoped they were ready to coach themselves. One of the 'what ifs' that we considered leading into Atlanta was the scenario in which the coaches for some reason couldn't be there one day. Would the players be able to look after themselves? I believe for a truly well-prepared team the answer should be yes.

In considering the obstacles that go along with chronic achievement, or maintaining winning performances over an extended period, we came up with the acronym 'TRAGEDY'. The letters of the word stood for some of the central issues that if not managed well could bring down a team that had climbed the mountain and wanted to stay there. For a coach the problem of maintaining a winning streak is age-old. We hoped that by confronting and addressing these matters head on we would be able to deal with the difficulties that face those aspiring to chronic achievement.

TERMINAL PLAYERS

'T' stood for 'Terminal players'. Sydney would cause some particular difficulties as a home Olympics as it was a catalyst for some senior players to continue when otherwise they may not have done so. Even in late 1996 it was clear that some would continue with Sydney as the final destination.

One of the problems with athletes who see the cut-off point is that they start preparing too early for retirement and the anticipatory slowdown begins well before the final match is to be played. They cease being curious about improvement, are often contented with their game as it is and are comfortable in what they do. In gardening parlance they are like the established lawn which becomes too thick and root-bound and is often spongy and sluggish in growth. Just as a thinning of the lawn can breathe life back into it, the comfortable established player needs room to spread out and grow. They need dynamism in their approach.

Essentially the terminal players were of three types in my view. First, there were those aging players who would be feeling the physical pinch as well as the call of other life experiences. Some were married or settled, some contemplated families, some had played more than a decade of top-level hockey.

The second and most worrying group were those who had played and won gold in Atlanta, and had slipped into a mid-career trough, despite having years of top-level play ahead of them. Perhaps the first victory had been a bit too early and they did not appreciate what they had done. It would hit them soon.

The third group were those who had missed out in 1996 who might lose volition if not rewarded and nurtured appropriately. Both young and old they might not want to risk the disappointment of another campaign.

Our antidote for the terminal player syndrome was fourfold. We needed to challenge each of these players with new tasks in their games. This could best be effected by playing a new structure. After Chris Spice left in 1997 we began to do this. It was also vital to challenge the players with a new position. In some cases this was undertaken from time to time. For others, a total position change proved valuable. The introduction of new players, of course, provided some of the principal stimulus. Nothing concentrates the minds of the senior players more than talented young athletes showing their worth. Finally, because we had a large group of players and changed selected teams regularly, the players appreciated that nobody was assured of a place.

I had been a terminal player myself in 1988 and I think I suffered from slowdown and pre-retirement 'grief' before the event. In the months before Seoul in 1988 I knew something was wrong but couldn't quite put my finger on it. In retrospect I think I would do things very differently if I got a replay. Unfortunately life doesn't offer those.

RECYCLING

'R' stood for 'Recycling'. The tendency to do what worked before is quite seductive. Indeed we see examples in sport and business all the time. 'It worked last time,' or 'We did it before,' are often used as the justification for actions. While one ought not discard proven methods lightly it is important to keep looking for improvement all the time. Only then do you make progress. In hockey the removal of the offside rule provided us with some interesting challenges and was fortuitous for it required both defenders and attackers to adjust their games quite dramatically. It certainly required us to review old methods thoroughly.

However, we were keen to shift the paradigm in any case, and a new structure or team formation was at the top of our list. Other things that we embarked upon involved employing a full-time video person, employing another assistant coach and developing new measures and statistical programs to better assess performance.

Trish Heberle came on board as our full-time video assistant. An experienced coach with the record of leading her South Australian Suns to a national title, Trish was much more than just a technician. Over the period she was seen as part of our coaching staff and her background offered much more insight than just her developing technical competence. She reorganised our whole approach to the use of this valuable coaching tool, implemented the introduction of digital technology and provided input to coaches and players that was valuable and pertinent. The benefit for Trish was that it gave her a break from her first love – coaching – yet it enabled her intimate access to our program. It was professional development for Trish as well as being a huge help to us.

Trish is now the head coach of the English program having been overlooked for a job in Australia. I suspect the knowledge she gained in our program will be very valuable to a country that could make significant progress in the next four years.

While much change is necessary one must also guard against changing those things that are working well. Thoroughly assessing the operating program, we aimed to keep and improve the good bits and replace the less productive bits. Winning in Atlanta didn't mean we had it all right, it only meant we had enough right. By 2000 that would not be enough! There was more to do.

In 1996, we went into the Olympics with a mission statement (see Appendix 5) that the team produced collectively in late 1995. By the time 1999 came around such an approach was not appropriate and early in 2000 we went through a process of defining our ethos. My very short statement was a variant of something that Spinoza had said: 'Excellence is as difficult as it is rare, live it every day honestly together until our task is completed . . . and then keep on living it . . .' I wanted the players to have something to continue with after the Games were over. Suffice to say in the discussions on this matter in February 2000 my attempt was shelved very early on! The girls wrote other words in the form of a short verse:

A honest belief, together we stand
there are no limits, no lines in the sand
accept the challenge with passion and trust
today, tomorrow till our flame becomes dust.

ACCEPTANCE

'A' stood for 'Acceptance'. Our opponents were saying it and I knew some players were thinking it. Every team that has achieved faces this way of thinking: 'It's someone else's turn', 'You've had a good run', 'The gap is closing'. These are all familiar manifestations of the theme but they are not necessarily valid.

My approach was to insist that the gap between ourselves and our opponents would only close if we stopped improving or slipped backwards. It was nobody's turn to win at the Olympics. It had to be earned. We had had a good run but it could continue if we improved more individually and as a team.

The demon of acceptance will always be there for the chronic achiever – you need to slam the door in its face when it turns up at the threshold. Don't deny its presence. Actively seek to frustrate it by continuing to improve. A team with a commitment to continuous improvement is not hard to coach.

GROUP DISINTEGRATION

'G' stood for 'Group disintegration'. This we believed would be one of our greatest problems. It is a common foe for teams that have done well. Individuals can become puffed up with their own importance. The media, family and friends, sponsors and managers all want to promote individuals from the team. More money is available and players have a profile. They are gold medallists. Some athletes become comfortable being a gold medallist and start living in the past.

This does not happen precipitously, it is insidious. A function to attend here, late to training there, a presentation to give and gradually the athlete is distracted. They become focused more on self and less on the group or team. The look too much outside the core of their sport and fall out of touch with what being very good entails.

Some do better than others, some are more marketable, some are in demand and tensions and frustrations creep into the group. Generally resentment festers slowly. From time to time critical incidents will expose the fractures and there will be alienation and loss of shared values, goals and direction. People start to blame one another when things go wrong rather than help to fix the problem.

Perhaps some of this is inevitable but our aim was to limit damage and to ensure our core values and direction were maintained. A number of strategies were employed to help to do this, but as important as anything was vigilance and recognition that this could happen. Open discussion about the manifestations of group disintegration and possible remedies for it was helpful in keeping the problem at bay.

Of course the introduction of new players and the task specificity of changing playing details helped to involve players in hockey again. However, the overall approach we adopted was to increase player involvement in team management. We believed that they ought to see the staff as facilitators, but the desire to learn and the discipline and drive to grow had to come from them.

Our approach to leadership and sharing that responsibility without a designated captain was an important part of the process of empowerment and developing group identity. The setting up of management committees and the players establishment in 2000 of a rotating management panel all gave effect to uniting the group in a common cause.

A potential problem identified in 1997 was the money available under the Medal Incentive Scheme from the Australian Olympic Committee. The decision for this to be shared amongst the whole group and not just the 1996 gold medallists was important to ensure team solidarity. Equally the players' decision, made early in 2000, to share the prize money from a Sydney medal equally amongst the whole group gave a good indication that there were shared values and direction on which we could count.

Of course from time to time stresses and pressures will tell in any group and manifest in tensions between players and staff. Selection, injuries, poor form, losing matches and outside pressures are all things that can cause disruption.

During 1999 Nikki Hudson (nee Mott) was suffering from a difficult to diagnose and long-standing knee complaint. Given the tensions involved with being away from her fiancé, Darryn, the injury and some inconsistent form, Nikki and I clashed when it was necessary to send her home from the Netherlands only a few days after arriving there. Nikki, who had been living in Toowoomba at the time, should not have flown to Amsterdam with us. She had not taken responsibility for her treatment and rehabilitation. Nikki's Medal Incentive Scheme payments were suspended and her future was threatened by the injury and her erratic efforts at rehabilitation.

Fortunately during the last four months of 1999 the physical problem was resolved and in 2000 Nikki returned to Perth with a more positive and refreshing attitude that saw her reach a level of fitness that was her best ever. Her efforts saw her payments restored and in Sydney in September she played some of her best hockey to be leading goal scorer in the Olympic tournament.

EXPECTATION

'E' stood for 'Expectation'. The view that 'We probably can win' and 'It'll be alright on the day' can be very dangerous. It can allow athletes to justify doing the minimum amount of preparation or only doing what worked before. The value of some poor performances cannot be underestimated in dispelling this comfortable thought. Our poor form in Glasgow and Amsterdam in May 2000 and the omission of some players from teams tended to focus the minds of those falling for comfortable expectation.

When we went via Glasgow to Amsterdam we didn't take our best eighteen players, and in the matches (where only sixteen could play) we never had our best line-up on the field. In Amsterdam we asked the players to take all the meetings and to be responsible for preparing for every match. This increased the stress on them and made the task of winning more problematic.

I was criticised for resting Alyson Annan and Rechelle Hawkes in major matches but always such things were done with an eye on the big picture in Sydney. I knew that we had to find out more about some of our developing players and the fierce competition in Amsterdam would be an important measure of their worth.

I went to Amsterdam not overly concerned about the outcome but hoping to discover depth and resilience. Having failed to reach the final there, I hoped that at least we would have removed any thought that 'It would be alright on the day'. The scourge of expectation had been dealt a telling blow!

In my notebook at the beginning of the year I scribbled two reminders to myself of this problem of expectation. The first was a quote from Shakespeare's *As You Like It*: 'Sweet are the uses of adversity.' The second came from an article I'd read in which the headline had captured my attention: 'I am acutely aware of the seduction of easy'. Taking short cuts and having an easy time was never going to be the best route that would prepare us for the Olympics.

DOUBTS

'D' stood for 'Doubts'. Doubts are always there. 'Can we do it?' 'Have we trained hard enough?' 'Is it possible to win again?' Everyone has these uncertainties and they are best faced up to and acknowledged. The battle between doubt and belief is there in every athlete and the process of outing our doubts is necessary.

Herb Elliott was unbeaten over the mile and 1500 metres in forty-two races yet he said his apprehensions fuelled his passion to train and compete. Our doubts are best directly acknowledged and rationally defeated. Properly directed they can inspire quality training and a fierce competitiveness. Allowed to fester they can strangle initiative and drive and cause us to play conservatively and without imagination.

THE 'YES' FACTOR

'Y' stood for 'Yes'. Given that about half the squad had played in Atlanta and been gold medallists there was a danger that their prior knowledge could overwhelm discussion or analysis. The tendency of the experienced players to try to convince the group that they knew best because they'd been there before had to be watched carefully. There was pressure on the new players to accept the views of the experienced medallists, to say 'yes' to their suggestions and ideas. Such acquiescence could be very dangerous!

Mostly one's memory of how something actually was is deceptive. Anyway we wanted to be wary of recycling. So we endeavoured to ensure that every view expressed was up for debate. Those who had been there before did not necessarily know all the answers and indeed often they were not remembering it as it had been. Every member of the group was encouraged to contribute.

And so we embarked on a course that hopefully would avoid 'tragedy'. There would be many pitfalls but we continued to endeavour to improve the team as we got closer to the time when final selection would occur. That was, as in 1996, very stressful.

I firmly believe our proactive approach to avoiding tragedy was important in keeping the program progressing. The mood of the group was at best one of humility, and when it slipped towards being proud and puffed up it was necessary to rebalance our priorities. Inevitably, in any program there will be an ebb and flow of fortune. Good management is usually able to choose when to reap and when to sow in such circumstances.

When I look back I can see many things we did not get right. Much of the stress in our coaching group came from within, but at least we were vigilant to the issues. In facing up to tragedy we ensured that we had direction and purpose between 1997 and Sydney 2000, and that our team at the Olympics was truly resilient.

PART THREE

17

What the Hockeyroos
Can Teach Business

During the past four to five years I have often been asked to speak to business groups and commercial organisations about my coaching experience and some of the values which underpinned the Hockeyroos' success. There appears to be a great deal of interest in this message. There are many parallels between sport and business and many lessons that each can learn from the other.

In business it is possible to make profits and grow without being the best. It is possible to be comfortable in the middle of the pack. Rarely would a sporting team be deemed successful without winning the premiership, gold medal or championship. Sport has an imperative of being the best which serves to mobilise resources and energies.

It is this focus on being the best that underpins the philosophy and behaviours of champion teams. It requires some of the important ingredients which can transform good business practice into best practice.

When I put my mind to what I thought was seminal to our success I came up with a handful of core values of a champion team. If these values pervade the actions and demeanour of any team it can be successful. These values define best practice whether it be in business or sport.

1 QUALITY

The best teams know quality, they practise it, stand for it and can reproduce it under pressure. It is their creed. As a coach you always aim to select and choose quality players but unless you are the manager of Manchester United you cannot have all the players you'd like. The draft structure or national boundaries make this impossible. Accordingly you have to develop quality and train it.

Quality skills, quality tactics, quality staff and quality administration do not happen by chance: they are conceived, trained, tested, chosen and organised. First you must build a sound platform from which to operate. In the same way businesses need quality products, systems, staff, ideas, research and administration. This discussion may seem obvious and yet many programs, teams and organisations seem to settle for second best. 'Close enough is good enough,' can easily slip into the pattern of behaviour, and corner cutting, arriving late, finishing early and procrastinating are seductive.

Leading into 2000, we coaches discussed what we might do to ensure the players owned the program and had control of it. We decided to give them 'wild cards' which they could use whenever they wanted time off or to miss training without a reason. The measure gave them the chance to opt out whenever they wished, no questions asked. We discussed the number of wild cards we should give each player for a six to eight-month period. Three to five? Maybe more? In the end Corinne Reid, the program psychologist, suggested they should be unlimited. This sent the athletes a clear message – they had plenty of autonomy. At the end of the year with twenty-five players in the squad only three or four wild cards had been used in total. There was no corner cutting or leaving early; training was where quality began and they wanted to be there.

2 TRAINING AND WORK ETHIC

At training quality was required, dev
enhanced. In the end, quality skills meant te
opportunities for our opponents. Only by requirin
ing would it be able to be reproduced under pressu
dependably.

Stephen R. Covey in his book *The 7 Habits of Highly Eff.
People* uses a quote from Aristotle. 'We are what we repeatedly a
Excellence, then, is not an act but a habit.' Training at the edge of
our capacity ensured that we made improvements as the athletes
training together competitively pushed one another. To get an
appropriate training effect you must make training harder than the
game. The workload was continuously monitored by our physiolo-
gist, Steve Lawrence from the Western Australian Institute of Sport,
to ensure that we worked harder than would be required in competition. Continuously monitored and evaluated, the athletes were
conscious of the standard desired.

Any business or organisation wanting to be good must invest in
training and preparation to ensure staff can handle any situations
that arise. Quality staff who are well trained and diligent are crucial.

3 FLEXIBILITY

In business they call it multiskilling. Athletes must be able to cope
with changes and be able to do more than one job in order to give
a team flexibility. The Hockeyroos were expected to have more than
one string to their bow. They were required to play on the right or
left, to defend and attack.

This started at training and continued in practice games and full
internationals. During a match, injuries, interchange or the opposition's success often required players to change or vary their role,
position or method. Without flexibility teams are too predictable
and cannot cope with new and different problems or replace absent,
out of form or injured players.

sinesses must have contingencies which allow them to manage situations themselves. Being able to replace a sick employee or al with a crisis or win challenges requires flexibility in the work-orce and systems. Training and recruitment ought to reflect such needs. Our athletes were expected to be able to do their jobs as well as someone else's. At times we played one player short to test our ability to fill the gaps and handle adversity.

4 GROWTH THROUGH ADVERSITY

Perhaps more than most activities sporting contests throw up doses of adversity. The experience is personal and individual at times and at other times it is a team experience. Because of the public nature of performances in sport the stress of failure, mistakes, disappointment or poor performance is very real. It can hurt.

Athletes, the good ones, learn from their mistakes, and grow in stature and experience from such situations. Ability to analyse and evaluate is crucial and mistakes should be considered learning opportunities.

Often the best and most telling lessons a business can learn come from the mistakes that are made. Whether in strategy, recruitment, advertising or product development it is rare to get it right first time every time. These experiences and failures should make us more aware of the pitfalls and more alert to the opportunities ahead and how to take advantage of them.

In 2000, when some of the Hockeyroos were perhaps a little too sure that things were going okay, we lost a sequence of games in May and June. It was a stressful experience and initiated an intro-spection and examination of our approach that also was stressful. It reminded us of how hard it was to win and the need to push harder and do more. Worthwhile goals are never easily achieved. I firmly believe that experience in mid 2000 put us back on track for our performance in Sydney in September.

5 BREADTH OF LEADERSHIP

Value the contributions of all. Every team member has something to contribute and an inclusive approach will reveal this. Only with a depth and breadth of leadership throughout the team or organisation can you be consistent.

Every Hockeyroo was encouraged to behave like a leader. That didn't mean giving orders but it meant taking responsibility for getting their jobs right and for the team working co-operatively. It meant dealing with problems as they arose and taking responsibility for them.

With a critical mass of leaders you can deal with every crisis. Throughout the workplace you want employees who take responsibility and solve problems rather than referring work to others or simply crying 'Too hard!' Athletes on the field of play cannot refer difficult situations on to someone else – they need to make decisions, judgments and act.

Most often in business it is an accumulation of small episodes of incompetence or indecisiveness that will lose you a customer. Similarly on the sporting field opponents score as a result of consecutive episodes of incompetence and indecisiveness. In a positive sense winning a customer or scoring a goal are outcomes born of consecutive episodes of competence and decisiveness!

6 CONTINUOUS LEARNING

The Japanese call it *kaizan* – an attitude of continuous improvement. The Hockeyroos were encouraged to have their eyes peeled for ideas. You learn from other sports, other teams, opponents, other coaches and other areas of human endeavour.

In business, airlines learn from the hospitality industry lessons about catering and bookings in order to improve their services. Every business monitors its competitors and parallel businesses to seek an edge. The work environment is in continuous flux and it must be monitored.

Just as our mistakes can teach us, so can our successes. Just as other sports and areas of endeavour can teach us, so can we conceptualise and imagine improvements and change. The search for progress and development must never cease.

We should actively take risks to find out about ourselves and our opponents. By experimenting with different tactics, different formations, different combinations of players and different approaches to leadership, training and team management, the Hockeyroos created their own learning environment.

It is necessary to ask questions, test the assumptions and myths of your sport or business and imagine other ways to do things. By practically opening up the debate and including the ideas of all those involved we are able to expand the ways of doing what we do. Without taking risks and experimenting with new and different methods we do not expand the boundaries for our learning. The attitude behind the saying 'If it ain't broke, don't fix it' is one of conservativism and fear rather than openness and willingness to grow.

7 WILLINGNESS TO PUT THE TEAM FIRST

This is not a concept that comes easily to Australians in my experience. The rugged individualist bucking the system is almost an Aussie icon. It is the reason that often teams I played in were not efficient against the Europeans with their rigid, structured, disciplined approach. Brilliant individuals can never make a difference in team games unless they are also an integral part of the structure of the team. Without co-operative, co-ordinated strategies that utilise individual abilities for the team's good, you will not get the best outcome.

In our game we scored by getting a number of pieces right consecutively and we were hurt by opponents when consecutive mistakes were made. Any of the events in the chain can contribute to the failure or success of the team. Individual performances are thereby directly linked to the team outcome. It is the same for business where each employee's contribution plays a role in the business outcome. A poor telephonist or sloppy salesperson will not assist even if you have a quality product to sell. Everyone must play their part.

I am often asked whether coaching a women's team was more difficult than a men's team. My response is to say that I thought the women in my team were more willing to work for the team than is often the case with men. For good or ill women are often socialised to sublimate their own ambitions for the benefit of the family and maybe that is what I saw in many of my players. Clearly they were less egocentric and more team-centred than men's teams often are.

Sharing the load on the field was expected, and by using interchange it was necessary. Of course in team sports participants should understand that the win or loss is a collective experience. The glory or gloom is shared together, and while playing well in a losing team is better than playing badly in a losing team it doesn't beat the feeling of a win.

In business such an approach is not so defined. Surely though every employee ought to share the rewards of successful enterprise – by ensuring this one is more likely to achieve harmony and teamwork.

8 COMMON GOALS

In 1976 at the Montreal Olympics Australia won just four medals: one silver medal and three bronze. It was the nadir of Australian Olympics performance. Twenty-four years later in Sydney we would win fifty-eight medals, sixteen of them gold.

The performance of our athletes in Montreal was the catalyst for the establishment of the Australian Institute of Sport in the early 1980s. While a much needed idea for a country wanting to be excellent in sport, it was conceptually flawed in that the facilities were concentrated in Canberra far away from Australia's population centres.

Slowly a more decentralised model is evolving and the concept is being refined. Notwithstanding these difficulties the Australian Institute of Sport has been an important factor in the turnaround of Australian sporting fortunes.

In the same way that the macro fortunes of Australia's sports system were turned around, the fortunes of individual teams, companies and businesses get turned around by having a strategic plan.

The dream that we set our sights on becomes the goal and then the plan of how to get there is conceived. Without the dream, without the goal, we are often purposeless and erratic and our efforts can be easily dissipated.

I was only a young schoolboy when President John Kennedy made the famous commitment in May 1961 to land a man on the moon before the decade was out.

I believe this nation should commit itself before this decade is out to landing a man on the moon and returning him safely to the earth.

We choose to go to the moon in this decade and do other things not because they are easy but because they are hard.

Because that goal will serve to organise and measure the best of our abilities and skills.

Because that challenge is one we are willing to accept, one we are unwilling to postpone and one which we intend to win.

In 1995, the Hockeyroos took part of Kennedy's words in their mission statement (see Appendix 5) formulated in November prior to starting preparation for the Atlanta Olympics.

The part of it that is most relevant, I believe, is 'that goal will serve to organise and measure the best of our abilities and skills'. The goal committed to and shared by a team can be the catalyst for individual and collective development. Step by step, often with small increments, one can get closer and closer measuring and evaluating all along the way.

In sport often the final judgments are made on just one performance or one event. That will cause distortions and sometimes a great upset occurs. The topsy-turvy of the score in low-scoring sports can be frustrating, but if the measure of quality is performance over time then such happenstance can be accommodated. Thankfully the outcomes in business are usually more even in measurement and management. They don't usually rely on one final event to determine their worth.

Unquestioningly a shared set of goals and a thorough plan implemented and evaluated progressively underpin the best achievements in sport. When France won the soccer World Cup in 1998, they were one of the few teams that had a four-year plan in which the coach as 'managing director' was able to implement his strategy over time. More than half the teams in that competition had appointed their coach less than a year before. Australia went for a part-timer! Competent as he may have been the plan was flawed and we didn't even get to the finals.

9 HONESTY

Candour is a critical part of the functioning of the best sporting teams. This does not mean one speaks without thinking first or without considering sensitivities. What it does mean is that coaches, players and administrators alike should be careful about being duplicitous or misleading. I might add that my experience in politics where a somewhat different ethic often applied merely confirmed the efficacy of this viewpoint.

Without open and honest communication it is too easy to misread or misinterpret messages. The players deserve to know where they stand, what is expected of them and what the consequences may be for their performance. Sometimes a player may do everything asked of them and more and still not gain selection. This is because the landscape of performance is relative and continually in flux. Every athlete lives with this knowledge and while the professional squad member at least has their future secured via a salary package, the semi-professional often risks more. Individual athletes suffer similar fates. Recently Grant Hackett broke a world record in the 800 metres freestyle. Unfortunately for him in the same race Ian Thorpe was four seconds ahead and Hackett's brilliant swim only took second billing.

In the interactions between athletes, coaches and administration, the requirement for honesty is central. Openness to criticism or willingness to change requires it as a bedrock value. The media report that will invariably upset or distract is often a distortion of reality. Only the trust earned through honesty will ensure that such events are kept in perspective. Honesty with one's self, of course, is a principle of the best performers. They do not cheat themselves by cutting corners at training. They do not seek unfair advantage in their sport and in competition. They seek to lift the performance of those around them with their approach. They provide an openness to criticism of their own game and true reflections on the team's performance.

These messages are often uncomfortable but the value of distress has already been described. It is distress that often brings about change and improvement. Of course the really honest player evaluates themselves even at the best of times in a critical way.

Some readers might think this account is naive and facile. My response is that in the end we usually reap as we sow. I have made most of the mistakes one can imagine in a life and usually they occurred because I deceived myself or others. I think one gets to a stage in life when one is willing to reflect honestly and admit such things.

The public, the shareholders, team-mates, family members, loved ones will forgive mistakes but will find duplicity or untruth harder to digest. False promises or unrealistic assertions create an environment of expectation which is fanciful – beware!

10 HUMILITY

This quality follows from honesty. It is a quality that underpins diligent training, a positive approach to learning and improvement and disciplined play and lifestyle.

As previously discussed, it is often said of great teams that they are arrogant and dismissive of their opponents. This is a misinterpretation of what is going on. Great teams respect the game and its culture, they understand the vagaries of sport and its nuances and they respect their opponents. Quality opponents expand the range of qualities of a great team. Great teams are assured, aggressive, competitive, determined and optimistic but they are not arrogant.

The Hockeyroos aimed to dominate our opponents. We planned to play aggressively and at high tempo. An opponent who could beat us would have to match and exceed our quality and persist longer than we were able to. If they were then victorious, they had surely earned their success. To be really good, of course, they would have to do it over time. Not just once.

Humility, a sense of your own vulnerability and an honesty about your performance and training are central to continued excellence for they fuel the wish to keep improving and learning which are crucial if your enterprise is to grow and develop. If you think you know all the answers my response is to look deeper. You will always find room for improvement.

18

Champions

A year or two ago Richard Aggiss surveyed fifty prominent hockey people and asked them to submit in rank order their twelve best Australian male players. Former Australian captains, coaches, players, officials, umpires and supporters were included in the survey. Thirty-three people responded and I was most pleased and surprised to be selected by this process as a member of the hockey legends. The team I chose was not the same as that selected by this process but it was reasonably close.

I thought those with a hockey bent might find it interesting to see what my views were on such a team. Who would I include and why? Equally the exercise for female players might be of interest given my experience with the Hockeyroos during the past decade. Additionally I thought I might conjecture about the outstanding international players I've encountered in the game.

However before I embark on that quite narrow hockey exercise, it may be of interest for many if I describe what it is that I believe makes up a champion. What are the ingredients of greatness from my perspective and how do I measure some of the greats of the last forty years? Indeed the task of measuring the quality of those outside that era would be too difficult for me and would necessarily rely on the interpretation and witness of others rather than my own experience. Such presumption I would rather avoid. Thus any athletes whose brilliance shone before 1960 would not make my best list. The likes of Sir Donald Bradman of course would be an omission because of this cut-off point, although he would feature at the top of any all-time great list.

I make no apologies for not including horses or jockeys in my list as I have no expertise and little interest in this area. Equally, my knowledge of and interest in motor sports being what it is I have made no observations. Michael Doohan and Jack Brabham clearly have been very special. I consider boxing an unfortunate sport that I do not understand and therefore have not included it. Likewise yachting is not something that excites me yet I, like most Australians, was uplifted by the special events of September 1983 when Australia won the America's Cup. Accordingly I have chosen to confine my conjectures to man versus man or woman versus woman or team versus team activities.

What are the things I look for in my champions? The same things that are the ingredients of any ideal player.

First, I look for athletic gifts including speed, strength, agility and endurance. Every event tests all of these to some extent. All are essentially God-given, although nurtured and respected all can be significantly improved with the exception perhaps of speed.

Next, technical skills such as balance, fluency and a capacity to reproduce the highest quality skills under pressure are the hallmark of my champions. Usually the very best players have flawless basics, the product of diligent preparation. Additionally they are able to produce exquisite moments of brilliance which distinguish them from sport's tradesmen.

Tactical nous encompasses judgment, timing and decisiveness. Great champions are able to seize the initiative, read the play and change the course of events by their interventions.

Sustained quality performances, or longevity, is a characteristic of all my champions except for Herb Elliott. Although undefeated over a few years he did retire early. However what was remarkable was that his times were still competitive many decades later. That is durability in another form! All of those mentioned performed well at the big events – that is the mark of a champion.

Competitive edge is an all-encompassing term that takes in a champions' capacity to compete in all circumstances, both good and bad. These athletes never gave up. They were and are persistent, resilient, brave and determined. They dominated at times and they also handled adversity and the extreme pressure of competition at the highest level.

Following are my lists of ten champion Australians and sixteen champion international athletes. I'm sure you will cheer some on my lists and disagree vehemently with other choices.

MY TEN BEST AUSTRALIANS (SINCE 1960)

Greg Chappell Greg was all round the best Australian batsman I have seen, though Steve Waugh is not far behind. I suspect Greg will have averaged more than Steve Waugh when Steve finishes. Not as good as some off the back foot, not as spectacular as Kim Hughes was sometimes, not as destructive as Doug Walters in full flight, not as nimble as Neil Harvey against spin, but all things included Greg was the best performed and most consistent.

He was compact, thorough, upright, correct, patient and at times punitive. Often for Western Australia I fielded close to the bat when he came in for South Australia or Queensland. His foot work was neat and crisp and he played very straight, always building an innings and always punishing bad bowling. He was also a brilliant fieldsman and more than useful medium-pace bowler.

Margaret Court (Smith) Margaret Court won twenty-four grand slam titles (11 Australian, 5 French, 3 Wimbledon and 5 USA titles) and was our greatest ever woman tennis player. This does seem incompatible with the impression, often given, of a nervous and inconsistent competitor! Tall, athletic and powerful, her game was ahead of its time.

Betty Cuthbert Brilliant in 1956 when she won the 100 and 200 metres and a relay (4 x 100 metres) gold medal, it was her comeback in 1964 in the 400 metres that sealed Betty Cuthbert's greatness. It also put her in my post-1960 timeframe.

Herb Elliott Herb Elliott was my first hero in sport. As an eight-year-old, my first Olympic memory was of his performance in Rome. I saw it on newsreel footage at the movies and listened to the radio reports of his triumph. We had no television. Forty-two times undefeated at the mile and over 1500 metres speaks for itself. He stands as our greatest male athlete on the track.

Dawn Fraser Dawn Fraser defended her 100 metre freestyle Olympic championship twice and set world records. She is a swimming legend and deservedly one of our greatest ever Olympians.

Cathy Freeman Women athletes have outperformed our men on the track. Freeman's two world championships and a silver and a gold at the Olympics put her right up there. I believe she could still be running in the Olympics in Athens in 2004 – a performance there could really exalt her. With no disrespect to Karrie Webb who was chosen by some as our best performed athlete in 2000, Freeman would have got my vote. Notwithstanding a doubtful world record time set fifteen years ago by Marita Koch in the days of drug-fuelled Eastern bloc performances, Cathy is running great times and dominating her event.

Rod Laver Twice a grand slam winner in 1962 and 1969, the left-hander from Rockhampton dominated the game as amateur and professional. Australia's best ever male tennis player was also part of five successful Davis Cup teams.

Dennis Lillee The Western Australian cricketer was pound for pound the most penetrating and menacing fast bowler during the last four decades. Had it not been for World Series Cricket, he would be our greatest wicket taker in tests.

Kieren Perkins One win in the 1500 metres freestyle was magnificent but to defend an Olympic gold is the ultimate. That Kieren nearly did it again in Sydney was extraordinary. That would have been the stuff of legends. Murray Rose was not selected for the Olympics in 1964, despite special performances that year. Had he competed and performed, he would have made the list. He was clearly of Perkin's quality.

Shane Warne Warne changed the nature of cricket when he arrived on the scene. He changed it for the better and has kept doing it for a decade. I still believe he should have some more in him – I hope I am right.

Notwithstanding some of his off-field antics, his control, variety, consistency and penetration have been exceptional. At a time when spinning was passé, Warne dared to do it and succeeded in a unique way.

MY BEST IN THE WORLD (SINCE 1960)

Viv Richards Thankfully, I did not field close to the bat when Viv burst on to the scene in Australia in December 1975. Playing against Western Australia he hit 175 in a display of power and panache that took one's breath away. In the covers it was not so bad as he tended to hit square or straight that day and often he hit it over your head anyway! Richards in his time was the most potent scorer in cricket, a game he and his West Indian team-mates would dominate for a decade.

A brilliant fielder whether catching, stopping or throwing and a tidy off spinner, he won matches with his bat whether in the one- or five-day game. While Barry Richards, Sunil Gavaskar and Brian Lara are all great, Viv Richards and Sachin Tendulkar are the best I've seen. For me they are more consistent or more destructive than the other three.

Sachin Tendulkar Tendulkar is simply the best batsman in the world at the start of the twenty-first century. This Indian player has time, is balanced, is aggressive and consistent. His footwork and quickness are exceptional and he deserves the accolade of being the player most like Bradman. I expect he will end his career with an average close to 60. He is a true artist to watch in both one-day and five-day cricket.

Sir Garfield Sobers Sir Garfield Sobers sits next to Don Bradman in any list of all-time great cricketers. The West Indian could bat, bowl (medium pace and spin), and field like a genius. His brilliance ignited that memorable test series between Australia and the West Indies in 1961.

Wayne Gretsky Gretsky, a Canadian, is acknowledged in North America as the greatest ice hockey player of all time. He was a high-scoring, match-winning, long-lasting champion. Gretsky raised the standard and expectations of his sport and then continued to play at the exalted level for his whole career. There were none better in his sport.

Eddy Merckx Eddy Merckx of Belgium won the Tour de France five times, from 1969–1972 and in 1974. He won a record thirty-five stages in the Tour and also won three world championships. It is the world championships that give the nod to Merckx over Miguel Indurain and Bernard Hinault who both also won five times in the Tour.

Jack Nicklaus Nicklaus dominated golf for a couple of decades and his record of majors won (18) put him in a class of his own. He was also runner-up eighteen times. He hit long, found the greens and finished superbly. The record of Nicklaus is only now being challenged by Tiger Woods, another American. Woods will have to keep doing it for the best part of the next decade to pass Nicklaus. On present indications he might do so comfortably, but Nicklaus has the runs on the board! However, Woods's grand slam suggests he may make it.

Three soccer players make my list as it is the biggest game in the world.

Pele The Brazilian maestro could do it all – gymnastic, inventive, brave and explosive. He could pass, use his head, score and eliminate. Pivotal in two World Cup wins – 1958 and 1970 – he is incontestably the greatest player of the era, and most believe the greatest of all time.

Franz Beckenbauer Franz has done it as a player and as a coach. In 1974 his German team was victorious in the World Cup final in Munich's Olympic Stadium. In 1966 as a young player he had experienced defeat at the hands of England. In 1990, as coach, he was on hand to see Lothar Matthias lift the trophy aloft in Rome. The 'Kaiser' was at the centre of the best German teams over three decades.

Diego Maradona The flawed genius was simply a magician with the ball in 1986. His skills were nearly singlehandedly responsible for giving Argentina a World Cup triumph. He is one player whose faults I find myself overlooking in the face of his majestic skills on the ball and his one-touch perfection in controlling and passing the ball. In that World Cup tournament in 1986, he played as well as I ever saw anyone play the game.

Steven Redgrave Five consecutive gold medals at the Olympics is just unbelievable in such a physically taxing sport as rowing. At Atlanta and Sydney this ageless athlete showed that technique, timing and teamwork were more important then youthful power. Surely he will retire now! He has.

Martina Navratilova In women's tennis I cannot separate Steffi Graf and Martina Navratilova. Both were brilliant, quick, powerful and dominated the game in their time. However, I went for Navratilova given her doubles record and nine Wimbledon titles. Billie Jean King is up there too but I thought Martina changed the way women approached the game with her physical presence.

Pete Sampras In tennis it is hard to go past Australian Rod Laver whose record is incomplete only because of his professional years. However Pete Sampras, with the most grand slam titles, has got to be up there. Bjorn Borg, John McEnroe and Andre Agassi haven't as many titles but were or are great.

Mark Spitz Mark Spitz won nine Olympic gold swimming medals, two in 1968 and seven in 1972 in Munich where he dominated in an incredible way. His performance in those Games marks him as the greatest swimmer I have seen.

Michael Jordan Michael Jordan is another who dominated his sport in an exceptional way. His athleticism was extraordinary. That plus great skill, a competitive bent and fine team-mates meant the Chicago Bulls were the greatest team in the National Basketball League. Jordan, like many great champions, seemed to lift those around him. That is the mark of the very best.

Jackie Joyner-Kersee Jackie won medals at three Olympics in long jump and defended her heptathlon title in 1992. A world record holder in that all-round test of athleticism in 1988 and 1992, she could claim a title as the best female track athlete in that period.

Carl Lewis In athletics Carl Lewis, with nine gold medals including his unparalleled long jump streak (he won gold in 1984, 1986,

1992, 1996) and a bundle of world records, stands alone in the modern era. While Michael Johnson's 200 metre and 400 metre wins in 1996 were followed by gold in the 400 metres in Sydney and Edwin Moses's dominance of the 400 metre hurdles was great, Lewis was a greater all-rounder who lasted and lasted.

Presently in Australia we have a number of emerging champions in a variety of sports. Karrie Webb is certainly pre eminent at golf already. Ian Thorpe appears well on the way. Lleyton Hewitt is threatening to win a grand slam and the likes of Aaron Badderley are on the horizon. Lauren Jackson shows the potential to dominate women's basketball. We should be patient with these prodigies and the real test of their greatness will be their ability to endure. With someone like Brett Lee already there are concerns about his 'soundness' as a long-term prospect. He may need to re-invent himself as Lillee had to do during his career. However I am not into speculation and I have too often seen precocious talent lose its way at the highest level. Though Mark Bosnich may be very wealthy I am not sure you could say that he has fulfilled his potential.

To complete this chapter I have indulged myself by assessing my time in hockey over the past three or four decades and the performances of those champions I have seen in that sport. No doubt those close to hockey will enjoy reading my views on the champions I have seen in hockey. However I will begin with the survey conducted by Richard Aggiss to find the best twelve Australian male players of the century. The thirty-three respondents each voted for twelve players in order. The first selected received twelve votes and the last one vote. Accordingly, the maximum number of votes available to any selected player was 396. I was surprised and delighted by the outcome! Here are the first twenty so selected:

1. Richard Charlesworth   347
2. Julian Pearce   280
3. Paul Dearing   176

4.	David Bell	149
5.	Brian Glencross	147
6.	Don Smart	140
7.	Ron Riley	120
8.	Terry Walsh	115
9.	Ken Wark (jnr)	99
10.	Mark Hagar	90
11.	Bob Haigh	89
12.	Des Piper	88
13.	Ray Evans	86
14.	Trevor Smith	58
15.	Jim Irvine	56
16.	Peter Haselhurst	52
17.	Michael York	49
18.	Eric Pearce	46
19.	Pat Nilan	40
20.	Colin Batch	35

Fourteen of this group made my top eighteen, and sixteen were in my top twenty. My preference is to select a group of sixteen as are allowed at major competitions. For completeness I would have two reserves as for all competitions except Olympic Games, eighteen players are now allowed. Accordingly these are my selections as the best men and women to play for Australia in the last four decades.

MY AUSTRALIAN MEN'S HOCKEY TEAM OF THE ERA 1960–2000

Strikers: Don Smart, Ron Riley, Terry Walsh
Attacking midfield: Trevor Smith, Ric Charlesworth, Colin Batch, Peter Haselhurst
Defensive midfield: Jay Stacy, Julian Pearce, David Bell
Defenders: Bob Haigh, Ken Wark, Craig Davies, Michael York
Goalkeepers: Damon Diletti, Paul Dearing
Reserves: 17 Mark Hagar, 18 Grant Mitton.

The best Australian men's team from those I have seen was very difficult to select. At the front Smart was exceptionally skilled, quick, could play in midfield and was a goal scorer. Riley, at times narrowly focused, was highly skilled with exceptional change of pace and direction and was the standout goal scorer at three Olympics. Walsh, especially before injury, was powerful and explosive, a great opportunist around goals.

I picked Trevor Smith in attacking midfield with myself, Haselhurst and Batch, though he could have been selected further back. He was easily in our best half-dozen ever in my view. Batch scored, penetrated and could play striker. Haselhurst, not quick but with exceptional ball control, had a great all-round game. I tried to develop an all-round game that had attacking and defensive elements. I think there's a place for me! Julian Pearce leads the defensive midfield. Our greatest centre-half he was brilliant in reading play and passing, and had strength, vision and toughness. Jay Stacy must have a place and I think this position would be best for his wonderful passing over distance. David Bell could attack and go forward as well as provide the deftness of a quick-footed defender.

At the back I have three former fullbacks: Ken Wark, Craig Davies and Michael York – with Bob Haigh our greatest left side defender. Wark's speed complements Davies's tackling, cover and reach while York is versatile and at home anywhere in defence. Paul Dearing was exceptionally brave and talented and Damon Diletti has been the best of the contemporary keepers playing in the 1992, 1996 and 2000 Olympics.

Brian Glencross perhaps misses out to the more athletic Davies and Des Piper would have been exceptional as a midfield reserve. I suspect I never saw the best of these two even though I played in Australian teams with them. However, as my two extra I chose the attackers Mark Hagar, a prolific scorer, and Grant Mitton our best ever right wing, but not in the top sixteen because his career was not as extensive as others. He had great penetration and at his best was unstoppable with his pace and reach.

MY AUSTRALIAN WOMEN'S HOCKEY TEAM OF THE ERA 1960–2000

Strikers: Katrina Powell, Jackie Pereira, Nikki Hudson
Attacking midfield: Alyson Annan, Sharon Buchanan, Rechelle Hawkes, Marian Aylmore
Defensive midfield: Kate Starre, Lisa Carruthers, Renita Garard
Defenders: Michelle Hagar, Jenny Morris, Liane Tooth, Wendy Pritchard
Goalkeepers: Rachel Imison, Kath Partridge
Reserves: 17 Michelle Andrews, 18 Shirley Tonkin.

My best Australian women's team includes at least four players who could play in Athens in 2000 – not a bad start for building the present team.

At the front I have Katrina Powell and Jackie Pereira, both very quick and brilliant goal scorers and opportunists. Nikki Hudson (Mott) is another sort of striker. A competent scorer but not prolific she can turn the best defences inside out with her control and balance. If she continues to improve she will be exceptional as she has pace and athleticism and a very powerful goal shot.

The next line is all class. Annan, Buchanan, Hawkes and Aylmore are all different, all brilliant. The first three, who played in my teams, I have discussed elsewhere in this book. They are all skilled technicians, playmakers and midfield schemers with Annan having the added potency of her brilliant goal scoring. Marian Aylmore led the team in the early 1980s. She was small but very quick and skilled at eliminating opponents. In any era she would have been a champion. Only motherhood prevented her playing in 1988.

The defensive midfield includes the guile of Renita Garard, the combativeness and endurance of Kate Starre and the fluency and penetration in passing of Lisa Carruthers. All are dual gold medallists at Olympic Games.

In defence I have chosen Michelle Hagar and Wendy Pritchard as the wing defenders. Both were athletic, skilled and fierce competitors. Jenny Morris and Liane Tooth, two more dual gold medallists, finish off the defensive line. Tooth played across two eras and her thoroughness and reliability were exceptional. The combination with the more adventurous Morris is irresistible. In goals Imison and Partridge edge out Clover Maitland. Imison can be our best ever if she lasts. Presently that honour lies with Partridge – less gifted than Imison but more thoroughly professional at this stage.

For my reserves I would choose Michelle Andrews and Shirley Tonkin. Michelle, a gold medallist in Atlanta was a brilliant scorer and match winner, unfortunately was defeated by the wear and tear of competition and did not make it to Sydney. Shirley Tonkin was the best player around when I watched women's hockey in the late 1960s and early 1970s. Unable to compete very much internationally, she had great skill and strength and was a goal scorer but could also play midfield. She was, in her time, outstanding. Her older sister, June Capes, was by all accounts equally brilliant. I hardly saw her play; however, two of her daughters, Lee Capes and Michelle Hagar, were gold medallists in Seoul. Some have suggested Shirley Francis was special but I didn't see her play and so she was not considered. Tracey Belbin and Juliet Haslam could not displace my defenders but they were close, as was Elspeth Clement who was quick but sometimes erratic. Tracey and Elspeth were gold medallists in Seoul. Eight of that team are in my twenty!

To name eighteen non-Australians over my time is more difficult. In the women's game I must in fairness restrict my timeframe to the 1990s onwards, for my knowledge of earlier times is limited.

Strikers: Heike Laetzsch (Ger), Natascha Keller (Ger), Mijntje Donners (Neth), Karina Masotta (Arg), Huiping Yang (China)
Midfield: Eun-Jung Chang (Korea), Luciana Aymar (Arg), Carole Thate (Neth), Anna Lawrence (NZ), Britta Becker (Ger)
Defence: Jeannette Lewin (Neth), Cecilia Rognoni (Arg), Eun-Jung Cho (Korea), Lisanne Lejeune (Neth), Chang-Sook Kwon (Korea), Sonia de Ignacio-Simo (Spain)
Goalkeepers: Hillary Rose (GB), Elena Carrion (Spain).

In the men's game I can go back to the 1970s to select my best non-Australian eighteen.

Strikers: Samiullah Khan (Pak), Stefan Blöcher (Ger), Hasan Sardar (Pak), Teun De Nooijer (Neth), Dhanraj Pillay (India)

Midfield: Mohamed Shahid (India), Shahbaz Ahmed (Pak), Juan Escarre (Spain), Mansoor Hussain Jnr (Pak), Stefan Veen (Neth)

Defence: Naeem Akhtar (Pak), Michael Peter (Ger), Munawaruz Zaman (Pak), Ties Kruize (Neth), Carsten Fischer (Ger), Ajitpal Singh (India)

Goalkeepers: Ian Taylor (GB), Ronald Jansen (Neth).

Some of these players in the midfield or as strikers could have played in either line.

A difficult job, I wonder what hockey followers would think?

19

Let Sport own Sport

One of the country's foremost writers, David Malouf, wrote in the *Australian* on 1 January 2001, about Australia's progress since Federation. He did not, unlike many others, undervalue the role of sport in the development of our nation.

> Sport has continued to be the place where we are most aware of ourselves as a people; and when we consider the alternatives there can be few healthier or more benign, more civilised ways in which a nation might discover a sense of itself than 'at play' – at competitive play with friends and neighbours. Those who baulk at the role sport plays in our life, who think of it as adolescent and low-brow to invest so much spirit in what is merely physical, miss the point and miss it badly. There is something about the encouragement to individual excellence within a discipline of team loyalty and fair play that speaks strongly to our sense of how a society at large might work.

Malouf makes a valid argument and one which should be taken seriously. I am not one who ascribes to sport's mythical qualities of healing and health or a pivotal place in society. I have always thought that our lives are embellished by the mix of a number of inputs. For many, sport provides part of that mix of activity and intellectual stimulation. In this I agree wholeheartedly with Malouf.

For me sport has always been a cerebral activity which combines the mental challenge of competition and strategy with the physical requirements of execution in a hostile yet ultimately benign (usually no one dies!) environment. For me, therefore, chess, enjoyable enterprise that it may be, is not a sport. What team sports require is the additional element of co-operation and co-ordination, so important in almost any activity in which we can become involved.

Others, I think, have gone too far in their claims for sport. I well remember listening to Peter Ueberroth, the Chairman of the Organising Committee of the Los Angeles Olympic Games, as the athletes stood in the middle of the stadium at the opening ceremony in 1984. He described the assembled athletes as the 'best hope for the future of mankind'. When I surveyed the crowd of runners, swimmers, jumpers, pugilists, bicycle and horse riders, spear throwers, ball hitters and kickers, I could not help thinking he may have been exaggerating!

By nature, most Olympic athletes are pretty one-dimensional during the competitive stage of their lives. This is not a criticism, merely an observation of fact. However, most who play sport do not aspire to Olympic feats; most are delighted to enjoy time together with team-mates and friends in healthy, stimulating contests that measure personal skills and co-operation. Long may this continue. As long as we can enjoy tennis with our friends without being too worried about the score it will be so. Bowls, golf and veterans' sports of all varieties allow for this as we grow older.

However, it is at the junior end that we must be vigilant. Modified junior sports programs are creative and can achieve our aims but the overzealous coach or parent will continue to present a risk. We should always encourage the joy of involvement and the satisfaction of learning and improving rather than the expectation of winning.

At the elite level we have seen a revolution in sport during the last three decades. The changes have been extraordinary in their dimensions and reach and their impact. The world's major sporting carnivals have become media and business events in which television, and therefore sponsorship and advertising, are the key players. Athletes receive incredible amounts of money. Many make in a year the wages of a lifetime's work for a competent university-trained professional. Like the money given to entertainers and some business leaders these figures reflect an unreality that often nurtures only a fleeting grasp of real people's economics.

Even in a game like Australian Rules Football where over six hundred athletes receive on average about $120 000 annually, the sums appear large to the ordinary punter. An Australian representative team in any code of approximately thirty to forty players would consist of the really elite athletes in that sport, those of the stature of Steve Waugh, John Eales, Michael Klim or Cathy Freeman. That leaves, say, 560 sub-elite athletes who probably earn on average $100 000 per year. That's pretty good when you're not even in the best forty in the country!

Of course these figures are chickenfeed compared with those earned in the United States and Europe where baseball, gridiron, basketball, soccer, boxing and athletics can reward their athletes so exceptionally.

The large payments made to Australian sportspeople should come as no surprise as it is something that has been heading our way for decades. The template was established in the United States many years ago and as with many things it is the model we slavishly follow.

This year at the Australian Tennis Open we had the absurd spectacle of Yevgeny Kafelnikov complaining about prize money in tennis. A multi-millionaire from the game, he was thankfully put in his place by a more balanced Andre Agassi who suggested that Kafelnikov should use his money to buy some perspective!

It is really scary that some athletes who are paid exorbitant sums of money think that they actually earned it! Some entertainers, actors and business people also think that, just as someone who buys and sells expensive real estate for a living thinks they earned their million dollars in commission. In defence of real estate agents at least they must perform to get paid. Increasingly athletes are demanding appearance money and long-term contracts without performance criteria. The world is full of fantasy. I would argue very strenuously that the teacher in the classroom adds much more value to our society.

It is relevant to speak about entertainers because in a very real way that is where sport is going. The contests in sport are pure drama and the outcome is always unknown (or at least it should be). My concern is that those who control the money will want to increasingly control the outcomes.

Money certainly has the potential to corrupt sport and distort the values which have been central to it for many decades. During the last couple of years a game we thought was solid and incorrupt-ible has shown itself to be rotten from the very top down. Cricketers the world over have shown what can occur in a culture of greed and excess.

I know that sport must remain relevant and contemporary. I am not advocating some march back to the past but I am advocating a stance for values in the games we play and the games that the world watches and enjoys. Those who administer sport are aware of the pressures. I am not sure that many of them have the courage to stand up to the media and money moguls of this world.

Already we have seen the paucity of leadership evidenced in the International Olympic Committee (IOC), the International Amateur Athletic Federation (IAAF), the International Cricket Council (ICC) and the International Football Federation (FIFA). These organ-isations are bedevilled by intrigue and laden with anachronistic structures and attitudes. In recent decades they have started to realise the power of the games they control. Yet they are incapable of getting their own organisations to function effectively. How then can we believe they will be able to operate in the best interests of their sports?

FIFA's decision on the venue for the 2006 World Cup hung on the arbitrary whim of a lone official who acted outside the direction of his national organisation. At least that is what we are supposed to believe. The IOC's Olympic host city bidding process remains open to abuse and distortion. Match fixing has neutered the ICC, and the IAAF appears impotent at best or unwilling at worst in its endeavours to legislate against performance-enhancing drugs.

The challenge is for the management and administration of sport to guard its principles and ideals from the evils of market forces, from voracious sponsors, from agents and managers who see sports as their cash cows and from media moguls who want its drama, brilliance and glory as a vehicle for programming and subscribers.

'Fat chance,' you might say and I suspect that is the case. Sports fall into one of two categories: they are already of mass media interest and on the media payroll or they are of no media interest and struggling to survive. Perhaps those struggling are the lucky ones for at least they still have autonomy. Unfortunately, too often their management is as mediocre as their public profile.

Of the others, the management is often as valueless as the overseers who control the money. This is not an optimistic picture and it is one that might not improve. That sport should own and control sport is idealistic and increasingly unlikely. Soon most major events will only be available on television if you are on cable. The pay TV operators know you will pay the subscription because that is the experience in the United States.

There is one cause for optimism. Most of us are far from elite and as such will never be part of the entertainment embodied in modern elite sport. We will only be spectators. However, we might still want to play, compete and be part of a team. While we are able we will join clubs and enjoy playing sport ourselves. Our children will want to join in too and sport and its values could survive at this level. I suspect the media and monied forces won't want that. They'll want you in front of the telly eating their pies and drinking their beer.

If they win the battle then humans will start to change – to look different. Already obesity is an increasing problem for young people. As we use our bodies less to exercise and 'live' our daily lives, we will change. Instead of walking to the shops, too many of us will drive 500 metres to buy a litre of milk. We will take out expensive gym memberships but won't walk up a flight of stairs.

Dr Roger Bannister was an elite athlete in another time. He was the first man to run the mile under four minutes (on 6 May 1954). He strove for excellence in running and he believed in the 'whole' man. He expressed a similar sentiment.

> Each of us has to find this activity for himself . . . The important thing is that we should perform ourselves rather than watch others. By absorption in the pursuit we forget ourselves and it fills the void between the child and the man.

As a player and as a coach I have been involved at the elite level of sport. It was fun and it was a great working environment for the athletes were highly motivated. I suspected then, and I think it is probably true, that the athletes who invested so much to be Olympians valued their involvement much more than many highly paid professionals. It seemed unfair that they received so little tangible reward, yet probably the benefits for them, in their growth, maturity and values were a significant gain. If karma exists then it must be so.

20

A Change of Pace

It was during 1999 that I decided finally that I would not stay with the Hockeyroos. I suspect many of them were relieved to hear it. For me it was eminently sensible. To stay on after Sydney would have been folly indeed.

In 1993 I had believed that the building of a team to its peak in international hockey would take about five or six years. I thought in the Olympic cycle of four years some things would be left undone. I believed two Olympic cycles would almost be too much. The danger of burn-out would be severe.

So it was that in 1999 I announced my plans to stop at Sydney. There were a number of reasons for this. While I tried to give opportunities to every athlete I believed that the athletes who had been with me deserved to be judged by another head coach.

I said to the players at the beginning of 1999 that they could build the foundation of a Sydney success during that year. The improvements and refinements that we would make in 1999 would be the basis of our game in 2000. Large changes in technique, fitness, tactics and teamwork would be difficult in 2000. That would be a year for fine-tuning rather than quantum shifts. The message was emphasised, but I know not all of the players approached 1999 that way. However for some like Angie Skirving and Rachel Imison that year was crucial for development. Others with a more mature game used it to catch their breath preparing for what was ahead in 2000. Certainly the last half of 1999 was pretty light. I wanted the players well rested away from the game before 2000's program began.

Within myself I knew that the job was taking its toll and I decided that in 1999 I would take my foot off the accelerator. During the last part of the year I handed over many of the coaching duties to Frank Murray and Bob Haigh. The players didn't need to hear too much from me and I was keen to freshen up for the difficult year ahead. I think it was a very wise move.

In September 1999 another distraction arrived. I had discussions with the Australian Cricket Board regarding the coaching job in cricket following Geoff Marsh's sudden exit. Malcolm Speed and I met in an airport lounge to discuss the possibility.

I had many years earlier enquired about the original coaching job which Bob Simpson had won. I still have the letter from David Richards which recorded my interest and asked me to consider the position. In the end the timing made the job out of the question – I was in the Parliament – and similarly in 1999 I indicated that I felt obligated to complete my Olympic contract. We had put in too much time together to not see it through.

While the money was better in cricket, the job with the cricket team appeared to me to be too demanding for one person to carry for any extended period of time. I indicated to Mal Speed that I thought the one-day, test, Second XI (Australia A) and Under 18 jobs needed to be integrated in some way and the load shared. Just as the demands on Geoff Marsh had proved enormous, I thought someone like John Buchanan with a young family would easily be burned out if the job was to remain unchanged. However, John, in my view, was the correct choice as coach. His enemy will be the demands of the job and establishing some team practices that might be resisted by a conservative sport with very highly paid athletes.

Knowing that I would be finishing at the Olympics took some weight off my shoulders. Unlike a player who might suffer the sense of loss when their career is ending, it allowed me to attack the job while looking forward to a break afterwards. If I wanted there could be more coaching jobs ahead at a later date.

My plan for 2001 was to have a sea change in my life. I would finish my university studies, have some quiet time at home, perhaps write this book and do a little speaking to allow me to earn enough to get by. Lawrie Lawrence had advised me some time ago that there was much more money in talking than in coaching! His dynamic personality and over the top manner are beyond me, but I have found it an interesting sideline.

The arrival of Oscar in October and Carmen's consequent change in circumstances made another income source desirable. Following the Olympics a number of football clubs approached me regarding the possibility of involvement. Given my desire not to leave Western Australia, Fremantle and the West Coast Eagles were the only feasible options. I had discussions with both clubs and pretty soon after the Olympics again found myself wrestling with the issue of another job. I was keen to have a break and insisted that formal involvement would not start until 2001.

The West Coast Eagles are a team in transition. One suspects that they did not pay enough attention to succession in the late 1990s and they are now paying the price. I felt for coach Ken Judge as he has a hard road ahead. The senior players are worn out and their vibrant young ones like Ben Cousins, Michael Gardiner and David Wirrpunda cannot do it alone. I thought Judge had a good handle on where he was going and the team's list, if it held up, was superior to Fremantle's. Ken Judge was enthusiastic about my possible involvement and I very nearly went there. In the end I saw it as a lesser challenge because the club had experienced a decade of good performance whereas the Dockers had no record or experience of success. Accordingly I thought it would be good for me to take the chance to look closely at such a club.

As a player I had experienced the frustration of not being able to beat some teams. Indeed all through the 1970s we only beat Pakistan twice in about a dozen encounters. I know what it can be like to build up a team when you are off the pace. By the 1980s there were young players in the Australian team who had never lost to Pakistan in a dozen encounters!

Fremantle were welcoming and I started in my role as 'high-performance consultant' on 8 January 2001. In many ways that was too late to have much impact on what happened at the club this season as we started playing matches just one month after I began and the basic structure and plans were already in place. My role is to observe and advise on every aspect of the club's activity. Certainly I expected it would take many months to get a handle on the nuances of the AFL. I knew the players from approximately twenty hockey nations, but knowing 600 AFL football players takes some homework.

Six years without an involvement in the finals leaves scars and changing the culture of the group is not an easy task. While our 2001 season has been disappointing it was not surprising as many of our key players are very young and we are not yet resilient enough. Indeed I indicated in my meeting with Fremantle's board in 2000 that we could win less games and still make some progress in changing the culture of the club. In 2000 we had been fortunate to win eight games. Our percentage of 70 reflected a very poor season.

Having been at the club for some months, I believe we have players from which a strong team can be built. I am more confident than I was at the beginning of my involvement when I was concerned that we may not have had a good enough group. There are many ways in which we can improve – the challenge will be to put them all in place and the aim must be to eventually build one of the best clubs in the country. It will not be easy.

Coaching is a very stressful and demanding job and those involved walk a tightrope which is intimately connected with the performance of the players. Football clubs try to run their business and often their boards are not aware of the elements that make up the performance of a team. Performance is multi-faceted and there are any number of aspects which need attention in order to optimise it.

Damian Drum in the last year of his contract with Fremantle was under a great deal of pressure given our start in the 2001 season. While the media and others often wish to set the agenda regarding the coach, they are probably not the most expert or objective observers and they certainly don't have the inside knowledge of what is going on at a club. Watching what Damian faced I feel reassured that I have chosen to take a break from coaching for a while! Coaching can be a fragile existence.

I presume the decision by the board to change coach half way through the season reflected their intention to clear the decks for next season as they did not see Damian as their coach in 2002. Such a move, however it is handled, is always problematic and underestimates the difficulty a new coach might encounter coming in from outside. Certainly such a move can further destabilise the club. It also might dangerously signal to the players that they may not be centrally responsible for performances. Nothing could be further from reality.

Even very good coaches can get sacked. After 1996 I was asked to conduct a coaching forum at the Australian Institute of Sport. Many of the coaches at the AIS attended. Of all those I came into contact with at the seminar I was most impressed by Erkin Shagaev, then the recently appointed coach of the Australian men's waterpolo team. Erkin, from Uzbekistan, was a highly credentialled coach from the former USSR. He asked the best questions and appeared insightful and competent in his approach. There was an authority in his manner yet after coaching Australia to a best ever semi-final at the World Championships in 1998 Erkin was dismissed.

In my view the decision was crazy and I said so at the time. Erkin's tough uncompromising approach was exactly what men's waterpolo needed. Their poor performance in Sydney at the Olympics did not surprise me. I am glad to see that Shagaev has been reappointed following Sydney. I hope he gets the chance to build a team for Athens. His story shows that any coach's tenure can be fickle even outside the big-money environment of the AFL or NRL.

I expect the Hockeyroos to continue to be successful because I know how good our squad was. My aim was always to build in a margin for error that would allow us to consistently win major titles. In doing this I believed depth and internal competition were indispensable ingredients.

While preparing for the Olympics last year we had a squad of twenty-five players. The nine who were not successful in getting to Sydney will form a very solid phalanx of players in the next team. Between them they have many hundreds of games of experience already. Those who continue, and I expect at least half a dozen will, are already outstanding. When one adds to that group some very talented juniors who will doubtless emerge then you have a potent team – a team with momentum and an awesome reputation.

I believe we have in place the players and the structures to continue to dominate, and the arrival of fresh coaches with new ideas and a different approach will embellish what is there.

I do not know whether I will ever coach at that level again. You have to live the job and immerse yourself in it completely to really do it justice. At the moment I do not have that energy. Perhaps a few years out of coaching will recharge my batteries.

Certainly my present position allows me to continue learning about sport in a more relaxed and different environment. My university studies are challenging and stimulating and I feel comfortable with my new family situation. Still I think I have made my life a little too cluttered. I hope in the next couple of years to have a long sabbatical overseas, I look forward to that possibility. Presently a relaxing year in Italy perhaps writing, travelling and reading is envisaged. Nothing more than that is planned. However no doubt there will be some interesting proposals that might come my way.

Central to my view of sport and coaching has always been the view that one needed to risk losing to win. You should never fear losing to the extent that you aren't aggressive and assertive enough to win. In a game like cricket that means making balanced declarations sometimes and setting attacking fields with fieldsmen in catching positions. In the co-operative team ball sports it means letting players express themselves and trying to score heavily as well as stopping opponents. Often teams get this balance wrong.

Just a few weeks before Sydney I received a letter from Meg Wilson, who was the past president of Women's Hockey Australia. Meg wrote to wish the team well before the Olympics as she had done before every major competition. Women's hockey under Meg had taken a risk on me. I know sometimes she cringed at my ideas but she, like the present president, Pam Tye, had thought the risk calculated. Successful teams take risks, many risks. The risks are calculated and the best teams get the calculus right. The Hockeyroos developed into such a team!

AFTERWORD

A Player's Perspective on Selection

In his book *Diplomacy*, former US Secretary of State Henry Kissenger wrote:

> Intellectuals analyse the operation of international systems; statesmen build them. And there is a vast difference between the perspective of an analyst and that of a statesman. The analyst can choose which problem he wishes to study, whereas the statesman's problems are imposed on him. The analyst can allot whatever time is necessary to come to a clear conclusion; the overwhelming challenge to the statesman is the pressure of time. The analyst runs no risk. If his conclusions prove wrong, he can write another treatise. The statesman is permitted only one guess; his mistakes are irretrievable.

Coaches and athletes in sport are the statesmen. They can prepare and be ready for the contest but when the game begins they are subject to the vagaries of time. They must act and usually there is no chance to do it again or try another way. The problems of competition are imposed upon them. Time is an ever present enemy. You only get one go at it and mistakes are often irretrievable.

The analyst is analogous with the media or the commentators and administrators – those who live off the game but are never measured themselves. They are never on display or at risk of losing. They can try another way because their investment in the outcome is not their own sweat and blood. They are spectators, not participants; they do not put their expertise on the line or stand to be judged as do those who compete in the contest.

Another American statesman put it more succinctly.

It is not the critic who counts; not the one who points out how the strong have stumbled . . .The credit belongs to those in the arena . . . who at best know in the end the triumph of high achievement; and at worst, if they fail, at least fail while daring greatly; so that their place shall never be with those timid souls who knew neither victory or defeat.

US President Theodore Roosevelt at the Sorbonne, Paris, 1910

In January 2001, I contacted Katie Allen. Travelling in a Kombi van in Tasmania, she was winding down after a hectic and topsy-turvy year. I asked her if she might write a few hundred words about how she felt at the time of Olympic selection. Selection is the moment of truth for all those who have put their whole lives into the dream of being an Olympic athlete.

Katie, a keen wordsmith and the resident team poet, agreed to do so but in the months following her response was not forthcoming. She had writer's block, she said! At the beginning of April on the day I submitted this manuscript Katie's story arrived – all 1800 words of it!

Hence this Afterword. Katie's perspective is that of an athlete who missed out. That of a wonderful young woman whom I would be proud to call my daughter. All who aspire to be coaches should read what Katie says, and always be mindful of their position of influence. We should exercise our best judgment always in all matters pertaining to our charges. It is a solemn responsibility indeed.

Here is Katie's story.

In sporting circles, selection is somewhat of a dirty word. In our squad, its mere mention was enough to set most of us into a severe spin. We were transformed from a group of relatively relaxed, confident people to twenty-five insecure, highly stressed individuals. The impact of our erratic behaviour was often far-reaching. For example, in the weeks leading up to selection of an Australian women's hockey team, Western Australia allegedly recorded its highest levels of road rage, chocolate consumption and domestic arguments. In other words, if you knew anyone involved in a Hockeyroos selection you would either lie low for a while or make time to attend their therapy sessions.

Unfortunately selection was a necessary part of what we did. There were twenty-five players and just sixteen places to fill. In some ways it was a bit like having your wisdom teeth come through; there's a lot of pain and not enough room. It was one of the most difficult things we would face, both as individuals and as a squad.

When I think back on all this, I am reminded of a quote that will stay with me forever. It was from a time when slavery still existed in the southern states of America. A woman addressed a group of slaves as they considered escaping their oppressive life. She said to them, 'You are not guaranteed success, but I still encourage you to walk forward into the danger.'

Perhaps for us, making ourselves available for selection was like walking forward into our own kind of danger. A danger that required you to put yourself on the line. Quite literally I guess since every selection involved the daunting task of ringing Women's Hockey Australia to see if you'd made the team. Although we repeated this process a number of times, it didn't seem to lessen the impact of each call. For me, two in particular come to mind.

The first was back in 1996. Following six months of full-time training in Perth, we travelled to Holland to play our last international series of games before Olympic selection. At the end of the series I decided to stay on and relax for a few days . . . at least, that was the plan. Instead I found myself slightly troubled. Something had nagged away at me since the last game and only then, as I counted down the final minutes before I made *the call*, did I know exactly what it was. Doubt. All of a sudden I had this horrible feeling that I wasn't going to make it.

I restlessly paced my hotel room, waiting for 3 am to roll around since that was the time they'd given me to call. I dialled the number. This next part I will never forget. I stated my name and waited for what seemed like an eternity; I could actually hear the lady on the other end desperately searching for it on the list she had in front of her. But given that my surname begins with 'A', it didn't take me long to realise that I'd been left out of the 1996 Olympic team. This was my first real experience of selection . . . and it sucked.

Before this I'd never really thought about missing out or not getting what I'd worked for; it just kind of happened. I'd been cruising along believing wholeheartedly that if I wanted something badly enough and did everything I could to get it, it would happen. So all of a sudden, with a few apologetic words on the end of a phone line, my idealist beliefs were completely crushed. I felt like I'd failed. I'd not only let myself down but everyone who'd supported me or taken an interest in my hockey since I'd first picked up a stick. Now they'd never get the chance to see me at the Olympic Games.

This disappointment and sadness overwhelmed me for days; it seemed to be all I could think about and the only thing that mattered. I cried and cried and when I stopped crying I started hating myself and when I grew tired of that I took up hating the coaches for losing faith in me and putting me through this hell.

Just when I thought things couldn't get any worse, they did. Training resumed a few days after I returned from Holland. One of our first commitments was a fitness test where you basically run until you can't run any more. Unfortunately I didn't make it that far. As soon as it got hard I pulled out. I just couldn't handle it and for a minute I didn't care. Then I felt ashamed. I was supposedly this tough, uncompromising player and here I was giving up. I spent the rest of the session crying in the toilet and the rest of the year (and most of 1997) struggling with what it all meant. I had not anticipated how much my omission was going to affect me.

In fact the next couple of years were full of incidents like this. I seemed to be questioning every aspect of myself and what I was doing or feeling. I couldn't be bothered doing anything and didn't see the point since obviously nothing I did was good enough anyway. I either tried desperately to prove myself or didn't try at all. This in turn made me a nightmare to play with and to be around. In fact I should probably take this opportunity to apologise to anyone who knew me during this period of my life.

The second phone call happened on 8 August 2000. I caught the midnight horror flight from Sydney to Perth the night before just so I could be in familiar surroundings when I discovered my fate. I stared out the window and began to reflect on my year and what I'd gone through to get to this point. I remembered at least three times when I'd seriously considered quitting and in some ways I felt lucky to have made it as far as I had already. I wanted to play so badly, but this time I knew the reality of being part of such a strong squad. I might not make it.

At the beginning of the year our psychologist Corinne had questioned me about the year ahead. She'd asked me whether I would still go through with it if I knew then that I wasn't going to go to the Olympics. As well as making me squirm (my typical response to a question from our shrink), it forced me to look at why I was doing all this. If it was just to go to the Olympics then maybe I was setting myself up for failure. Maybe I needed to judge my success on something more than this. That's when I made a commitment to myself to value those moments and hours and days between selections, the ones that usually get forgotten. Things like hanging out with my friends, eating breakfast on my back verandah and above all having the opportunity to play the game I love at the highest level. Whatever the final outcome, it had to be worth the effort I was about to put in.

After much contemplation, my answer was yes. I still wanted to proceed regardless. I felt like I had something unique to offer this group of people whether I was selected for the Olympics or not. It was as simple as that.

Despite all these philosophical thoughts, I spent the rest of the flight either in tears at the prospect of another missed Olympic selection or momentarily regaining my composure in an attempt not to give up until the very end. Unlike 1996, I didn't have a definite feeling either way, which left me with only one option. Sit back, order a glass of red and wait.

I arrived home around 1 am and decided not to set an alarm in an ambitious attempt to sleep in as long as possible. Unfortunately it was not to be and I found myself wide awake well before the designated ringing period of 7–7.30 am. Again there was not much I could do except wait and it was still a bit early for red wine. So with the cordless phone in my grasp I closed my bedroom door and sat on my bed. I could do this, I felt strong, I was in control, hockey wasn't everything, it was just another team, it was only the Olympics, I was ready . . . Who was I kidding? I'd never been so nervous in my life.

Seven o'clock came and went and on my bed I remained. The phone was now out of my grasp and being stared at from a distance. The swear words started to flow thick and fast as did the thoughts of not making the call in the hope that it would all blow over. I didn't want to know. At least now, in the safety of my bedroom, I hadn't missed out.

I had run out of stalling time. It was now fast approaching 7.30 am, and I had a matter of minutes before the team list would be released. I'd then have people ringing me regardless. So I had no choice but to make *the call*. I got through straightaway – I guess I must have missed peak time – and eventually managed to get my name out. After one last moment of doubt – I think it went something like, Shit, did she say congratulations or commiserations? – I knew that I would be going to the 2000 Olympic Games.

In both cases, I had done the hard work to prepare and was good enough to be selected. But I can see now that there was so much more to it than that, otherwise our entire squad would have made it. We all possessed our own unique strengths and qualities. However, you could never control how well other people played or whether your strengths complemented those around you. I discovered through selection, as the wise lady said, that you are never guaranteed success. No matter how much you have done or how much you think you deserve it, some things are out of your hands.

So why do it? Why put yourself on the line when the outcome is uncertain and there is a chance you may suffer great disappointment?

Well, all I can say is why not. It takes courage to know you might fail at something and still do it, to see the possibility in your opportunity and go for it. And aside from that, I honestly believe that not being selected has been just as important to me as being selected (although I certainly didn't think so at the time). Only through missing out have I begun to appreciate what happens in between making those calls, and to learn that the destination is only part of the journey. The words 'value every incident' will remain forever etched in my memory.

APPENDIX 1
Ric Charlesworth's Record in Sport

HOCKEY

Club A grade
Cricketers 1968–79
University 1980
Suburbans 1981–82
Cricketers/Wolves 1983–88
Captain and Captain/Coach of Cricketers and Suburbans 1976–78, 1981
Life Member of Cricketers Hockey Club.

State
Junior Under 16s 1966–67
Colts Under 21s 1968–71 (captain 1971)
Seniors 1971–88 (captain 1974–77, 1981–84) (twelve times national
   champions)

International

1972–88	Played 227 matches (more than 130 as captain, 1977–84)
	Scored 90 goals for Australia
World Cups	1 gold and 2 bronze medals
	1975 Kuala Lumpur (5th)
	1978 Buenos Aires (bronze medal)
	1982 Bombay (bronze medal)
	1986 London (gold medal)
	1986 World Cup Player of tournament and leading goal scorer in the tournament
Olympics	1972 Munich (5th)
	1976 Montreal (silver medal)
	1980 Moscow (selected)
	1984 Los Angeles (4th)
	1988 Seoul (4th)
Champions Trophy tournament	1980–88 Gold, silver or bronze medallist at each

Selected in various world teams between 1976 and 1986

CRICKET
Club A grade
West Perth 1969–70, 1976–82
University 1970–76 (premiers 1974–75)
Captained both clubs

West Australian Cricket Association First grade batting average
1975–76 (59.5)
1976–77 (78.8)
1981–82 (55.8)

State (First Class)
Western Australia 1972–79, 47 matches, 2327 runs at batting average
  30.2, 35 catches, captain in four matches
Sheffield Shield winners in 1972–73, 1974–75 (did not play), 1976–77
  and 1977–78 seasons.

AWARDS
- Olympians Medal 1980 (Fairest and Best Perth Classic League)
- Western Australian Sportsman of the Year Award 1976, 1979, 1987
- Lindy Award 1986
- Jaycees Outstanding Young Australian Award 1984
- Advance Australia Award 1984
- Order of Australia 1987
- Australian Coaching Council Team Coach of the Year 1994, 1996, 1997, 1998, 1999, 2000
- Inducted into Sport Australia Hall of Fame 1987
- Inducted into Hall of Champions, Western Australia, 1995
- Western Australia Sports Champions of the Year Awards, Western Australian Coach of the Year 1994, 1995, 1996, 1997, 1998, 1999, 2000
- Confederation of Australian Sport Coach of the Year 1996, 1997, 2000
- 2001 Citizen of Western Australia in sporting contribution category

COACHING EXPERIENCE
1971	Cricketers Under 14s (result 2nd)
1972	Cricketers Under 14s (result 1st)
1975	Western Australia Senior state team as captain with withdrawal of Merv Adams (result 1st)
1976	Cricketers Senior Men's 1A Team (result 1st)
1977	Cricketers Senior Men's 1A Team (result 1st)
	State Under 21s Team (result 3rd)

1978	Cricketers Senior Men's 1A Team (result 2nd)
	State Under 21s Team (result 2nd)
1979	Cricketers Senior Men's 1A Team (result 1st)
1981	Suburbans Senior Men's 1A Team (semi-finalists)
1990	Westside Wolves Under 13A girls (result 2nd)
1991	Westside Wolves Under 15 girls (result 1st)
1992	Westside Wolves Under 15A girls (result 1st)
1993–2000	Australian Women's Hockey Team

ADMINISTRATION

| 1984–92 | Board member of Western Australian Institute of Sport. Reappointed 2001 |
| 1994–97 | Board member of Australian Sports Commission |

COACHING ACCREDITATION

| 1993 | National Coach Accreditation Scheme Level III |
| 2000 | International Hockey Federation Master Coach |

APPENDIX 2
Hockeyroos' Win–Loss
Record 1993–2000

ALL GAMES PLAYED, INCLUDING OLYMPICS AND WORLD CUPS

	Played	Won	Lost	Drew	For	Against
1993	19	14	3	2	57	21
1994	37	27	6	4	90	30
1995	32	30	1	1	94	23
1996	32	26	2	4	115	31
1997	23	19	1	3	75	17
1998	44	33	6	5	161	47
1999	37	27	6	4	128	42
2000	29	22	5	2	94	28
TOTAL	253	198	30	25	814	239
% or ave goals per game		78.3	11.9	9.8	3.22	0.94

OLYMPIC GAMES AND WORLD CUPS

	Played	Won	Lost	Drew	For	Against
1994	7	5	1	1	17	5
1996	8	7	–	1	27	5
1998	7	7	–	–	33	8
2000	8	7	–	1	25	6
TOTAL	30	26	1	3	102	24
% or ave goals per game		86.7	3.3	10	3.4	0.8

CHAMPIONS TROPHIES

	Played	Won	Lost	Drew	For	Against
1993	6	5	–	1	18	3
1995	6	5	–	1	12	4
1997	6	4	1	1	13	4
1999	6	5	–	1	25	8
2000	6	4	2	–	17	6
TOTAL	30	23	3	4	85	25
% or ave goals per game		76.7	10	13.3	2.83	0.83

APPENDIX 3

Hockeyroos' Record by Country 1993–2000

(Two matches or more)

	Played	Won	Lost	Drew	For	Against
KOREA	30	22	4	4	109	44
NETHERLANDS	28	15	6	7	63	38
ARGENTINA	27	19	4	4	69	32
GERMANY	26	19	2	5	59	22
NEW ZEALAND	18	17	1	–	64	16
SOUTH AFRICA	18	13	3	2	49	14
SPAIN	17	13	1	3	67	9
CHINA	16	16	–	–	68	15
GREAT BRITAIN	13	11	2	–	32	13
ENGLAND	13	8	3	2	33	17
USA	12	11	–	1	44	5
INDIA	8	6	2	–	21	7
SCOTLAND	6	6	–	–	29	5
CANADA	5	5	–	–	22	3
JAPAN	4	3	1	–	14	3
IRELAND	3	3	–	–	12	0
RUSSIA	2	1	1	–	12	3

APPENDIX 4
Hockeyroos'
Competition Results
1993–2000

INTERNATIONAL COMPETITION 1993
KOREAN TEST SERIES   SYDNEY   MAY 1993

12/5/93	Aust v Korea	3–3	
14/5/93	Aust v Korea	2–1	
15/5/93	Aust v Korea	1–2	1 win, 1 draw, 1 loss

JAPAN SERIES   TENRI/OSAKA   JUNE 1993

5/6/93	Aust v Korea	4–1	Tenri
6/6/93	Aust v Spain	8–0	Tenri
8/6/93	Aust v Japan	1–0	Tenri
10/6/93	Aust v Spain	6–1	Osaka
12/6/93	Aust v Japan	1–2	Osaka
13/6/93	Aust v Korea	0–3	Osaka 4 wins, 2 losses

PRE-CHAMPIONS TROPHY TOUR   BISHAM ABBEY/VUGHT AUGUST 1993
Tests

12/8/93	Aust v Netherlands	0–0	Breda
14/8/93	Aust v Netherlands	3–2	Vught
17/8/93	Aust v Great Britain	2–0	Bisham Abbey
18/8/93	Aust v Great Britain	4–0	Bisham Abbey 3 wins, 1 draw

4TH CHAMPIONS TROPHY   AMSTELVEEN, NETHERLANDS AUGUST 1993

22/8/93	Aust v Great Britain	2–0	6 wins
23/8/93	Aust v Spain	8–1	
25/8/93	Aust v Germany	1–0	
26/8/93	Aust v Korea	4–0	
28/8/93	Aust v Netherlands	2–1	
29/8/93	Aust v Netherlands	5–4	final: 1st Place Penalty strokes 4–3

1993 AUSTRALIAN WIN–LOSS RECORD

Matches played	Win	Draw	Loss
19	14	2	3

INTERNATIONAL COMPETITION 1994

INDIA/SOUTH AFRICA TOUR   DEHLI/CAPE TOWN/ JOHANNESBURG   FEBRUARY 1994

17/2/94	Aust v India	2–0	Delhi	
19/2/94	Aust v India	4–1	Delhi	
20/2/94	Aust v India	1–0	Delhi	
22/2/94	Aust v India	0–1	Delhi	3 wins, 1 loss
27/2/94	Aust v South Africa	2–1	Cape Town	
1/3/94	Aust v South Africa	3–0	Cape Town	
4/3/94	Aust v South Africa	1–2	Johannesburg	
5/3/94	Aust v South Africa	0–0	Johannesburg	2 wins, 1 draw, 1 loss

5 NATIONS TOURNAMENT   BUENOS AIRES   APRIL 1994

12/4/94	Aust v South Africa	4–0	
14/4/94	Aust v USA	4–0	
16/4/94	Aust v England	2–0	
17/4/94	Aust v Argentina	2–2	3 wins, 1 draw

Tests

19/4/94	Aust v South Africa	2–0	
20/4/94	Aust v Argentina	3–0	
22/4/94	Aust v Argentina	0–1	2 wins, 1 loss

INTERNATIONAL TRI-SERIES   SYDNEY   MAY 1994

Tests

| 12/5/94 | Aust v Canada | 4–1 | |
| 14/5/94 | Aust v New Zealand | 5–1 | 2 wins |

EUROPEAN TOUR   SPAIN/GERMANY/GREAT BRITAIN MAY–JUNE 1994

21/5/94	Aust v Spain	3–0	Madrid	
23/5/94	Aust v Spain	5–0	Madrid	
25/5/94	Aust v Spain	0–0	Murcia	Penalty strokes 5–3
28/5/94	Aust v Germany	1–0	Braunschweig	

29/5/94	Aust v Germany	3–0	Braunschweig	
31/5/94	Aust v England	2–1	Lilleshall	
1/6/94	Aust v England	3–0	Lilleshall	7 wins

PRE-WORLD CUP TEST MATCHES   VUGHT/AMSTELVEEN
JULY 1994

| 8/7/94 | Aust v Netherlands | 1–1 | Vught | |
| 9/7/94 | Aust v Netherlands | 1–3 | Amstelveen | 1 draw, 1 loss |

8TH WOMEN'S WORLD CUP   DUBLIN   JULY 1994

13/7/94	Aust v Russia	1–2		5 wins, 1 draw, 1 loss
14/7/94	Aust v Argentina	3–1		
16/7/94	Aust v Spain	1–1		
18/7/94	Aust v Ireland	4–0		
20/7/94	Aust v Korea	4–1		
22/7/94	Aust v Germany	2–0	semi-final	
24/7/94	Aust v Argentina	2–0	final	Gold Medal

ANSETT AIR NZ TRI-SERIES   CHRISTCHURCH
NOVEMBER 1994

16/11/94	Aust v New Zealand	3–1	3 wins, 1 loss
18/11/94	Aust v Argentina	3–2	
19/11/94	Aust v New Zealand	4–0	
21/11/94	Aust v Argentina	2–4	1st place

1994 AUSTRALIAN WIN–LOSS RECORD

Matches played	Win	Draw	Loss
37	27	4	6

INTERNATIONAL COMPETITION 1995
TELSTRA 4-NATION TOURNAMENT   HOBART/ADELAIDE
MARCH–APRIL 1995

Hobart

30/3/95	Aust v New Zealand	1–0	Hobart	3 wins
31/3/95	Aust v China	3–2	Hobart	
1/4/95	Aust v South Africa	4–0	Hobart	

Adelaide

5/4/95	Aust v China	1–0	Adelaide	4 wins
6/4/95	Aust v South Africa	3–0	Adelaide	
8/4/95	Aust v New Zealand	3–0	Adelaide	
9/4/95	Aust v China	2–0	Adelaide	1st place

EUROPEAN TOUR   MAY–JUNE 1995

26/5/95	Aust v Scotland	3–1	Belfast	
27/5/95	Aust v Scotland	3–2	Belfast	
27/5/95	Aust v Ireland	4–0	Belfast	
28/5/95	Aust v Ireland	4–0	Belfast	
31/5/95	Aust v Belgium	8–0	Brussels	
3/6/95	Aust v Germany	4–3	Celle	
4/6/95	Aust v Germany	2–1	Celle	
10/6/95	Aust v Netherlands	2–1	Papendaal	
11/6/95	Aust v Spain	3–1	Amstelveen	9 wins

CANADA TEST SERIES   VANCOUVER   JULY–AUGUST 1995

29/7/95	Aust v Canada	5–1	
31/7/95	Aust v Canada	3–0	
2/8/95	Aust v Canada	6–1	3 wins

ATLANTA CHALLENGE CUP   ATLANTA   AUGUST 1995

6/8/95	Aust v Spain	1–2		2 wins, 1 draw, 1 loss
7/8/95	Aust v South Africa	0–0		
9/8/95	Aust v USA	4–0		
11/8/95	Aust v Spain	4–0	final	1st place

TELSTRA INTERNATIONAL SERIES   SYDNEY AUGUST–SEPT 1995

27/8/95	Aust v Great Britain	4–1	
2/9/95	Aust v Great Britain	2–1	
3/9/95	Aust v Great Britain	3–2	3 wins

5TH CHAMPIONS TROPHY   MAR DEL PLATA SEPTEMBER 1995

9/9/95	Aust v USA	2–0		6 wins
10/9/95	Aust v Germany	2–0		
12/9/95	Aust v Spain	1–0		
13/9/95	Aust v Korea	4–2		
16/9/95	Aust v Argentina	2–1		
17/9/95	Aust v Korea	5–4	Final: Penalty strokes 4–3	Gold Medal

1995 AUSTRALIAN WIN–LOSS RECORD

Matches played	Win	Draw	Loss
32	30	1	1

INTERNATIONAL COMPETITION 1996
TELSTRA INTERNATIONAL SERIES   ADELAIDE/PERTH
FEB–MARCH 1996
Adelaide

21/2/96	Aust v Argentina	2–2	
24/2/96	Aust v USA	3–1	1 win, 1 draw

Perth

28/2/96	Aust v Argentina	4–0	
2/3/96	Aust v USA	2–0	
3/3/96	Aust v Argentina	3–1	3 wins

ACCLIMATISATION CAMP   DARWIN   APRIL 1996
Tests

1/4/96	Aust v Japan	8–0	
2/4/96	Aust v Japan	4–1	2 wins

TELSTRA INTERNATIONAL SERIES   BRISBANE/CAIRNS
APRIL 1996

20/4/96	Aust v New Zealand	3–1	Brisbane		
21/4/96	Aust v Korea	2–0	Brisbane		
25/4/96	Aust v Korea	5–1	Cairns		
27/4/96	Aust v New Zealand	6–2	Cairns		
28/4/96	Aust v Korea	5–1	Cairns	final	5 wins

EUROPEAN TOUR   GREAT BRITAIN/GERMANY/HOLLAND
MAY–JUNE 1996

29/5/96	Aust v Great Britain	3–2	Reading	
30/5/96	Aust v Great Britain	3–0	Reading	
3/6/96	Aust v Germany	1–1	Frankfurt	
5/6/96	Aust v Germany	4–1	Neuss	
6/6/96	Aust v Netherlands	2–1	Tilburg	
8/6/96	Aust v Netherlands	4–0	Rotterdam	
9/6/96	Aust v Netherlands	1–1	Amsterdam	5 wins, 2 draws

XXVITH OLYMPIC GAMES   ATLANTA
JULY–AUGUST 1996

20/7/96	Aust v Spain	4–0		7 wins, 1 draw
21/7/96	Aust v Argentina	7–1		
23/7/96	Aust v Germany	1–0		
25/7/96	Aust v Korea	3–3		
26/7/96	Aust v Great Britain	1–0		
28/7/96	Aust v USA	4–0		
30/7/96	Aust v Netherlands	4–0	semi-final	
1/8/96	Aust v Korea	3–1	final	Gold Medal

6TH INDIRA GANDHI GOLD CUP   NEW DELHI
DECEMBER 1996

15/12/96	Aust v Russia	11–1		3 wins, 2 losses
16/12/96	Aust v China	6–2		
18/12/96	Aust v India	0–3		
21/12/96	Aust v Korea	1–2		
22/12/96	Aust v Korea	6–2	final	Gold Medal

1996 AUSTRALIAN WIN–LOSS RECORD

Matches played	Win	Draw	Loss
32	26	4	2

The Hockeyroos completed their best unbeaten streak of 41 matches during 1995–96.

INTERNATIONAL COMPETITION 1997
1997 TELSTRA SERIES   PERTH/SYDNEY/NEWCASTLE
MARCH 1997

Perth
14/3/97	Aust v Germany	2–2	

Sydney
| 16/3/97 | Aust v Germany | 4–2 | |

Newcastle
| 17/3/97 | Aust v Germany | 1–0 | |

Sydney
| 19/3/97 | Aust v Germany | 4–3 | 3 wins, 1 draw |

TELSTRA CHALLENGE   MELBOURNE/BRISBANE   MAY 1997

Melbourne
| 3/5/97 | Aust v New Zealand | 2–1 | |
| 4/5/97 | Aust v China | 5–0 | |

Brisbane
7/5/97	Aust v New Zealand	6–1	
8/5/97	Aust v China	5–0	
11/5/97	Aust v China	6–0	5 wins

TEST SERIES   SPAIN   MAY 1997

24/5/97	Aust v Spain	3–0	Madrid	
25/5/97	Aust v Spain	2–1	Madrid	
27/5/97	Aust v Spain	5–0	Madrid	3 wins

6TH CHAMPIONS TROPHY   BERLIN   JUNE 1997

1/6/97	Aust v Germany	1–1	5 wins, 1 loss
2/6/97	Aust v Netherlands	2–0	
4/6/97	Aust v Great Britain	3–0	
5/6/97	Aust v USA	5–0	
7/6/97	Aust v Korea	2–3	
8/6/97	Aust v Germany	2–1	Gold Medal

1ST KOREA TELECOM CUP   SEONGNAM   JUNE–JULY 1997

28/6/97	Aust v Canada	4–0	4 wins, 1 draw
30/6/97	Aust v Argentina	4–1	
2/7/97	Aust v England	1–1	
3/7/97	Aust v Netherlands	2–0	
5/7/97	Aust v Korea	4–0	Gold Medal

1997 AUSTRALIAN WIN/LOSS RECORD

Matches played	Win	Draw	Loss
23	19	3	1

INTERNATIONAL COMPETITION 1998

1998 TELSTRA TEST   PERTH   JANUARY 1998

30/1/98	Aust v England	1–0	
31/1/98	Aust v England	2–4	1 win, 1 loss

1998 TELSTRA TEST   PERTH/BUNBURY   FEBRUARY 1998

Perth

3/2/98	Aust v Netherlands	3–2	Perth	

Bunbury

5/2/98	Aust v Netherlands	3–1	Bunbury	

Perth

7/2/98	Aust v Netherlands	1–2	Perth	
8/2/98	Aust v Netherlands	6–0	Perth	3 wins, 1 loss

1998 TELSTRA CHALLENGE   SYDNEY/ADELAIDE
MARCH–APRIL 1998

Sydney

26/3/98	Aust v USA	4–0	
28/3/98	Aust v Argentina	1–1	
29/3/98	Aust v Germany	0–1	

Adelaide
1/4/98	Aust v Argentina	3–1		
2/4/98	Aust v Germany	3–0		
4/4/98	Aust v USA	4–1		
5/4/98	Aust v Argentina	3–2	final	5 wins, 1 draw, 1 loss

1998 TELSTRA SERIES V KOREA   CANBERRA/MELBOURNE APRIL 1998
21/4/98	Aust v Korea	9–2	Canberra	
23/4/98	Aust v Korea	3–0	Canberra	
25/4/98	Aust v Korea	1–1	Melbourne	
26/4/98	Aust v Korea	3–1	Melbourne	3 wins, 1 draw

1998 PRE-WORLD CUP TEST MATCHES   MILTON KEYNES MAY 1998
12/5/98	Aust v England	2–2	Milton Keynes	
14/5/98	Aust v England	5–2	Milton Keynes	
16/5/98	Aust v Netherlands	4–2	Utrecht	2 wins, 1 draw

9TH WOMEN'S WORLD CUP   UTRECHT   MAY 1998
20/5/98	Aust v Scotland	5–0		7 wins
22/5/98	Aust v China	7–1		
24/5/98	Aust v USA	6–1		
26/5/98	Aust v Germany	3–0		
27/5/98	Aust v South Africa	5–2		
29/5/98	Aust v Argentina	4–2	semi-final	
31/5/98	Aust v Netherlands	3–2	final	Gold Medal

1998 TEST MATCHES   SINGAPORE   AUGUST 1998
8/8/98	Aust v China	2–0	
9/8/98	Aust v China	2–1	2 wins

XVITH COMMONWEALTH GAMES   KUALA LUMPUR SEPTEMBER 1998
9/9/98	Aust v Scotland	5–0	
12/9/98	Aust v Malaysia	11–0	
14/9/98	Aust v Jamaica	12–0	
16/9/98	Aust v India	4–0	
17/9/98	Aust v Trinidad & Tobago	8–0	
19/9/98	Aust v New Zealand	7–3	semi-final

20/9/98	Aust v England	8–1	final	Gold Medal

TEST MATCHES AND TRI NATIONS TOURNAMENT
BUENOS AIRES/MAR DEL PLATA   DECEMBER 1998
Mini Tournament

| 3/12/98 | Aust v Argentina | 1–2 | Buenos Aires | |
| 5/12/98 | Aust v Argentina | 1–0 | Mar del Plata | 1 win, 1 loss |

Tests

| 6/12/98 | Aust v Argentina | 1–2 | Buenos Aires | 1 loss |

Tri Nations

8/12/98	Aust v Argentina	2–2	Buenos Aires	
9/12/98	Aust v Netherlands	1–1	Buenos Aires	2 draws
12/12/98	Aust v Netherlands	0–2	Buenos Aires	
13/12/98	Aust v Argentina	2–0	Buenos Aires	1 win, 1 loss

1998 AUSTRALIAN WIN–LOSS RECORD

Matches played	Win	Draw	Loss
43	33	5	6

INTERNATIONAL COMPETITION 1999
SOUTH AFRICA TOUR   CAPE TOWN/POTCHEFSTROOM/
PRETORIA   MARCH 1999

19/3/99	Aust v South Africa	3–0	Cape Town	
21/3/99	Aust v South Africa	1–2	Cape Town	
24/3/99	Aust v South Africa	4–1	Potchefstroom	
26/3/99	Aust v South Africa	1–2	Pretoria	
28/3/99	Aust v South Africa	3–0	Pretoria	3 wins, 2 losses

TELSTRA CHALLENGE   CANBERRA/PERTH   APRIL–MAY 1999
Tournament 1

29/3/99	Aust v India	5–1	Canberra	
1/4/99	Aust v Korea	8–0	Canberra	
2/4/99	Aust v South Africa	5–3	Canberra	

Tournament 2

5/4/99	Aust v Korea	4–0	Perth	
6/4/99	Aust v South Africa	3–1	Perth	
8 /4/99	Aust v India	5–1	Perth	
9/4/99	Aust v South Africa	5–0	Perth	7 wins

TELSTRA TESTS   TOOWOOMBA/BRISBANE   JUNE 1999

1/6/99	Aust v England	1–2	Toowoomba	
3/6/99	Aust v England	3–2	Brisbane	
4/6/99	Aust v England	3–0	Brisbane	2 wins, 1 loss

7TH WOMEN'S CHAMPIONS TROPHY   BRISBANE   JUNE 1999

10/6/99	Aust v New Zealand	5–1		
12/6/99	Aust v Germany	6–2		
13/6/99	Aust v Argentina	4–2		
15/6/99	Aust v Korea	6–0		
17/6/99	Aust v Netherlands	1–1	semi-final	
19/6/99	Aust v Netherlands	3–2	final	5 wins, 1 draw

TOUR OF EUROPE   NETHERLANDS/GERMANY/ ENGLAND/SCOTLAND   JULY–AUGUST 1999

19/7/99	Aust v Netherlands	1–3	Utrecht
31/7/99	Aust v Germany	1–0	Leverkusen
1/8/99	Aust v Germany	1–1	Leverkusen

FOUR NATIONS TOURNAMENT   MILTON KEYNES AUGUST 1999

4/8/99	Aust v Netherlands	3–3	Milton Keynes	
5/8/99	Aust v Spain	7–1	Milton Keynes	
7/8/99	Aust v England	0–2	Milton Keynes	
8/8/99	Aust v Netherlands	3–4	final (lost final in extra time on golden goal)	
10/8/99	Aust v Scotland	8–2	Edinburgh	
11/8/99	Aust v Scotland	5–0	Edinburgh	4 wins, 2 draws, 3 losses

OCEANIA SERIES   DUNEDIN/SYDNEY   SEPTEMBER 1999

8/9/99	Aust v New Zealand	1–0	Dunedin	
11/9/99	Aust v New Zealand	2–0	Sydney	
12/9/99	Aust v New Zealand	4–0	Sydney	3 wins

SYDNEY INTERNATIONAL   SEPTEMBER 1999

22/9/99	Aust v China	2–1	
23/9/99	Aust v USA	2–2	
25/9/99	Aust v Spain	6–0	
26/9/99	Aust v USA	4–0	3 wins, 1 draw

1999 AUSTRALIAN WIN–LOSS RECORD

Matches played	Win	Draw	Loss
37	27	4	6

INTERNATIONAL COMPETITION 2000

TELSTRA TESTS V KOREA   PERTH   APRIL 2000

14/4/00	Aust v Korea	3–1	
15/4/00	Aust v Korea	6–0	
17/4/00	Aust v Korea	3–0	
18/4/00	Aust v Korea	3–1	4 wins

PRE-CHAMPIONS TROPHY TOUR   GLASGOW   MAY 2000

21/5/00	Aust v Great Britain	1–3	
22/5/00	Aust v Great Britain	2–3	2 losses

CHAMPIONS TROPHY TOUR   AMSTELVEEN   MAY–JUNE 2000

26/5/00	Aust v New Zealand	4–1	
27/5/00	Aust v Argentina	3–0	
29/5/00	Aust v Germany	1–2	
31/5/00	Aust v Netherlands	1–2	
1/6/00	Aust v South Africa	6–0	
3/6/00	Aust v Argentina	1–0	4 wins, 2 losses Bronze Medal

(Gold–Netherlands, Silver–Germany)

PRE-OLYMPIC INTERNATIONAL MATCHES   SYDNEY JULY 2000

Tri nation series

2/7/00	Aust v Germany	1–1	
3/7/00	Aust v New Zealand	0–3	
5/7/00	Aust v Germany	5–0	
6/7/00	Aust v New Zealand	4–0	3 wins, 1 draw, 1 loss

Telstra Challenge

8/7/00	Aust v Germany	3–0	final

FOUR MATCH TEST SERIES V CHINA   SYDNEY   AUGUST 2000

1/8/00	Aust v China	5–2	
3/8/00	Aust v China	4–2	
5/8/00	Aust v China	9–0	
6/8/00	Aust v China	4–2	4 wins

**XXVIIth OLYMPIC GAMES SYDNEY   AUSTRALIA
SEPTEMBER 2000**

17/9/00	Aust v Great Britain	2–1		
19/9/00	Aust v Spain	1–1		
20/9/00	Aust v Argentina	3–1		
22/9/00	Aust v Korea	3–0		
24/9/00	Aust v New Zealand	3–0		
25/9/00	Aust v Netherlands	5–0		
27/9/00	Aust v China	5–1		
29/9/00	Aust v Argentina	3–1	final	(Gold Medal) 7 wins, 1 draw

2000 AUSTRALIAN WIN–LOSS RECORD

Matches played	Win	Draw	Loss
29	22	2	5

APPENDIX 5
Hockeyroos Mission Statement 1996

We will win in Atlanta by being the best we can be, because Olympic gold is the ultimate challenge in our sport. We will achieve this by playing beyond our previous performances and by never, never giving up.

I will be the best I can be by:

1 Continually *challenging myself* to go beyond my comfort zone
2 Making the necessary *sacrifices*
3 *Believing* in my ability and the strength of my purpose
4 Valuing *excellence, determination* and *dedication* in both training and match play
5 Having *faith* and *confidence* in, and being *supportive* of, my team-mates
6 Not making excuses but taking *responsibility* for my development, performance and for my lifestyle
7 Seeking feedback and making *contributions* to the program
8 Being *tolerant* of differences in others and *respecting* them for who they are and what they have to offer
9 Accepting disappointments and frustrations and overcoming them by *working together*
10 Having faith in the course of action chosen for the team and being *committed* to it knowing that it may not always be my preference.

We choose to do this thing NOT because it is easy but because it is hard.

APPENDIX 6
Hockeyroo Players
1993–2000

Katie Allen 1993–2000
Michelle Andrews 1993–2000
Alyson Annan 1993–2000
Debbie Barratt 1993
Tracey Belbin 1993
Nina Bonner 1997
Cat Brooke 1995
Sally Carbon 1993, 1994
Lisa Carruthers 1993–2000
Tammy Cole 1995, 1997, 1998
Kerry Crawford 1996–98
Melanie Dempster 1993–95
Christine Dobson 1993, 1994
Louise Dobson 1995–2000
Rachel Durdin 1998, 1999
Kelly Free 1997–99
Renita Garard 1994–2000
Tammy Ghisalberti 1993, 1994
Linda Harvey 1994, 1997, 1998
Juliet Haslam 1993–2000
Rechelle Hawkes 1993–2000
Nikki Hudson 1993–2000
Rachel Imison 1998–2000
Bianca Langham 1994–2000
Allison Lippey 1994
Alex Lupton 1998, 1999
Clover Maitland 1994–2000
Karen Marsden 1993–96

Claire Mitchell-Taverner
  1994–2000
Cindy Morgan 1998
Jenny Morris 1993–2000
Lorelle Morrisey 1993
Brooke Morrison 1998–2000
Bianca Netzler 1998
Janita Ogilvie 1997
Alison Peek 1993–2000
Jackie Pereira 1993–96
Nova Peris 1993–96
Katrina Powell 1995–2000
Kim Rayner 1993
Candice Ringrose 1998, 1999
Danni Roche 1995, 1996
Kate Sage 1995–97
Angie Skirving 1998–2000
Karen Smith 1996–2000
Carmel Souter 1998–2000
Justine Sowry 1993–2000
Kate Starre 1993–2000
Liane Tooth 1993–96
Julie Towers 1998–2000
Kristen Towers 1998–2000
Melanie Twitt 1998–2000
Kym Van Der Harst 1994
Simone Wallington 1994, 1995,
  1997

APPENDIX 7

Typical Weekly Programs
1996 and 2000

The following programs taken from a week in July 1996 and a week in June 2000 provide an example of a typical week for the Hockeyroos. The 1996 program contains some extra sessions (including a Parliament House function and a presentation from Mick Malthouse) as this week was very close to our departure for Atlanta. The 2000 week was not as close to the Olympics so it reflects a typical training week.

WEEKLY PROGRAM COMMENCING 17 JULY 2000

MONDAY	TUESDAY	WEDNESDAY	THURSDAY	FRIDAY	SATURDAY	SUNDAY
9.00 am Administration meeting	7.00–10.00 am Weights 3 groups	9.00–11.00 am Group training session	7.00–8.00 am Goal Keepers Weights	7.00–10.00 am Weights 3 groups	Goal Keepers Weights	
Active recovery Challenge Stadium (bring bathers and running shoes)	10.30–1.30 pm Light session Small group or individual	Yoga	9.00–11.00 am Video Sessions in parts	8.30–9.30 am Goal Keeper individual		
10.30–12.00 Staff meeting		Free	11.00–1.00 pm Light session Small groups or individual	10.30–12.30 pm Light session Set plays	Club fixtures or free day	Club fixtures or free day
Staff available (meetings)	Team activity only as required		1.30 pm Medical meeting Café Subiaco			
2.30–5.00 pm Group training session Yoga		Free	Staff available (meetings) Goal Keepers video	Free		
			7.00–9.30 pm Game			

WEEKLY PROGRAM COMMENCING 1 JULY 1996

MONDAY	TUESDAY	WEDNESDAY	THURSDAY	FRIDAY	SATURDAY	SUNDAY
8.00–9.30 am Yoga 136 Rokeby Rd Subiaco	8.00–9.00 am Active (own) recovery	8.00–10.00 am Group training	7.15–8.30 am Goal Keepers Weights	8.00–9.00 am Active (own) recovery	Goal Keepers Weights	
			9.00 Discussion session	9.00–10.00 am Psych weekly review		
10.00–11.00 am Training session Indoor – Lords	9.00–11.00 am Set plays and small games / As required or optional individual	10.00 am Meeting Mick Malthouse	10.00 am Player prep Tactics analysis	9.00–10.30 am Set plays As required or optional individual / 10.30–11.00 am Week review		
	11.30 am & 12.30 pm Weights/ circuits 2 groups	11.00–1.00 pm Psych available	11.00 am Video projects / 12.00–1.00 pm Individual training Coaches available	11.30 am & 12.30 pm Weights/ circuits 2 groups	Club fixtures or rest	Club fixtures or rest
2.00–3.30 pm Preview meeting	Free or 3.00–5.00 pm Computer course – Canning College (7 squad members)	1.00–2.30 pm Yoga	1.00–2.00 pm Parliament House Function / 3.30–5.30 pm Group training and game	Free		
3.30–5.30 pm Training Set plays or Optional individual						
Free	6.00–7.30 pm Psych session	6.00–8.00 pm Prep for Thursday Facilities open Coaches avail	Free			

Coach and Psychologist individual session to be arranged as required

As at 26 June 1996

ACKNOWLEDGMENTS

I began writing this book in November 2000 and completed the task by the end of March. Without the word processing skills of my partner Carmen Black I would never have made it. Carmen also provided valuable editorial support, criticism and advice throughout that time and the editing process. Her contribution has been inestimable.

Jacquie Brown from Pan Macmillan helped me to get started and crystalise an approach to writing the book. On her departure, as the book was taking form, Bernadette Foley continued that job and saw the project through. She guided me skillfully through the editing process. Additionally, Ian Heads offered great support and advice to a novice writer.

Judith Coen from Women's Hockey and Anne Konrath, my personal assistant at the Australian Institute of Sport Hockey Unit, were both helpful in providing detail and checking facts. Trevor Vanderputt provided useful information about the Anglo–Indian influence on Australian hockey. Wally Foreman, Glen Mitchell and David Hatt all helped me confirm my details and deliberations about Chapter 18.

I should also acknowledge all those who were part of the 'off field' team that stood behind our great team. Many are mentioned in the book but Ross Smith who oversaw our physiotherapy needs and Andrew Potter who was our principal medical resource (when the Adelaide Crows released him) were pivotal.

David Parkin and Wayne Bennett willingly agreed to provide comment for the cover and foreword. Both are busy men and outstanding coaches within their respective disciplines. I am honoured and grateful for their involvement.

Finally and most importantly, the central characters, the Hockeyroos. They were the inspiration for this book and provided much of the substance. I hope the book will provide a record of some of their successes just as it is a record of an important part of my life.

CREDITS FOR QUOTES

Page 64   Wayne Gretzky, quoted in Michael Lynberg (ed.), *Winning!: Great Coaches and Athletes Share their Secrets of Success*, Doubleday, New York, 1993, p. 14.

Page 98   John Wooden, *They Call Me Coach*, McGraw Hill, New York, 1998.

Page 99   Kareem Abdul-Jabbar, quoted in Michael Lynberg (ed.), *Winning!: Great Coaches and Athletes Share their Secrets of Success*, Doubleday, New York, 1993, p. 78.

Page 100   Alex Ferguson, *Managing My Life*, Hodder and Stoughton, London, p. 328. Reproduced with the permission of Hodder and Stoughton Limited.

Pages 105–106   Martina Navratilova, quoted in Michael Lynberg (ed.), *Winning!: Great Coaches and Athletes Share their Secrets of Success*, Doubleday, New York, 1993, p. 40.

Page 172   Alexander Haslam, et al. Abstract for 'Inspecting the Emperor's Clothes: Evidence that Random Selection of Leaders can Enhance Group Performance', *Group Dynamics: Theory, Research and Practice*, vol. 2, no. 3, 1998.

Page 228   David Malouf, 'Here We Are: Against the Plan and Against the Odds', *Australian*, 1 January 2001, pp. 2 & 13.

Page 233   Roger Bannister, *First Four Minutes*, Penguin, London, 1995, p. 220.

Page 241   Henry Kissinger, *Diplomacy*, Simon & Schuster, New York, 1994, p. 27.

Index of Names